Film Appreciation
Through Genres

Film Appreciation Through Genres

MICHAEL PATRICK GILLESPIE

McFarland & Company, Inc., Publishers
Jefferson, North Carolina

ISBN (print) 978-1-4766-7639-5
ISBN (ebook) 978-1-4766-3550-7

LIBRARY OF CONGRESS CATALOGUING DATA ARE AVAILABLE

BRITISH LIBRARY CATALOGUING DATA ARE AVAILABLE

© 2019 Michael Patrick Gillespie. All rights reserved

No part of this book may be reproduced or transmitted in any form or by any means, electronic or mechanical, including photocopying or recording, or by any information storage and retrieval system, without permission in writing from the publisher.

The front cover image is from *Barton Fink*, 1991
(20th Century–Fox Pictures/Photofest)

Printed in the United States of America

McFarland & Company, Inc., Publishers
Box 611, Jefferson, North Carolina 28640
www.mcfarlandpub.com

To Holly, Cole and William

Acknowledgments

I am very grateful to the many people who patiently have talked to me about film, guided my interpretations, and challenged some of the conclusions that I reached far too easily. In the process they have taught me a great deal. In particular, I would like to thank Lenny Abrahamson, Michelle Alonso, Ruth Barton, Mary Catherine Boden, April Bolet, Julius Cohen, Michael Creeden, Sean Crosson, Nancy Curtin, Maneck Darwala, Bob Dickerson, Tiffany Fajardo, A. Nicholas Fargnoli, Eugene Finn, the Rev. John Fitzgibbons, S.J., Natalie Foreman, Liz Gill, Ann Gillespie, Paula Gillespie, Gene Henderson, Adelaida Martinez, Aramis Martinez, John McCabe, Asher Milbauer, Ira Nadel, Kassandra O'Connell, Sunniva O'Flynn, Leigh Pike, Krista Ratcliffe, Albert Rivero, James Silas Rogers, Heather Russell, Andrew Strycharski, John Su, Jamie Sutton, Tony Tracy, Harry von Suskil, and my film studies students at Marquette University and Florida International University. There were more conversations than I can recall and many people who shaped my sense of film. I offer my gratitude to those individuals as well.

I also wish to acknowledge the support of Marquette University and Florida International University for grants each provided to support the research for this book.

Table of Contents

Acknowledgments — vi
Prologue: But First, a Brief Word — 1
Introduction: Do the Right Thing — 4
One. Once Upon a Time in the West: Westerns — 23
Two. Angels with Dirty Faces: Gangster Films — 55
Three. A Touch of Evil: Film Noir — 74
Four. Die, Monster, Die: Horror Films — 94
Five. It Came from Outer Space: Science Fiction Films — 121
Six. Monkey Business: Slapstick Comedies — 145
Seven. It Happened One Night: Screwball Comedy/Romantic Comedies — 173

Now What Am I Looking At? — 196
Glossary — 199
Chapter Notes — 219
For Further Reading — 223
Index — 227

Prologue
But First, a Brief Word

Let me begin by demonstrating my keen grasp of the obvious. A great deal has already been written about film from a variety of perspectives. Many books devoted to cinema scholarship focus on the history of its development, on its methods of production, and on theories of its interpretation. Numerous other books simply record—with varying degrees of insight—reactions to movies. I want to distinguish this book from either the adamantly academic or the intensely individual category. *Film Appreciation through Genres* discusses motion pictures in a way that is more than visceral but not quite cerebral. It highlights an approach to film appreciation that remains accessible to all levels of film enthusiasts and that distinguishes itself by an emphasis on thoughtful, individual responses. It is a book that takes film, but not itself, seriously.

The present book acknowledges that those of us who enjoy motion pictures usually have strong opinions about the worth of any movie that we have seen. Often we base our views on logical conclusions drawn from our observations. Many times we come to a fuller understanding of what we have seen by comparing our current assessment to those we have previously made of other movies. Some of us will go further, assessing a film's actors, its director, or even its writers. We might go on to contrast those efforts with the work of the same individuals or other figures working in any number of other movies. Some of us use terms like montage, cross-cutting, flashback, voiceover, *mise en scène* and others relating to the narrative and the production process to express our responses more precisely. All these methods are employed to varying degrees by those of us who take a casual, though not unsophisticated, approach to the analysis of what we see on the screen.

At the same time, untrained viewers can be limited by their own tastes and experiences like a casual wine drinker who enjoys a glass of house red without knowing why. As one becomes more interested in wine, one may make an effort to acquire skills which will make the tasting experience even more enjoyable. This can be done by learning about different types, different years, and different wineries. It does not automatically necessitate a significant investment in rare vintages or the construction of wine cellars, but it does require a commitment to comprehending how the experience comes about. The same holds true for films. A great deal can be gained through a fundamental understanding of the process without a commitment to the vocabulary and methods of formal film criticism.

To that end, this text demonstrates how one can come to a sophisticated comprehension of motion pictures through a clear sense of how movies come together. It fosters an informed approach to film appreciation that goes beyond individual preference and allows one not simply to understand what one enjoys but to comprehend the sources of that enjoyment by showing readers how to refine personal perspectives through a heightened awareness of common modes of production, familiar structural frameworks, and popular thematic features.

This does not mean teaching individuals how to understand movies. Most enthusiastic viewers have already mastered that ability. However, it does give them the means and perspectives to express with greater confidence what they have comprehended. Readers of *The New York Review of Books* can speak about a range of books reviewed there without having to read them all. Similarly, *Film Appreciation through Genres* gives nonprofessional viewers a way to talk about films without necessarily having seen the all movies that they choose to discuss. Insightful observations can come from simply keeping some key general concepts in mind when applying them to specific works under discussion. I believe that a simple and direct approach to film appreciation can bring this about.

Thus, the plan of this book is fairly straightforward. After an introduction giving an overview of Classic Hollywood Cinema, the form adopted in almost every film that has been made, seven chapters examine various genres: Westerns, Gangster Movies, Film Noir, Horror Films, Science Fiction, Slapstick Comedies, and Screwball Comedies.[1] Each talks about the general features of the genre, and then each offers examples from three variants or subgenres of the form—one generally drawn from films of the 1930s or 1940s, one from films of the 1960s or 1970s, and one from films made since 1980. The point is to show the consistency of generic elements from decade to decade and to offer examples of how readings of each of the subgenres could proceed. At the end of each section of a sub-genre, I offer a list of similar films. These compilations are by no means exhaustive. Rather, they aim to be representative and to stimulate readers to find other examples as well.

I understand that there is a certain looseness in my delineation of genres. That is intentional. I try throughout the book to maintain a tone that acknowledges the subjectivity that we all bring to the cinema. That is not a dismissal of academic rigor but a reaffirmation of the idea that one can think about movies in a critical way without adopting the formal approaches of scholars. I also understand that a number of additional genres could have been included. I quite agree, and would have done so were limitations of space not a consideration. As it stands, I have chosen a range of prominent genres as representative examples that will provide ample guidance for understanding other forms of film as well.

Let me add a few logistical comments for clarification. In general, when examining a particular film I identify the actor playing a certain role, and subsequently simply reference the character by his or her name in the film. Release dates of all films mentioned appear in parentheses after the film's title in the index. I have kept quotations from films to a minimum, and have used only those that I have directly transcribed from the scenes references. Throughout the book, when a particular cinematic characteristic is referenced, the title of a film that demonstrates that quality appears in parentheses. At the same time, of course, it certainly does not suggest that it appears only in the movie that is referenced.

In revising the book for publication I managed to catch and correct a few embarrassing mistakes in the details of some of my film descriptions: the actor who got a grapefruit in the face in *The Public Enemy*; what the thirty-nine steps signified; and a few others. There are probably more that I missed. If you find them, I would be grateful to you for taking the time to drop me a line to tell me: *Michael.gillespie@fiu.edu*.

Introduction
Do the Right Thing

Where Do We Stand

We spend a great deal of time talking about motion pictures. It may be over drinks after going to the movies. It may be at home after watching a film on a cable channel or through an on-demand feature. It may be during a random conversation on a date, during lunch at work, while waiting for an airplane to takeoff, or simply while passing the time with friends. A film discussion can be an icebreaker, a litmus test for compatibility, or a sure way to fill an awkward pause in a conversation.

Many intelligent, enthusiastic individuals approach conversations about films as an extension of the pleasures derived while watching them. Love for movies and enthusiasm for discussion makes many people want to attain a better understanding of what they have seen and to develop a greater skill in talking articulately about their experiences. This sophisticated midpoint between theorizing and plot summary is not as difficult to achieve as some might assume, and "it's so cool" should only be the starting point.

Classic Hollywood Cinema

Since their introduction just before the turn of the last century, the vast majority of narrative films have followed the same structure, a method that eventually came to be called Classic Hollywood Cinema.[1] Using that basic narrative form, a range of different types or genres emerged to explore particular themes and issues from clearly defined assumptions and perspectives. (I will talk about the most prominent genres in the chapters that follow.) In each of these categories, fundamental elements that make up any film adapted to the subject of the genre and took on increasingly complex significance, while maintaining the familiar structure that contributes so much to the understanding of a particular movie and to the expectations that viewers brought to all. Understanding these structures and elements enables one to speak with discernment about any number of movies, whether one has seen them or not.

Let me begin with the overriding concept that gives structure to all of these films: Classic Hollywood Cinema. Although that designation itself did not come into widespread use until the 1970s, the form—a standard, linear approach that emphasized narrative over other elements in the film—evolved quickly in motion pictures made in America by the Kalem Company, Biograph Studios, Edison Studios and numerous others from the first decade of the last century. Even before film companies moved to Los Angeles to take advantage of favorable weather and avoid copyright harassment from Thomas Edison, the straightforward, efficient method for managing a film's narrative established itself as the model that would shape work in studios around the world.[2]

Its structure both mimics and concentrates our everyday perceptions. It evokes a variety of realistic situations while focusing full attention on the resolution of a specific problem. It announces the difficulty early in the film, and it shapes all of the elements found in the movie in relation to resolving that problem. Though the form's narrative structure remains relatively straightforward and easy for viewers to follow, the very simplicity of Classic Hollywood Cinema plotline has always allowed creative filmmakers, through imaginative manipulation, to offer a sophisticated variations on the storyline. Looking at *The Wizard of Oz*, a popular film that continues to appeal to viewers eighty years after its first appearance, underscores the points I am making.

What We Learn from the Emerald City

Early on, the narrative of *The Wizard of Oz* introduces its central problem: Dorothy (Judy Garland) discovers herself in Oz and must find a way to get home. From that moment of revelation, the film follows a conventional linear timeframe with a clearly delineated beginning, middle, and end. As a result, even though the duration of Dorothy's visit to Oz might seem much longer than the period during which she remains unconscious in her bedroom on Aunty Em and Uncle Henry's farm, one never loses sight of the movie's chronological progression from the time she finds herself in Oz to the moment when she awakens in Kansas.

As the narrative unfolds the actions of a few central characters advance the plot or respond to conditions that relate to the problem. In an effort to discover how to return to Kansas, Dorothy and the friends she has met on her journey—the Scarecrow (Ray Bolger), the Tinman (Jack Haley), and the Cowardly Lion (Bert Lahr)—move steadfastly towards the Emerald City while simultaneously struggling against the machinations of the Wicked Witch of the West (Margaret Hamilton) and her minions who are determined to foil Dorothy's plans. Members of the supporting cast enhance efforts to resolve the central problem or illuminate subplots that complement the main issue driving the narrative. Thus, the Tinman, the Scarecrow, and the Cowardly Lion all want something from the Wizard (Frank Morgan), but their wishes and their actions are

The Cowardly Lion (Bert Lahr), the Tinman (Jack Haley), Dorothy (Judy Garland), and the Scarecrow (Ray Bolger) in *The Wizard of Oz* (1939).

incorporated into the larger issue that drives the storyline, Dorothy's overriding need to get back home.

The narrative in Classic Hollywood Cinema concludes when characters resolve the problem that has driven the action of the film. In *The Wizard of Oz* this occurs as soon as Dorothy realizes that tapping the heels of the ruby slippers together and expressing her sense of the primary importance of home will send her back to Kansas. Though the end can surprise no one familiar with Classic Hollywood Cinema's formulaic structure, a lack of suspense does not matter. The manner in which the story unfolds delights us time and again.

How Things Come Together

The clear organization provided by Classic Hollywood Cinema does not mean that the narrative will be simplistic. Indeed, many films regarded as masterpieces use its format as a familiar referential structure to ground viewers' perceptions of ingenious thematic and cinematic variations. For example, *The Third Man* relentlessly follows the problem-oriented narrative pattern at the heart of Classic Hollywood Cinema.

Everything relates to a single issue: efforts by a range of individuals to establish the true nature of Harry Lime (Orson Wells). The central figure, Holly Martins (Joseph Cotten), spends the entire motion picture on a Grail-like quest to square the facts of Lime's life in post–World War II Vienna with Martins' recollections of their friendship before the war. The story of Holly Martins' gradual realization of Lime's true and very complex nature, held together by scenes chronicling Martins' evolving point of view, serves as a model for the interpretive methods followed by most filmgoers: a steady linear process of accumulating information, relating one set of impressions to another, refining the opinions one has, and finding an overall unity in the implications of what one sees.

The depth of the relationship between Harry and Holly is amplified by representations of other complex characters. Lime's disaffected and vulnerable girlfriend Anna (Alida Valli) gives the viewer a sense of Harry's contradictory nature manifest through an amoral cosmopolitanism that the conventional Holly Martins resists acknowledging. Anna, who is both vulnerable and pragmatic, also nicely highlights the limits of Harry's benevolence and stands as emblematic of his coldblooded willingness to use any and all of his friends and acquaintances to forward his own ends. In a similar fashion, the calculating British officer Major Calloway (Trevor

Howard) shows that only a marginal difference obtains between Harry's callous determination to enrich himself and Calloway's ruthless manipulation of others and employment of any means at his disposal to capture Harry.

Classic Hollywood Cinema has always depended on more than thematic variations to create powerful films. It uses the expanded narrative possibilities of motion pictures to give new significance to or intensified the immediate impact of dramatic features long familiar in the theater. Understanding nuanced meanings of familiar terms will greatly enhance any film discussion. In the next section, I will elaborate on the particular significance of these terms in cinema.

A Closer Look at Some Common Terms

The famous UCLA basketball coach, John Wooden, would begin the first practice of every year with a session on how to tie a gym shoe.[3] Wooden won ten national titles with the Bruin teams that he coached,

Holly Martins (Joseph Cotten, left) and Harry Lime (Orson Wells) in *The Third Man* (1949).

and was not a man to engage in frivolous gestures. As he explained to his players, it is all too easy to take the familiar for granted and to overlook important aspects of even the most fundamental elements of one's surroundings.

I mention this as a prelude to a section explaining some of the key terms identifying concepts that combine into a unified impression of a film. I understand that many viewers are already familiar with the general use of these terms, but I think it useful to review their cinematic context to give a fuller sense of their functions. (An expanded list of such terms can be found in the glossary at the end of this text.)

The French phrase *mise en scène* (translated literally as "setting on stage") originated as a collective label for the elements that go into the staging of a play, and it has made an easy transition to the designation that encapsulates the orchestrated influence of major components in filmmaking: the composition of shots or scenes through the interplay of actors, setting, costumes, props, lighting, camera angles, sound, and editing. (Indeed, in French films the director is identified by this term, singling out the filmmaker as the one who has ultimate responsibility for coordinating all of the material elements that combine to create a motion picture: script, acting, cinematography, lighting, sound, and any other odds and ends.)

When watching a movie, individual viewers may give differing emphases to these elements. However, no one can apprehend a single shot or a specific scene, much less an entire film, without coming to some opinion on how these components work together. To that end, let's look at how each of these features contribute to a full understanding of the *mise en scéne* shaping any film.

It might seem self-evident to note that **actors** animate the lines that appear in the screenplay. However, their efforts extend well beyond giving voices to a script. Actors interpret the natures of their characters not simply in terms of behavior consistent with their backstories but they work to make their roles support and illuminate the unfolding narrative of the film. Thus, we should not consider the efforts of any one of them in isolation. Rather, each actor, from leading players to those with bit parts, stands as a contributing member of the company whose performances combine to shape a viewer's full sense of the narrative.

For a good illustration of this one need only consider the interactions that take place in the 1940 film *His Girl Friday*. In the opening scene, when Hildy Johnson (Rosalind Russell) strolls through the newsroom of *The Morning Post*. She exchanges a chorus of hellos from switchboard operators, reporters, and copyeditors and offers of a flippant condolence to the advice to the lovelorn editor whose cat has just had kittens, With every exchange, bit players contribute to the ethos of the journalistic world and enhance our sense of Hildy's uniqueness.

We also come to understand Hidly through the alternating the professional and domestic demands made by two other central figures in the film, her rapacious editor Walter Burns (Cary Grant) and her conventional, insurance agent fiancé, Bruce Baldwin (Ralph Bellamy). Conversely, as a fast talking dame, to use Maria Batista's brilliant characterization, Hildy strives to meliorate the naiveté of Bruce and mitigate the ruthlessness of Walter so that we can see complexities in both them and her. Over the course of the film, conversations with other reporters shows Hildy's humanity set in contrast to their heartlessness. At the same time, when interviewing key figures for her story on an impending execution, she shows an unrelenting determination to be the first to get the same facts that the other reporters are pursuing. In short, these various exchanges reveal not only the depth of Hildy's character but also demonstrate the manner in which even minor roles add complexity to the plotline.

In addition to developing through interactions of its actors, a motion picture grows out of the material context that surrounds the action. **Settings** can be created on a soundstage or brought to the foreground on location. In either case, their physical features stamp the action with a material context and a quantifiable specificity. Although the setting can be arrestingly monumental, like the scene in *North by Northwest* when Roger Thornhill (Cary Grant) and Eve Kendall (Eva Marie Saint) scramble over president's faces on Mount Rushmore, even the most understated can go well beyond merely providing a finite background to the picture.

Whether sparse, elaborate, or somewhere in between, they add emotional layers by evoking the viewer's own cultural, emotional, and intellectual associations towards the locations, and provide both support and contrast for the roles that the actors play. When filming his cavalry trilogy—*Fort Apache, She Wore a Yellow Ribbon,* and *Rio Grande* and indeed a number of other westerns that he made—John Ford did not on settle on filming the archetypal vistas of the open plains that characterize the landscapes of much of the actual west. Instead, he opted for the majestic backdrop of Monument Valley whose typography gives scenes in his films a magnitude and an exoticism that can dominate our sense of what we are seeing.[4]

In the example pictured here, the barren rock formations and the arid land underscores for viewers the unforgiving environment in which the film's narrative unfolds. The surroundings highlight the sense of iso-

On location in Monument Valley with Captain Nathan Brittles (John Wayne, kneeling in front of the regimental and national flags), Sgt. Maj. Michael O'Rourke (Ward Bond, to the right) and Lt. Col. Owen Thursday (Henry Fonda, to the left) in *Fort Apache* (1948).

lation and individuality that provide a thematic underpinning for Ford's productions. The starkness of the physical world emphasizes the ethos of rugged individuality that animates these narratives. And overall, the aridness, the size, the strangeness of the setting creates metaphysical associations with Manifest Destiny, rugged individualism, and bootstrap optimism that shape our sense of the American psyche.

Setting can also intensify our sense of an individual. In a memorable scene early in *Lawrence of Arabia*, Sherif Ali (Omar Sharif) appears as a dot in contrast to a bright blue sky and a desert shimmering with heat moving toward Lawrence (Peter O'Toole). The background of sand and sky intensifies our sense of the figure who gradually grows to a recognizable size. By the time Ali takes out his gun and shoots Lawrence's guide because the man without permission had been drinking from a well, the setting has already profoundly shaped our sense of the man.

Despite functioning on a much smaller physical scale, even elements that may seem at first to be no more than ancillary elaborations of the general tone of a motion picture, its **props** and **costumes**, for example, can go well beyond visual enhancement or utilitarian plot advancement. In *Rear Window* the temporarily wheelchair-bound L.B. Jefferies (Jimmy Stewart), a highly successful photographer, uses the camera that he normally wields on magazine assignments to cover breaking news around the world, to give him a magnified view of his neighbor's actions. Alfred Hitchcock, the film's director, allows Jefferies' camera to underscore his skill as a photographer while aiding his efforts at solving the mystery unfolding in a neighboring building. More subtly, but of equal or greater importance to our understanding, it also suggests the voyeuristic tendencies that lead him to his profession and that impel him to spy on the man in the apartment across the courtyard.

In *Beetlejuice* the plaid shirt and khaki pants of Adam (Alec Baldwin) and the gingham dress of Barbara (Geena Davis) highlight their ordinary, Norman Rockwell–like complacency. At the same time their dress emphasizes, in the same subversive fashion one can see in a Rockwell painting, a *faux* hominess covering a willfully naïve doltishness. This adds a wonderful level of irony even as it makes them perfect foils for Betelgeuse (Michael Keaton) and the Deetz family (Catherine O'Hara, Jeffery Jones, and Wynona Ryder).

Roles, locations, artifacts, and clothing make overt contributions to the ***mise en scène*** that unites elements into a film. Other devices, taken up in the next section, overlay the narrative to enhance specifics and to contribute to the broad interpretive understanding that viewers form as they watch films.

Technical Importance

Much the same is true for different elements grouped in the mechanical side of filmmaking. What we have loosely come to call **special effects**—a term that goes well beyond referencing the computer generated graphics of current action movies—has combined features unique to motion pictures to make powerful aesthetic impressions. Here are some important general categories.

Illumination is such an integral part of the movie experience that one can take for granted **lighting**, which can fluctuate between intrusive assertions of its presence to insinuations so subtle as to pass unnoticed. However it is employed, its impact remains profound. The position and intensity of illumination can seemingly add or subtract years to a person's age or radically affect the representation of a character or an image. Beyond that, over the course of a film, lighting can create emotional tones that profoundly influence a viewer's disposition.

It is most evident in the Film Noir genre. There, the stark contrasts established by the manipulation of darkness and shadow in a film like *Touch of Evil*, for example, heighten tension and intensify the psychological complexity of the drama. Conversely, the calculated emphasis on brightness and light in *L.A. Confidential* creates similar sensations through a self-conscious inversion of the conventions for illumination in that genre.

When used effectively, lighting goes well beyond its utilitarian function of illumination. It exerts an equally forceful, if seemingly understated, impact in emphasizing or masking features of characters, props, and settings. And it sets and sustains emotional tones that profoundly affect understanding.

In a similar fashion, **camera position** always does more than merely record the movement. It informs our conception of everything that occurs on-screen. This does not simply apply to the objects we recognize, but extends to the tone that we attach to a scene or even an entire narrative. Alternating shots can underscore feelings emanating from the cordial remarks of a friendly conversation to the harsh exchanges of a heated confrontation. It can create awe or disdain through a high or low angle shot. And it can suggest subtle aspects of characterization or narrative development through lingering on an object or a figure or by shifting quickly from one shot to another.

The single, extended take that opens the climatic scenes in *High Noon* moves the camera back slowly from a close-up of Marshal Will Kane (Gary Cooper) to a high angle shot of him standing in the middle of the deserted main street of Hadleyville. In the process, it presents a chilling summation of his situation. Initially the camera captures the fear and hesitation that run across Cooper's face as he realizes that he is about to confront four armed men. Then, as it moves above and away from him, it conveys a powerful sense of the isolation. Finally, it underscores the despair that he feels upon realizing that none of the townspeople will come to his aid.

Conversely, it can delay or confuse our sense of a character or of the action. With the exception of just a few shots, *Lady in the Lake* is filmed entirely from the perspective of its central character, Philip Marlowe (Robert Montgomery). Viewers see the world exactly as Marlowe does, and our sense of gradual understanding matches his as he struggles to solve the mystery of the missing woman. This point of view can have a profound psychological effect. Because we are accustomed to seeing all the elements in a scene, it becomes very easy to feel the same claustrophobia and confusion that dogs Marlowe throughout the narrative.

Sound has exerted a profound influence on one's impressions of a film. Because of the acclaim received by *The Jazz Singer*, the first feature length talkie, it is easy to assume that the introduction of dialogue into motion pictures was the most important contribution of sound made to picture production. However, its impact in fact is subtler and more detailed. Whether through a special effect that punctuates an event, music that cues emotions, or ambient noise that contextualizes the action, sound brings an unobtrusive yet insistent direction to interpretations of a scene.

The wail of a locomotive gives voice to the landlady's expression of horror as she discovers a dead body in *The 39 Steps*. The rapid bowing of a cello before each shark attack in *Jaws* builds tension well before the huge fish appears. And the background clamor of Manhattan in *Taxi Driver* underscores the cacophony that informs Travis Bickle's (Robert Di Niro) chaotic sense of his environment. All reflect aural coloring that vastly enhances our perception of what we watch on the screen.

From the *frisson* created in late nineteenth century audiences by Louis Lumière's *Arrival of a Train at La Ciotat Station* to the computer generated imagery of contemporary action movies, whether through the apparently seamless conjunctions of continuity or in the more self-conscious breaks of montage, **editing** prescribes the things we see and the order in which we see them. In many instances, it imbues a scene with spontaneity otherwise impossible to capture.

For example, deft cutting between Katharine Hepburn and Cary Grant arguing at the swimming pool in *The Philadelphia Story* creates a seamless naturalistic rendition of an exchange that in the absence of editing could not be shot without revealing the cameras photographing it. That smooth transition stands in sharp contrast to the self-consciously abrupt cross-cutting between the synchronous events of the baptismal ceremony and the executions of rival gangsters that take place at the end of *The Godfather*. There, movement between images of Michael Corleone's (Al Pacino) sacrilegious recitation of the Baptismal vows and his henchmen's killing men who threaten his power underscores the moral void of Michael's world with greater force than any words could.

Each of the elements mentioned above makes an integral contribution to what constitutes a motion picture, yet, as previously noted, a viewer derives impressions of a film from their amalgamation, what is termed

Arrival of a Train at La Ciotat Station (1896) was a 50-second French black-and-white documentary directed and produced by Auguste and Louis Lumière.

the *mise en scène*: the relationship of each to all the others. Film appreciation comes from understanding this interaction.

Genres as Organizing Points

Audiences tend to comprehend an individual work of art associatively, through the expectations that they have for particular groups or types and through associations with other works within that category. Leonardo da Vinci's *Mona Lisa* is a striking achievement in no small part because of the comparisons that it invites with other Renaissance paintings. The uniqueness of the music of Giacomo Puccini's *Madama Butterfly* becomes more apparent when one thinks of it in context with other late nineteenth and early twentieth-century operas. We understand how the lyricism of W.B. Yeats' poetry lifts our spirits in part because the verse of so many of his contemporaries fails to do so.

Talking about films in relation to one another makes sense because of this associative approach. It both highlights superior offerings and gives insights into the value of less than perfect works. In a study that emphasizes narrative, as this book does, examining genres—categories of films that share certain structural conventions and thematic patterns—serves as an efficient way to comprehend this method. While films in all groups follow the Classic Hollywood Cinema structure, each genre develops characters of plot, action, and production that are unique to its category.

Generic conventions in motion pictures set up as paradigms for organizing our initial impressions and for anchoring our specific sense of the film's meaning in previous viewing experiences. Genres should never become prescriptive templates for interpretations. Nonetheless, comprehending their defining features clarifies many of the instinctive associations that we make with particular types of movies.

Understanding these specific categories, informed by Classic Hollywood Cinema conventions yet with characterizing features unique to each enhances our ability to appreciate films. Comparing genres shows how the expectations for the narrative of a Western differ from those for a Gangster film, a Horror movie, a Slapstick Comedy, or any other form. This provides clear protocols for distinguishing one type of film from another. It gives a refined view of the shared characteristics of seemingly dissimilar movies. And it lays out many of the common expectations for all movies and recognizes the particular qualities that inform the way that we see certain kinds of motion pictures.

Points to Consider

Going back and forth from a general sense of film structure to the definitive characteristics of different genres requires a consistent approach to produce the clearest insights. This means using a systematic method of analysis. In that spirit, the following questions are not meant to form a series of instructions to be committed to memory and regurgitated on command, like Mr. Memory's performances in *The 39 Steps*. Rather, they reflect the stages of understanding common to most approaches to film interpretation. Even without having seen a particular film, having answers to these questions gives us something to say about it.

1. Does this film fit into an identifiable genre? Establishing the type of movie under consideration orients the viewer toward the boundaries, expectations, and assumptions that shape the narrative. For instance, in the opening credits and initial scenes, we encounter elements that place *The Maltese Falcon* in the Film Noir genre: the stylized music, the starkly lit image of the statuette of a black bird, and the introduction of the tough-talking detective rolling his own cigarettes all serve as markers to highlight the conventions of a particular kind of film. (Even without knowing the specific term, experienced filmgoers will recognize the features of Film Noir: the alienated anti-hero, operating according to a personal code, at odds with the views of corrupt or indifferent individuals and social institutions.) With that in mind, we very quickly characterize Sam Spade, Brigid O'Shaunnessy, Joel Cairo, Myles Archer, Kasper Gutman (Humphrey

Bogart, Mary Astor, Peter Lorie, Jerome Cowan, Sidney Greenstreet), and all of the other figures encountered in the film. We expect to find them shaped by alienation, and we are not surprised to see a tone of world-weariness and evidence of disillusionment running throughout the dialogue. Nonetheless, even as conventions set boundaries for our interpretation, they do not prescribe specific reactions to characters. For example, different viewers may interpret Sam Spade as idealistic, cynical, corrupt, or something else entirely. The genre does not tell us how to assess his nature, but it does provide guidance into the motivations of individuals operating in the unique world of this type of film.

2. **How is this motion picture similar or dissimilar to other films in this category?** The patterns to which narratives conform often affect a viewer through their associations with other films that one has seen. Understanding the generic echoing allows one to draw on experience with other films. A Western made in the 1990s, *Tombstone*, for example, engages the viewer in part because its storyline, sets, and costumes play off the conventions that one has seen established and upheld in predecessors—like *The Man Who Shot Liberty Valence*, *Shane*, or *The Westerner*—even as it makes a unique statement. Since we have experienced similar representations in the codes of plot, typography, and dress, we have already a sense of how to approach and interpret the movie we are watching. Even more striking, a film that both makes such references and plays against them—*Django Unchained* is a good example of this in the Western genre—has a powerful effect upon our conceptions. The contrasting ways by which conventions can provoke responses illustrate how generic expectations do not prescribe what we will understand in a specific film but rather how they offer parameters within which our imaginations can work. Nonetheless, recognizing those iconographic affinities remains an important interpretive gesture.

3. **What key concern shapes the narrative?** In classic Hollywood cinema, the issue or problem that drives the action of a motion picture has a pronounced impact on all other elements shaping one's interpretation. In John Ford's *The Quiet Man*, for instance, the central character, Sean Thornton (John Wayne), makes it clear from the beginning that he is returning to Ireland seeking respite from his brutal life in America. (The quest nicely mirrors and contrasts Dorothy's quest in *The Wizard of Oz*.) He is determined to see his birthplace, Innismore, as an Edenic alternative to the city where he grew to manhood, Pittsburgh, with its hellish steel mills. Local residents have their own view of Innisfree, and their responses to Thornton's attitudes range from bemused tolerance to sardonic dismissal.

In *The Quiet Man*, however, Ford also uses sets and setting as a skillful suggestion of the complexities imbedded in its thematic issues. Early on, for example, when Sean Thornton pauses on a scene stone bridge to look at his parents' former home, the establishing shots are all clearly set outdoors. (Ford filmed his exteriors on location in Cong, Ireland.) However, the close ups of John Wayne, the actor who plays Thornton, recalling his mother's sentimental memories of Ireland were clearly shot on a soundstage. The visual artificiality erodes some of the legitimacy of Thornton's ingenuous feelings. For their part, viewers may choose to interpret this image in a serious, a comic, or an ironic fashion—or even in some mixture of each. In any case, the response viewers make to the Irish landscape that is now identified as a central feature of the film is inexorably influenced by our interpretations of Thornton's dreams and aspirations. The rolling panoramas continually remind us of Thornton's quest, and challenge us to affirm or to deny its efficacy. The one thing we cannot do is ignore its centrality to the analytic process.

Sean Thornton (John Wayne) and Mary Kate Danaher (Maureen O'Hara) in *The Quiet Man* (1952).

4. What attitudes or assumptions does the narrative foster? The way that we understand the plot, especially as it is initially presented, raises specific expectations that shape our subsequent assessments of the characters and the action. In the opening of *The Untouchables*, for example, a Capone henchman, after Frank Nitti (Billy Drago), menaces a speakeasy owner. After he goes, viewers see a young girl holding a satchel, left behind by Nitti, just before it explodes in front of the speakeasy. The sympathy that this emotional (some might go so far as to say manipulative) representation creates for Eliot Ness (Kevin Cosner) and his men and the concomitant abhorrence that it generates for Nitti, Al Capone (Robert Di Nero) and the rest of his gang inform the viewer's judgments for the remainder of the film. Consequently, when Ness and others operate outside the law by going so far as to make members of the Capone gang victims of felonies, our opinions of either group remain the same. For instance, in the climactic scene in which Ness kills Frank Nitti in cold blood by throwing him off the roof of the Chicago Criminal Courts Building, Ness' act completely reverses the behavior that viewers would typically expect from confrontation between a criminal and an officer of the law. Brian de Palma, the film's director, has invited us to see mitigating circumstances by having Nitti mock Ness over the death of his friend, Jim Malone (Sean Connery), and has suggested an emotional distance to events by having Ness flippantly describe Nitti's whereabouts after throwing him off the roof: "He's in the car." (The location of the gangster's body is on top of a vehicle in the street below.) Nonetheless, a full interpretation keeps in mind a film's manipulative tendencies.

5. What salient details advance our understanding? Because of the way narrative unfolds in a movie, its details not only condition our sense of a particular scene but go on to shape our overall response to the film. In *The Sting*, for example, viewers quickly understand the central issue that drives the action—the need to find a way to gain revenge, through trickery, on a violent and unpredictable character. Early on the film signals the pattern of deception that characterizes everything the main characters do. Harry Gondorff (Paul Newman) shows Johnny Hooker (Robert Redford) how to appear to other card players to be drinking straight gin when in fact consuming a watered down concoction only mildly alcoholic. As plans to implement the deception of this individual move forward, the complexity of the preparations—enlisting confederates, finding the appropriate props and locations, charting the movements of various characters involved—provides as much entertainment as will the successful conclusion of these efforts. (Indeed, any filmgoer familiar with the genre will anticipate the outcome of the action, and therefore will derive more pleasure from understanding how it comes about than from the finale, which he or she intuited from the start.) At the end of the film, when Gondorff and Hooker rise up after apparently being shot and killed, they are simply playing out the patterns of illusion and trickery introduced early in the narrative. The more aware the viewer becomes of the function of details surrounding the sting, the more satisfying the viewing of its dramatic enactment will be.

6. How do the characters function? The representation of characters within a film is informed but not prescribed by the central feature of classic Hollywood cinema: the problem. To comprehend the behavior of Ripley (Sigourney Weaver) in *Alien*, for example, we relate her role to the problem of dealing with the ravenous creature found roaming through the ship that hurtling through space. We may begin by contextualizing Ripley through the first dramatic encounter, and the one that precipitates the central problem of the film. When Dallas (Tom Skerritt) and Lambert (Veronica Cartwright) attempt to bring the injured Kane (John Hurt) back to the ship, Ripley refuses to let them past the airlock. She steadfastly follows established procedures to prevent contamination. When she is undermined by Ash (Ian Holm) simply opening the hull door, we see the frustration she will face throughout the film as she struggles to impose the rule of order over that of emotion. The complexity of Ripley's experiences and the ambivalence that she expresses toward the mission and toward those who undertake its execution open several possible options for reading her character, but they all relate to the central concern of how to survive in this hostile environment. (A feminist interpretation that takes gender conventions and conflicts into account further enhances and complicates one's interpretation.)

At the same time, while the threat of extermination posed by the voracious creatures encountered on the ship intensifies individual assessments of Ripley, it does not in itself cause us to see her in a particular fashion. In fact, while the solution to the central problem—how to escape from or destroy the predatory alien—stands as fairly cut and dry, the path to resolution offers multiple interpretive possibilities. In the end, Ripley's willingness to improvise to survive suggests a reversal in attitudes.

7. What are the extra-textual ramifications? The impact of the cultural context of the film upon the story and the characters demands some consideration. The movie *Animal House* succeeds to a large degree because of the brilliant characterizations of individuals like Larry Kroger (Tom Hulce), Dean Wormer (John Vernon), Bluto (John Belushi), and any number of others. Much of their comedic appeal, however, emerges from the atmosphere that surrounds them at the fictional Faber College and the small town in which it is located. In scene after scene, the film evokes and parodies cultural attitudes of the early 1960s. The motion picture derives its humor from the way that characters play off these attitudes, and our assessment of figures in it turns upon their own willingness to defy or conform to the conventional mores established by the narrative.

Any sophisticated film will presents a myriad of complex cultural details. The erudite viewer has become adept at identifying the significance of these details and arranging them in a meaningful fashion. What this question aims to do is break down the way that arrangement occurs so that readers will come away with a clearer sense of how they come to understand films.

One

Once Upon a Time in the West
Westerns

A General Sense of the Genre

From the release in 1903 of *The Great Train Robbery*, through John Ford's cavalry trilogy of the late 1940s and early 1950s, to Scott Cooper's 2018 production, *Hostiles*, filmmakers insistently reinforce the idea that the Western stands as a quintessentially American form of motion picture. It is tied to the distinctive geography of the North American continent. It sets its action against the background of United States history over a period roughly dating from the late eighteenth to the end of the nineteenth century. And it highlights popular assumptions, beliefs, and perceptions that grew out of the cultural community of nineteenth-century America and that, however anachronistic they may seem to some contemporary viewers, continue to shape our sense of ourselves.

Bandit (Justin D. Barnes) in *The Great Train Robbery* (1903).

The Physical World

The range of diverse and panoramic settings which one encounters in Westerns emphasize a sense of the awe-inspiring power of the land. Though generally concentrating on the Great Plains, the Southwest, and to a lesser degree Texas, filmmakers also set Westerns in the Pacific Northwest, the Black Hills of the Dakotas, and even across the borders to Canada and Mexico. The breadth and diversity of that area produce a multiplicity of geographic features. (A few films that otherwise qualify as Westerns—like *Drums along the Mohawk*, *The Fighting Kentuckian*, and *The Last of the Mohicans* in any of the versions, 1920, 1936, 1970, or 1992—take place east of the Mississippi in the late eighteenth or early nineteenth century, but these are the exceptions that prove the rule.) As noted in the introduction, John Ford's motion pictures made Monument Valley synonymous with the Western landscape. Likewise, the vast open space of the Great Plains, the majesty of the Rocky Mountains, and the arid pueblos of the Southwest have also become signature locations.

The viewer's full sense of this world, however, goes beyond its materiality. The sheer size of the West conveys a vast sense of emptiness that creates a profound feeling of human isolation, both from the terrain and from the other creatures inhabiting it. However, as any number of filmmakers have demonstrated, that impression of immensity does not immediately stipulate a single response. Indeed, the striking features of the topography alternately highlights both the independence and the vulnerability of those who occupy this space. Thus, an image of an imposing mesa in the middle of a flat vista invites a range of impressionistic responses to the isolation, grandeur, and ominous tone of the country. A shot of a rolling prairie, a mountain crag, or a river canyon can induce the same effect. The viewer might easily see these panoramas as indicative of an individual's safety from the intrusive demands of society or read them as evidence of a person's vulnerability amid such awe-inspiring landscapes (*Jeremiah Johnson*).

In addition to location, the climate serves as a key factor in the Western. Scenes of the oppressive heat in the great deserts, the astounding violence of storms on the plains, and the suffocating weight of mountain snow punctuate Westerns, and relentlessly redefine the position of humans in this world. The colossal aspects of the weather remind viewers of the relatively diminutive position of the players on the screen even as this environment underscores their courageousness in facing such extremes (*The Revenant*).

Like the setting, the distinctive costumes of individuals in Westerns invite us to make associations specific to the genre. No one can see John Wayne on a poster advertising *Rio Bravo* and doubt for a moment the type of picture being promoted. The Stetson hat, the leather vest, the boots and spurs, and, most of all, the gun belt and Winchester proclaim a cinematic world unique to the Western genre.

These items are not simply the accessories of a particular culture. They are the articles needed to define one's nature and to make one's way in this world of very specific demands and conditions. Even the clothes of characters appearing in films set on the plains of Africa, in the rain forests of South America, or on the outback of Australia do not convey the same assertive cultural presence that one sees in the cowboy couture. Heroes, villains, and ambivalent characters: while their moral dispositions may vary radically, their clothes assert that all are firmly located within the same highly specific cultural system of values.

The historical setting (as distinct from the physical one) also remains an important if implicit influence on this categorization. With the exceptions noted above of films dealing with discrete events, like a campaign in the French and Indian Wars or the siege of the Alamo, Westerns mainly fall in the period between the end of the Civil War and 1900. A few—like *The Wild Bunch, Butch Cassidy and the Sundance Kid, McCabe & Mrs. Miller,* or *The Shootist*—straddle the two centuries, but, when they do, they emphasize a sad, even nostalgic, perspective that laments the passing of an era. Films located in the West but taking place significantly after the turn of the century—like *Giant, Hud, The Last Picture Show, Raising Arizona, Blood Simple,* or *No Country for Old Men*—almost always fall into other generic categories, though associations with the Western, intended and unintended, inevitably accrue.[1]

The distinction remains important. The distance between the Western's time period and the viewer's day-to-day experiences fosters a romantic conception of the characters and events in these movies not immediately evident in other types of motion pictures. Even films offering a sardonic representation of the genre's ethos, like the so-called spaghetti Westerns of director Sergio Leone, derive their corrosive force from the romantic expectations that adhere to this format.

Cultural and Aesthetic Context

The material presence of the West in many of these motion pictures can lead one to forget the pivotal function of imaginative license in the structuring narratives in this genre. Directors and actors from the 1960s and 1970s—Sergio Leone, Sam Peckinpah, and Clint Eastwood, to name just a few—have contributed to an evolving concept of the complex ethos of Westerns.[2] However, all of these men owe the inspiration for their work to the great actors and directors of the twenty-year period from the late 1930s to the late 1950s—like Howard Hawks, Fred Zinneman, John Ford, Gary Cooper, Henry Fonda, James Stewart, and of course John Wayne. They showed how imaginative approaches could both fulfill generic expectations and create unique narratives.

The impact of early filmmakers is such that any Western produced since the end of the Eisenhower era, while by no means committed to replicating the features of the early classics, cannot escape comparison to the model established well over half a century ago. Some motion pictures—like *Once Upon a Time in the West*—present this quite starkly as a struggle between civilization and savagery, but the finest Westerns take this conflict even further to explore the psychological, emotional, and moral fissures within the seemingly homogeneous society that claims the allegiance of the central character. In *The Ox-Bow Incident*, for example, the conflict turns on value systems in flux, and it features individuals struggling to decide when traditional values must be enforced and when they must be cast aside to accommodate demands of expediency and a

Clint Eastwood in *A Fistful of Dollars* (1967) demonstrating how he succeeded John Wayne as the prototypical Western hero.

mistrust of established institutions. (In a neat reversal, in the earlier film, Henry Fonda plays a young cowboy deeply conflicted by contrasting values. In the later one, Fonda is an aged, villain with no concern for morality.)

Like accounts based upon the myths of other eras, the narrative of a Western outlines an implied or overt quest seeking affirmation of the putative values of society. As a film like *The Searchers* makes abundantly clear, however, the nature of that quest and the values informing it are continually under threat of revision. Ethan Edwards (John Wayne), in his obsessive commitment to finding his niece who has been carried off by Comanches represents both a man determined to uphold personal values that have become corroded by racism and self-hatred. He barely bothers to conceal the lust he feels for his brother's wife. He reflexively bullies those weaker than himself, and celebrates strength over intelligence, compassion, or empathy.

Ethan's behavior, in fact, parallels that of his nemesis, Scar, the Comanche who led the raid on his brother's ranch. In consequence, viewers cannot admire Ethan without implicitly endorsing the character of Scar. Nor can they condemn Scar's behavior without opening Ethan's char-

Ethan Edwards (John Wayne) in *The Searchers* (1956).

acter to the same judgment. (Ethan's eventual acceptance of his niece who has been a Comanche captive for five years seems an artificial change illogical in light of his behavior throughout the rest of the narrative.) At the film's end, standing framed by the ranch house door but not invited to enter, he is cut off from the society that ostensibly celebrates his manliness. He is a bitter parody of the ideal of rugged individualism that animates so many Western characters.

At the same time, one cannot simply dismiss the conventional value system at the heart of the genre: one that privileges honesty, morality, and courage. Even in motion pictures that putatively critique this code with individuals seemingly operating either marginally or completely outside this code—like *A Fistful of Dollars*—the central characters fall back into patterns of heroic behavior—gestures, often fatally doomed from the start, that nonetheless assert a commitment to the moral code of behavior that defines their identities. In this fashion, the narrative of the Western benefits greatly from its willingness to incorporate conflicting impulses within the mythic format.

Key Elements in Plot and Characterization

However one perceives its mythic overlay, the follows the classic Hollywood cinema narrative formula laid out in the introduction. It organizes the action around a central problem or issue that drives the action of the film. This condition in turn influences the representation of characters whose natures evolve in response to the problem. And finally, whatever subplots arise do so in relation to that central issue.

In any Western, very specific imaginative principles shape the construction of the narrative, and, with some variation, its plot unfolds with a comfortable predictability. The key issue in this type of film will almost always turn on a clash of societal values. It may be seen in the unbending, prescriptive ethos of the East running up against the necessarily more pragmatic mores of the West. It may become apparent in the confrontation between the domesticating impulses of a person from town trying to curtail the independence of someone accustomed to the freedom accorded by the isolation of the plains. It may be embodied in the more dangerous clash between one way of life and another—farmers and ranchers, bandits and peace officers, cowboys and sheepmen, cavalry and indigenous peoples, and numerous other polarities—each seeking control over the same space, the same institutions, or even the same people. Whatever the issue is that provokes it, in every case an unmistakable turbulence of conflicting values roils the narrative of every Western.

In such a world of emergence and struggle, labels—especially as applied to individuals—become more and more important for enforcing a measure of stability, just as they provoke variable responses from viewer to viewer. Even pejorative terms like tinhorn, drifter, gunslinger, half-breed, tenderfoot, and dancehall girl give people a handy reference point for categorizing and understanding one another. At the same time, as Westerns relentlessly demonstrate, these designations inevitably oversimplify the nature of major and minor characters, provoking misperceptions that sometimes produce catastrophic results.

The distinctiveness of individuals becomes most apparent in any interpretive efforts to distinguish good from evil, particularly because of the way those concepts regularly shift within the framework of the genre. As often as not, conventional institutions—the Church, the legal system, even the family—prove inadequate to the task of offering useful moral direction or social guidance in a turbulent and unpredictable world. Instead, personal inclinations, sometimes seemingly little more than instinctual responses, serve as the forces driving behavior.

Individuals may offer lip service to essentialist ideals, those rigidly defined standards of behavior imposed without regard for their stereotypical connotations. More often than not, however, one comes to understand the values embraced by the central characters and to delineate the guidelines that the plot offers for judging their actions through a complicated series of incidents that underscore the way conflicting principles within the Western ethos clash. Thus, at the beginning of a film, goodness and evil may seem easily discernable traits, but, as the narrative unfolds, individualism—often synonymous with self-interest—blurs the distinctions.

The narrative of a Western will often highlight the relativism of ostensibly definitive values by embodying the impulse to resolve moral ambiguities within the struggles of its central character. Often this is a figure like Alan Ladd's title character in *Shane*. In that film, he uneasily straddles the physical, spiritual, and emotional division between the paradigmatic Anglo-American communities of settlers that he encounters and the untamed world that circumscribes it.

While films in many other genres self-consciously contrast the attitudes and behavior of the central figure with those of society as a whole, the Western makes a more refined distinction. There, the central figures do not simply strain against the limits of society—as is the case in Gangster

Joey Starrett (Brandon de Wilde, left) and Shane (Alan Ladd) in *Shane* (1953).

films, for example—or self-consciously move to its margins—as in Film Noir. Rather, in the Western they oscillate between the polarities of civilization and savagery, and more often than not show equal sympathy for both. As a result, characters endeavor, often with only mixed success, to reconcile opposing values through synthesis, or at the very least, mutual accommodation.

One sees this in the popular perceptions imposed upon John Wayne based upon an amalgamated sense of the characters he often portrayed. Ignoring both American history and the range of roles taken by Wayne, contemporary Americans who seek to identify with what they presume to be the Western ideals more often than not have a highly reductive sense of the values professed by his characters. Those who celebrate the unswerving probity of "the Duke" (a nickname that John Wayne favored throughout his film career) often forget the confused and tortured nature that highlighted his portrayal of emotionally crippled Ethan Edwards in *The Searchers* or the self-destructive, megalomaniacal impulses that gave a tragic quality to his depiction of Thomas Dunson in *Red River*. Even as the Ringo Kid in *Stagecoach*, a film discussed in detail later in the chapter, his character evinces at best a highly subjective sense of right and wrong.

This moral ambivalence within a so-called Western paragon is nowhere more apparent than in the movies that Wayne made late in his career—*True Grit, The Cowboys, The Shootist,* and *Rooster Cogburn*. Each motion picture flirts alternately with parody and self-aggrandizement, but all offer interesting comments on the way that Wayne and his contemporaries like James Stewart (who appeared with Wayne in *The Shootist* and earlier in *The Man Who Shot Liberty Valance*) and directors like John Ford, Don Siegel, and Howard Hawks shaped viewers' perceptions of the genre while tempting the hasty to oversimplified generalizations. In fact, as Wayne and other actors show in their fine performances, the most interesting figures in Westerns are not those blindly adhering to simplistic codes of behavior but rather those who confront the limitations of their values and struggle to find accommodation within the world around them.

The unique position occupied in Westerns by this central figure and his (or much less frequently her) distinct relationship to competing worlds encompasses a variety of attitudes and enables a range of figures to assume this role: marshal, outlaw, rancher, farmer, cavalryman, native American, drifter, townsman. The dominating feature of their identities, however, remains consistent: they take the position of a moral sounding board within the film. This does not mean that they are the most virtuous individuals in the cast of characters. Rather, it underscores the fact that their position on the margins of both worlds gives them the best ability to highlight and at times to resolve the central issues that propel the narratives.

In a manner similar to the Film Noir hero I will discuss in Chapter Three, in the Western, the misfit/hero derives identity and worth from the ideals of the world from which he nonetheless segregates himself. He adheres to societal values that are often mocked or at the very least ignored by the more pragmatic behavior of the community around him. In extreme cases, the Western hero cannot bear the double standard and abandons communal life. This makes him indisputably the product of a particular time and place but, at the same time, not a figure molded by the exigencies of that world. (Superheroes—Batman, Superman, Spiderman—find themselves in exactly this situation, and as a result their films are often represented as mixed-genres.)

In fact, the main character's uniquely Western values—mixing loyalty and individualism, courage and discretion, pride and diffidence—underscore his distinctiveness and shape his responses to whatever specific issue propels the action. Often a veneer of coarseness makes his principles difficult to discern immediately. Indeed, we generally find the actions of the central figure conditioned by the untamed habits that society seeks to banish. On the occasions when he does become domesticated, a sense of defeat, even if understated, informs the film's conclusion. Most importantly, in almost every instance, he mediates between the conventional distinctions of savagery and civilization, presenting an alternative to the extremes of each.

Because isolation features so prominently in this definition of identity, villains in Westerns often prove difficult to distinguish from heroes. Both manifest individualism antipathetic to the communal mentality of most other figures in the film. Both operate on the margins of a society that could not accommodate the extremes of either personality. Indeed, films like *Tombstone, The Good, the Bad, and the Ugly*, and *Pat Garret and Billy the Kid* all feature central characters whose defining traits put them closer to the antagonists who confront them than to the communities that witness their struggles. Additionally, as in *My Darling Clementine*, the society represented in Westerns manifests, at best, the flawed embodiment of the hero's ideals. Because, like the villain, he cannot compromise, he remains on its periphery, where we find Rooster Cogburn in *True Grit*.

This begs the question, what does distinguish the heroes and the villains? In the end, it is the same feature that drives the plot: the civilizing impulse. Villains in Westerns do not simply resist the social values of civilization. They give no indication that they feel any attraction whatsoever for the rewards that society offers to those who assume the guise of upright individual. Indeed, like the gangsters of the next chapter, they derive a distinct advantage from ignoring the social restraints that appear to guide everyone else's behavior. The hero, on the other hand, may never accept socialization by the frontier community, but he acknowledges the value of its ideal form even as he often rejects the less than ideal manifestations of it. (I will return to this distinction in the next section of this chapter when discussing the concept of rugged individualism.)

Issues

As noted earlier, with a few exceptions, Westerns take place in the mid-to late nineteenth-century. They coincide with the era of the massive transcontinental migration propelled by the alternately optimistic and desperate expectations of the European-Americans who crossed the country: It was an America fleeing the psychological trauma of the aftermath of the Civil War and at the same time buoyed by the optimistic belief in the opportunity for a new beginning in a world untroubled by the restraints and problems of the East. Such conditions created an oscillating mindset of profound insecurity battling with ebullient self-confidence.

The primary concept shaping this world was an endorsement, sometimes casually implicit and at other times ferociously explicit, of the idea of Manifest Destiny, the nineteenth-century belief in the inevitable and morally justifiable expansion of the territorial boundaries of the United States to encompass the entire continent. Although the unapologetic chauvinism in *How the West Was Won* presents this view most directly, this presumption of entitlement informs almost any film involving migration, occupation, or domination of the land. In the most simplistic renditions, a missionary-like zeal characterizes this movement, presenting itself as bringing civilization to a savage land, and it puts the putative civilizers in opposition to everything they encounter. This dichotomy appears most starkly in settlers-versus-Native Americans movies, but even the films that pit cattlemen, miners, farmers, or sheepmen against one another— for example, *Shane*, *Heaven's Gate*, or *Pale Rider*—express the struggle in terms of the inevitable advance and evolution of civilization opposed by those committed to conditions as they are. The few motion pictures that sympathetically examine the consequences for earlier inhabitants of this seemingly irresistible force for change—*Dances with Wolves*, *A Man Called Horse*, and *Broken Arrow* are three notable examples—generally lament the loss of the indigenous way of life, but do not refute the logic that impels characters moving toward change.

Corollaries of Manifest Destiny emerged as the concepts of Rugged Individualism and the Bootstrap Theory which idealize self-sufficient determinism and presume that anyone who embraces a life of diligence and hard work will have a chance for success equal to anyone else's. Their buoyant sense of optimism makes these views seem attractive. At the same time, one needs to consider carefully the implications that turn these views into a determined pursuit of self-interest.

Rugged Individualism and the Bootstrap theory legitimize an overall approach that enables its possessor to operate successfully, free of restraints imposed by society, in any endeavor. Indeed, it becomes a point of honor to do so. Nonetheless, the inclination towards self-absorption can lead to alienation. The rugged individual must retain at least an emotional attachment to that society or run the risk of becoming a renegade. This creates a paladin-like mentality (the name self-consciously adopted

Stands with a Fist (Mary McDonnell) and Lt. Dunbar (Kevin Costner) in *Dances with Wolves* (1990).

by the complex gunfighter played by Richard Boone in the popular 1950s television series *Have Gun, Will Travel*). At its best, as embodied by James Stewart as Lin McAdam in *Winchester '73*, whose independence embraces an implicit obligation to uphold a moral position even in an atmosphere of cynicism and relativism. At its worst, this inclination produces a tyrannical determination to impose his views upon the community, like Judge Roy Bean (Walter Brennan) in *The Westerner*.

In its most positive representation, the Rugged Individual stands apart from society but never feels indifferent to it. There this empathy for communal values, rather than a strict adherence to them, serves as an important feature distinguishing heroes from villains in classic Westerns, where frequently the difference between the two does not rest upon clearly defined legal statutes. Instead, these labels testify to a willingness to assert independence while safeguarding those unwilling or unable to defend their own rights. A film like *Hombre* puts both the heroic stance of John Russell (Paul Newman) and the villainous one of Grimes (Richard Boone) outside the communal patterns of behavior. Russell, however, retains a regard for the abstract virtues of society while Grimes contemptuously preys upon its material weaknesses.

This conflicted impulse to remain outside the community while endorsing, from that position, concepts of integration and collective achievement becomes most evident in the way that Westerns affirm the American Dream, the rags-to-riches imagery that holds out the promise that anyone has a chance for personal success. Films from *The Virginian* to *Wyatt Earp* feature characters who see America as a place where the individual can rise through determination, ambition, and courage. Occasionally, movies like *The Magnificent Seven* also emphasize the need for the individual to act within the community, especially in the face of a hostile environment that is both natural and man-made. More often than not, however, one finds the protagonist working in isolation self-consciously outside the system. Consequently, for most motion pictures in this genre what sets the central character's actions apart from renegades and desperadoes comes not so much from an inclination for violating rules but from a motivating idealism that other, more cynical, characters do not share.

The source of uneasiness in the relationship between the hero of a Western and the society that surrounds him turns on the force that shapes most of the action. More than any other genre, save perhaps Gangster films, violence stands as a key factor driving the development of the Western narrative. It occupies a paradoxical role in its effect upon the tempo and direction of everyday life, both accelerating the course of events and paralyzing ordinary activity. Violence remains abhorrent to the society that champions the orderly routine of communities seeking to tame savagery. At the same time, it functions as an inherently necessary response to the chaos that individuals encounter in a new environment seemingly without laws or ethical standards.

More insidiously, Westerns often suggest that violence represents the natural response to the challenges one faces. It lurks beneath society's surface in a Darwinian "survival of the fittest" representation of the chauvinistic philosophy of Manifest Destiny and the slightly more benevolent Bootstrap Theory of achievement. In short, violence asserts itself as the most prominent characteristic in defining the Western ethos, even as it stands out as the element whose features society continually strives to efface. Assessing the function and legitimacy of violence in a Western stands as an ongoing challenge for every viewer.

However, change in the Western community or in the individual does not inevitably come about through physical force, for the genre also continually endorses the concepts of emergence, rebirth, and transformation. The West embodies possibilities, the chance for peoples to recreate themselves. In consequence, the notion of identity becomes a fluid matter. On the one hand, in a land of possibilities a man or a woman can leave behind the characterizing features of the East and take on new roles. On the other hand, the provisional nature of so many of the social institutions that have sprung up in this new environment continually erodes a stable sense of self. As a result, flux is the paradoxically consistent feature within the Western narrative.

Indeed, Westerns espouse a range of attitudes and opinions often far less conservative, in the sense of the term connoting stability and resistance to change, and more unpredictable than many modern viewers realize. In a film seemingly dominated by stereotypes and clichés, John Ford's *The Man Who Shot Liberty Valence*, a subversive dialectic invites viewers to look beyond the dominant chauvinism and see an insistent critique of sexism, hierarchy, hypocrisy, and racism: The typical Western hero, Tom Doniphon played by John Wayne, triumphs over Liberty Valence, the archetypal badman, played by Lee Marvin, by shooting him from ambush. The idealistic Easterner, Ransom Stoddard played by James Stewart, finds that the values of society have no impact in a violent world and in the end gains acclaim through a misappropriated act of heroism. Hallie Stoddard (Vera Miles) chooses the man who teaches her to read over the Western type who aspires to be the patriarch. And, in every scene in which he appears, Pompey (Woody Strode) the black servant of Doniphon consistently shows more dignity and understanding than his employer. The inherent ambiguity of the film's narrative is summed up in a single phrase when Maxwell Scott (Carlton Young) says after interviewing Stoddard: "When the legend becomes fact, print the legend." Whether or not Ford intended to challenge so many assumptions about Western archetypes is unimportant. The ability of sophisticated moviegoers to apply a nuanced interpretation shows the strength of the narrative in resisting any single point of view as the dominant reading.

Specific Application

Despite the subgroups identified within this chapter, a fundamental structure for narrative and characterization that varies little from picture to picture emerges for Westerns. One sees in *Stagecoach*, *High Noon*, and *Unforgiven* essentially the same story of struggle for self-definition by a character keenly aware of the demands of the world around him. All three films show a person seeking to uphold a system of values, albeit often highly subjective, while at the same time following fundamental instincts for preservation in a hostile environment. Violence remains a common feature in all three. What distinguishes these motion pictures and each of the sub-groups they represent from one another is the moral foundation that provides the basis for the central character's self-identification.

That is to say, each film represents a different approach to justice and community by the individual who chooses to oppose a strong, malevolent force that acts as a law unto itself and in every case because of these choices finds himself outside the boundaries of society. In *Stagecoach*, men have murdered The Ringo Kid's father and brother with impunity, and Ringo undertakes the task of meting out the justice that the legal system has failed to administer. In *High Noon* the Miller gang challenges the efficacy of broadly accepted civic values, and, despite being killed in the process, their threat exposes the town's hypocrisy and lack of real commitment to those values. *Unforgiven* offers a starker and at the same time more complex moral struggle grounded on the uneven, idiosyncratic application of communal values, and it challenges the viewer to judge the appropriateness of applying any ethical code within the Western genre.

Stagecoach

This motion picture was produced in 1939 under the direction of John Ford. It featured a highly respected cast—including Claire Trevor, Thomas Mitchell, John Carradine, and Andy Devine—in a story that highlights the promised potential for change that makes life in the West attractive. *Stagecoach* marked the emergence of John Wayne from parts in B-films (he had already appeared in over eighty movies in this category) to a role that gave him the status of a bona fide Hollywood star. The film relies on conventional Western costumes and props and a montage emblematic of the Western's landscape to establish a sense of place in the minds of viewers. However, it does so through a narrative that examines key features of the highly complex social structures at the heart of every Western to forestall simplistic generalizations about characterization and action.

The movie's opening shots—with the backdrop of Monument Valley, the scene of the cavalry camp, and the image of the telegraph line that ceases transmission after sending a single, fateful word, "Geronimo"—invoke familiar iconographic markers signifying the isolation and vulnerability of those living in the West. First impressions in any motion picture can hold a great deal of significance, but these initial scenes in particular allow one to explore just how viewers respond to the Western genre. Each is suggestive without being prescriptive. Each image relies upon impressions that viewers bring to the film to create a complete meaning. And opportunities to review the impressions derived from each will recur over the course of the motion picture in a fashion that underscores the complex attitudes being explored in the movie.

Stagecoach moves from simplicity to complexity in a deliberate, methodical fashion. It first introduces a series of characters living on the margins of society who at first glance reflect little more than stereotypes. When the stage which gives the movie its title leaves the town of Tonto, its passenger list contains a cross-section of failures, scoundrels, and outcasts: Dallas (Claire Trevor), a prostitute; Hatfield (John Carradine), a gambler; and Josiah Boone (Thomas Mitchell), a drunken physician—"the dregs of the town" by Doc Boone's own admission. As a counter balance

Stagecoach (1939): (left to right) Samuel Peacock (Donald Meek), The Ringo Kid (John Wayne), Buck (Andy Devine), Dallas (Claire Trevor), Marshal Curley Wilcox (George Bancroft), Lucy Malory (Louise Platt), Lt. Blanchard (Tim Holt), Sgt. Billy Pickett (Francis Ford), Ellsworth Henry Gatewood (Burton Churchill), Hatfield (John Carradine), and Josiah Boone (Thomas Mitchell).

it also presents a cross-section of what the town would call respectable society: Lucy Mallory (Louise Platt), the pregnant wife of a cavalry officer; Henry Gatewood (Berton Churchill), a banker; Samuel Peacock (Donald Meek), a timid whiskey salesman; Curly Wilcox (George Bancroft), the sheriff; and Buck (Andy Devine), the stagecoach driver.

Though this film and others in this subgroup play upon such types to establish both communal parameters and a social pecking order, their subsequent action always tests the efficacy of hasty generalizations based upon such constructions. Much of what follows in *Stagecoach* highlights the abilities of marginalized figures to form an effective, if transitory, community more adept at providing nurture and identity than the established cultures from which the characters have fled or have been expelled. Additionally, the film explores the questions of how far individuals can go in recreating themselves within this evolving society and of how permanent such recreations will be.

The belief that misfits, or at the very least marginalized individuals, have the ability to come together to form a community equal or superior to the seemingly legitimate society of the town propels the narrative action throughout this subgroup. Films like *Silverado*, *Posse*, and *The Angel and the Badman* all valorize this concept. Because whatever triumphs these groups realize often prove to be transient, their achievements highlight the fact that the ideals valorized, often in name only, by more established societies lack the lasting cohesive force many assume them to have.

Films in this subgroup always begin by emphasizing the initial isolation of these marginalized individuals. This occurs abruptly in *Stagecoach* with in the expulsion of Dallas and Doc Boone from Tonto. In short order, the narrative quickly introduces a factor that precipitate the move toward community. It might seem to be the shared threat from Geronimo's marauders, but in fact it comes from a surprisingly benevolent source, an outlaw who has recently escaped from prison and boards the stage after it has left town. The Ringo Kid (John Wayne) is a young man whose incarceration at the age of seventeen makes him understandably unaware of the nuances of social intercourse. He enters the group with a keen sense of his status as an outsider but also with a natural equanimity that makes him blithely ignorant of the subtler cultural and class distinctions observed by others. This proves an essential trait for advancing the action.

Ringo becomes a catalyst. In his repeated efforts to insure that Dallas receives the same treatment as Lucy Mallory, he shakes the complacent social stratification that had settled on the party. After the gambler Hatfield has given water to Mrs. Mallory, Ringo asks, "Ain't you forgetting the other lady?" While his behavior at first may seem cloyingly ingenuous, in fact, Ringo embodies the power of characters in Westerns to reconfigure perceptions of the world to suit their current needs. When Dallas presses him about his ignorance of her past, he replies, "I know all I wanna to know." Over the course of the film not just Ringo the escaped convict, but Dallas the prostitute, Hatfield the gambler, and Doc Boone the drunkard all redefine themselves by being able to demonstrate their value to this makeshift community. In doing so, they challenge the legitimacy of the unshakeable convictions that gave the so-called respectable ladies of Tonto the moral authority to condemn these characters early in the film.

Negotiating cultural differences to reach satisfactory social accommodations is a theme repeatedly asserted in this type of Western. In *She Wore a Yellow Ribbon*, ex-Confederates join with troops who served on the Union side during the Civil War to form a formidable cavalry unit. In *The Cowboys*, an aging rancher molds a band of children into a group of ranch hands able not only to do the daily work of tending cattle but also to regain the herd after it has been stolen by bandits. Perhaps most uniquely, in *Red River* a more complex process unfolds. First Tom Dunson (John Wayne) shapes the loosely knit group of cowboys into a community dominated by his authoritarian ways. Then his foster son Matt (Montgomery Clift) reconfigures the group into a more egalitarian society. In some way all of these instances echo the experiences of the travelers between Tonto and Lordsburg. Mutual dependence eventually overcomes initial obstacles to facilitated co-operation, but with the community based upon contingency there is often little indication that it will survive beyond immediate needs.

Stagecoach reminds viewers of the haphazard, even capricious, nature of Western societies. The passengers are thrown together by the coincidence of the decision each has made to travel at that time. Their interactions are affected not only by their personalities but also by the events that overtake them: the difficulty of travel over rough terrain, the danger of attack from Apache war parties, and the birth of Mrs. Mallory's daughter. While they learn a measure of tolerance and experience the benefits of cooperation as they commiserate over the discomforts of the trail, see that the mother and child are safe, and fight off the attack by hostiles, the question of whether they coalesce as a community remains open to interpretation, and therein lies the film's great achievement.

When the cavalry saves the coach from the indigenous marauders, *Stagecoach* seems in danger of coming to a stereotypical Western ending. However, Ringo's determination to go on to Lordsburg to kill the men who murdered his father and brother not only continues the action, it disrupts any effort to come to an easy resolution of the central issues. This determination to pursue a vendetta reminds viewers of the anarchy just below the surface of the world of the Western and of the still only sporadically successful efforts of its social institutions to impose order and justice.

Civilization itself seems at best an impermanent and superficial condition. At first glance, Lordsburg appears as open and raucous as Tonto was law-abiding and tranquil, yet parallels between the two obtain. In many ways, the same narrowness and intolerance characterize the dominant attitudes in both settlements. One can see them as alternative versions of the same corrupting aspect of urban life when contrasted with the liberating experience of living on the range.

Indeed, the practical and compassionate approach to justice and fairness that the makeshift community of travelers employed seemingly has no place in bastions of civilization. The Ringo Kid can find justice for the murder of his father and brother only by shooting down their killers. The sheriff of Tonto, Curley, who has sworn to arrest Ringo, in part at least because he fears that The Kid will die trying to avenge his loss, allows him to go free, presumably because Ringo, having survived the shoot-out, is no longer in danger. By the conclusion of the movie, the narrative leaves the viewer with the message that one can only escape the corrupting elements of society by fleeing from civilization. For those familiar with this type of Western, it is hardly an unexpected gesture.

Such films commonly have characters turning their backs on established communities. Shane, in the movie of the same name, leaves the farm of the family who took him in once the cattle baron has been defeated. Ethan Edwards, in *The Searchers*, returns to the wilderness once his niece has been brought home. And perhaps most famously, John Dunbar (Kevin Costner) in *Dances with Wolves* achieves a full sense of his humanity and an awareness of community only when free of civilization's formal trappings, at least in the sense of the European-American heritage. These departures are not always a mark of bitterness. As often as not, they reflect a character's resignation that the frontier community around him can never escape the flaws of the human position.

Thus, *Stagecoach* is not simply a motion picture fueled by cynicism. In its own fashion, it embodies the sentiments implicit in any number of Westerns that seek to define the features of the ideal society. It forwards many of the concepts discussed earlier in the chapter—adherence to the Bootstrap Theory, belief in the Melting Pot, even an endorsement of the concept of Manifest Destiny. At the same time, through the imperfections of the central characters and the failings of the world that judges them, the film rejects the simplistic pieties suggested by its iconographic opening. Instead, by the conclusion of the movie, *Stagecoach* has acknowledged the fragility and transitory nature of community even as it has celebrated its noblest elements.

The action of *Stagecoach*, and of other films in this Western subgroup, turns on the question of whether or not individuals or events can reconfigure a community, even if that involves only a temporary change, like that formed by the travelers on the stage. The bonds that emerge while the passengers are sharing water, helping to deliver the baby, or fighting off the Indian attack suggest the possibility of breaking the inhibitive and selfish patterns of behavior that characterize towns like Tonto and Lordsburg. However, as the flights from civilization noted above emphasize, those communal ties last no longer than the trials and dangers that the passengers must face.

All this clearly acknowledges the limitations of change. The temporary community of the stagecoach passengers dissolves when individuals move off into a larger, more permanent society. The Ringo Kid and Dallas have defied convention and fallen in love, but freedom and happiness for them only comes outside of the community. The beneficence of Curley has "saved them from the blessings of civilization," allowing them instead to go off to live on the Kid's ranch "on the other side of the border," a vague boundary that stands as much a psychological delimitation as a physical one. In the end, although the status of the dominant culture remains unchanged or even unchallenged, the benefits of community seem ambiguous at best.

Thus, at its conclusion, *Stagecoach* very subtly reaffirms the attitudes introduced in the early scenes of the motion picture. The inexorable movement of Easterners and Eastern standards into the West and the displacement of all previous settlers and their values—from native Americans, through fur traders, to ranchers and cowboys—is an undeniably acknowledged certainty, though tempered by momentary tolerance. *Stagecoach*, at least, offers some alternative for individuals who wish to resist this amalgamation. As we will see in the following discussions, most Westerns at their conclusions do not evince even this minimal amount of guarded and qualified optimism.

Although it stands as a wonderful achievement, *Stagecoach* by no means presents a prescriptive mold for the Western concerned with the construction of community. Other examples of this category include motion pictures as diverse as *Red River, The Angel and the Badman, Shane,* John Ford's cavalry trilogy—*Fort Apache, She Wore a Yellow Ribbon,* and *Rio Grande—Silverado, Dances with Wolves, The Searchers, A Man Called Horse, The Cowboys, Jeremiah Johnson, The Man Who Shot Liberty Valence, Posse,* and *Once Upon a Time in the West.* As with the other subgenres, placing specific films in one category or the other is in many ways a subjective decision. This grouping and the others in this and subsequent chapters serve as starting points for more refined comprehensions of the genres.

High Noon

High Noon, a 1952 film directed by Fred Zinnemann, stars Gary Cooper as Will Kane, a man stepping down as marshal of Hadleyville, and Grace Kelly as Mrs. Amy Foster Kane, the woman whom he marries at the opening of the film. Like *Stagecoach*, it evokes characteristics that one finds in all Westerns—a celebration of individualism, an optimistic sense of the possibility of new beginnings, and the inevitable conclusion that violence ultimately determines the course of one's life.

At the same time, *High Noon* presents a much darker and far more fatalistic view of the world than the communal-oriented movies represented by *Stagecoach*. Even the most cynical travelers on the stage to Lordsburg acknowledged the possibility of the temporary formation of a community. The behavior of the townspeople in *High Noon* argues strongly against the idea that such a genuine collective spirit can ever exist. Films in this subgroup focus not so much on a character's need for an ideal society but upon the isolation of the idealistic individual from the ordinary, deeply imperfect community.

The passengers in *Stagecoach* ultimately show an ability to suspend the narrow-minded attitudes and biased inclinations they derive from the dominant culture and to work in a cooperative fashion, sacrificing individuality for the good of the whole. In *High Noon*, the people of Hadleyville take the opposite tack. When the peace and tranquility of their town are threatened by lawlessness, they exude a veneer of civic concern, aiming to shield themselves from criticism, while in fact endeavoring to distance themselves from any concerted communal action. From the beginning to the end of the film, nearly to a person, they behave in a self-centered, selfish, and at times self-deluding manner, suppressing any trace of group loyalty in favor of overbearing self-interest. When Will and Amy Kane leave Hadleyville at the end of the movie, unlike the Ringo Kid and Dallas, they are not fleeing the high-minded restraints of community but rather escaping the horrific consequences of living in a town without genuine moral values.

High Noon, in direct contrast to *Stagecoach*, unfolds almost exclusively in town. Three men gather at the railroad station in Hadleyville to meet the train carrying the newly paroled Frank Miller. It is obvious to all that they have come together to carry out the vengeful murder of Will Kane, the man who sent Miller to prison. Everyone in Hadleyville recognizes the intentions of the Miller gang, yet only Will Kane shows any willingness to face them.

This is typical of the self-righteousness masking self-interest that characterizes the townspeople in the other films of this group. The citizenry in *McCabe & Mrs. Miller* show more concern for the fire in the church which they do not attend than they do over the death of McCabe, whose whorehouse and saloon many have patronized. The inhabitants of *Rio Bravo* simply ignore the plight of the lawmen cornered in the sheriff's office by ranch-hands determined to release their boss's son. The mob that hangs the innocent cowboys in *The Ox-Bow Incident* claims to be seeking justice, yet the film shows a range of men acting out of a series of craven needs. In every instance the issue remains the same. The narrative examines the question of whether an individual or even a handful of people can sustain the ideals that the community pretends to endorse but refuses to uphold.

Perhaps the most striking aspect of the critique of society offered by *High Noon* is its ability to evoke the unrelieved isolation of individuals in this seemingly close-knit community. Although the motion picture's opening seems to celebrate a supportive and relaxed social world, the fractured nature of the town and its ambiguous attitude towards its marshal quickly become clear. The Babbitt–like boosterism of the first few scenes quickly dissipates, and contradictory attitudes emerge. The degeneration of rugged individualism into grasping, and often cowardly, self-interest that stands as a common if chilling theme of such Westerns as *The Naked Spur* and *3:10 to Yuma*, but nowhere is it represented with greater subtlety or power than in *High Noon*.

From the opening scenes, though admittedly perhaps not immediately evident, the film manifests the fractured nature of the community. Because Amy Foster Kane is a Quaker, her marriage to Will does not take place in the town's Protestant church, where many of the citizens are in attendance for Sunday worship. Further, though scarcely 11:00 a.m., the town saloon appears as crowded as the church's service. (The passage of time is carefully recorded in scene after scene by shots of a ticking clock, and the film's eighty-five minutes of running time coincide with the period that elapses from the Kane wedding to the concluding shoot-out.) The bluff good nature of the men who have gathered to witness the civil ceremony that unites Will and Amy proclaims an active communal fellowship. Nonetheless, that feeling quickly dissipates when it becomes evident that, despite an earlier decision to leave, Kane now plans to fight Frank Miller and his thugs in Hadleyville and to call upon his wedding guests publicly to support him in the confrontation.

Further, through a concerted effort to avoid easy delineations of good and bad, the film makes interpretation of the community's behavior a highly subjective process. It does not simply contrast a courageous and idealistic Will Kane with the craven and cynical townspeople. Both Kane and the townspeople see themselves caught up by events of the day. Kane feels that, if he does not face the gang now, they will pursue him wherever he goes. The townspeople see themselves as being unfairly involved in Kane's troubles. After all deliberations are completed, neither Kane nor the citizens of Hadleyville believe that they have any choice in how they respond to the threats of the Miller gang.

The film provides a particularly interesting analysis of the relation of individual scruples to communal attitudes. (Indeed, the structure of the story self-consciously echoes Hollywood's timorous response to the contemporaneous efforts of the House Un-American Activities Committee to investigate claims of Communist influence within the motion picture industry.) In other films involving the confrontation of lawmen and criminals—like *Tombstone, My Darling Clementine, Wyatt Earp,* and *The Gunfight at the O.K. Corral*—townspeople more often than not form little more than a bland backdrop for the conflict between good and evil. These films manage to highlight the isolation of the individuals facing the formidable odds against overcoming the villains who seek to take their lives, but they do not attempt to capture the keen sense of loss felt by the man who realizes, as does Will Kane, that the world from which he derived his values has proven not simply inadequate or even indifferent, but hostile to their application.

High Noon makes this revelation all the more poignant by underscoring the limitations of the central character. Early on, in explaining his decision to remain in town to confront Miller, Kane declares, "I'm not trying to be a hero." Rather, he follows a pragmatic approach to what he must do. Seeing a confrontation with the Miller gang as inevitable, Kane prefers

Will Kane (Gary Cooper) in *High Noon* (1952).

to take his chances in a place where he expects his friends will support him. In this fashion, he articulates the faith in community upon which the films in the *Stagecoach* category rest. In *High Noon* and other films in its group, however, the narrative offers overpowering proof that such faith is misplaced.

The chilling revelation that gradually emerges in *High Noon* is that, while all others in the town feel that they have no greater latitude for action than Kane, their behavior traces far more self-deluded choices. The script deftly uses interactions between Kane and the "select men of the town"—the very people whom the mayor had pledged to safeguard Hadleyville for the twenty-four hours that will elapse between Kane's resignation and the arrival of the new marshal—to articulate a range of motivations for self-preservation. Judge Percy Mettrick (Otto Kruger), the man who married Amy and Will, is the most honest, and perhaps the most cynical, of the group. He quickly decides to leave, declaring his belief that the shaky structure of civilization upon which the town rests cannot resist or overcome the unbridled savagery of the Miller gang. Sam Fuller (Henry

Morgan) bluntly refuses to see Kane, and compels his wife to lie about his whereabouts, asserting to her that any other course of action would put her at risk of becoming a widow. Martin Howe (Lon Chaney, Jr.), the former sheriff, wallowing in self-pity and despair, tells Kane that the job of a peace officer is a thankless task for which he has no further appetite. He then, in perhaps the most manipulative gesture of the film, uses his infirmities as an excuse for abandoning his friend, claiming that if he joined Kane the marshal would be too worried about Howe's safety to fight effectively.

The most disturbing rationalization for not assisting Kane, presented with crushing irony in the town's church, comes from Jonas Henderson (Thomas Mitchell playing against the type that he had established in *Stagecoach*). After hearing Kane's appeal to the congregation and seeing indications that some are considering offering their support, Henderson steps forward to preach the gospel of self-interest. He begins by praising Kane and all that Kane did to bring order to the town. He then shifts the discourse to speak about how "people up north" will react adversely to a gunfight in the town. He goes on to say that if Kane were not in the town when Miller gets off the train, there would be no trouble for the town. Henderson concludes his oration by a reversal of the sentiments invoked when he opened it, telling Will to leave town. "It's better for you, and it's better for us."

Together these four men embody the social institutions that define the nature of Hadleyville, and by extension their reasons for refusing to help articulate diverse manifestations the town's attitude of self-preservation above all else. If they stand as the public rejection of Kane's plea, other characters embody a personal rebuff. Harv Pell (Lloyd Bridges), the town's deputy and Kane's closest colleague, demands reciprocity for his cooperation. When Kane cannot guarantee that Harv's assistance will insure his promotion to marshal, Harv refuses to step in.

Helen Ramirez (Katy Jurado), the lover first of Frank Miller, then of Will Kane, and finally of Harv Pell, has long occupied the role of an outsider that Kane is now thrust into. She clearly articulates her position and her attitude toward the community that Kane has sought to preserve in a powerful exchange with Amy Kane that begins: "I've always hated this town. To be a Mexican woman in a town like this." Helen goes on to show her clear sense of Kane as one of the few real men in the town, and she berates Amy for deserting him. At the same time, the distance that she feels as Kane's jilted lover extinguishes any sympathy for him. As she curtly tells Amy: "He is not my man." Though Helen implies that she would come to Kane's aid if they still had a romantic attachment, a similar tie is, for a time at least, insufficient to convince the newly married Amy Kane to ignore her Quaker pacifism and support her husband. These complex psychological representations allow the narrative to acknowledge the nobility of Kane's code of behavior even as it rejects the possibility of a broader community embracing this code, or at least defending it when put to the test.

Inevitably, Kane goes out alone to face the Miller gang. As noted in the Introduction, the brilliant shot of Kane stepping out into the street—beginning with a close up that shows his twitchy, edgy demeanor and gradually pulling back and up to a distant image of a tiny man alone in the street of a seemingly deserted town—sums up the physical and psychological position in which Kane finds himself. During the desperate battle that rages between Kane and the Miller gang, only Amy Kane makes a clear choice regarding her values, but even her choice raises difficult questions. When she shoots in the back one of the men trying to kill her husband, she rejects the limitations of a religious belief that would prevent her from defending someone she loves. It remains for viewers to decide whether that act represents the triumph of loyalty and concern in a world consumed by self-interest, or shows a capitulation to the code of violence that has had a corrosive effect on nearly everyone in the film.

Kane and Amy succeed in killing the four men who have come to Hadleyville to take his life, but one can hardly see the film's ending as triumphant. In the final scene, as people pour out of their homes and fill the street with bustling activity, Kane with obvious contempt throws his marshal's badge into the dirt at the feet of the townspeople and then climbs into a buckboard. Leaving Hadleyville in silence, Kane condemns the spirit of community in unspoken language far harsher than any speech he might have uttered. Indeed, in the isolation that he has been forced to face that morning, one can claim that, psychologically at least, his defeat stands as significant as that of the men in the Miller gang who lie dead in the street.

Like every film in this subgroup, *High Noon* measures the impediments to the achievement of communal ideals raised by practical, even pragmatic, concerns. Other motion pictures that offer diverse perspectives on this issue include *Tombstone, My Darling Clementine, Rio Bravo, Broken Arrow, The Bravados, McCabe & Mrs. Miller, The Ox-Bow Incident, 3:10 to Yuma* (both versions), *Wyatt Earp, The Naked Spur, The Gunfight at the O.K. Corral,* and *The Magnificent Seven.* Despite the diversity among these titles, all focus attention on the struggles that arise in the clash between ostensive collective principles and the pragmatic mores of a particular society.

Unforgiven

Unforgiven, directed by Clint Eastwood and released in 1992, centers its narrative on a reformed gunfighter, Will Munny (played by Eastwood), now trying to make a living raising pigs on the Kansas prairie. As John Ford did in so many of his movies, Eastwood's film, set in 1881, uses breathtaking landscape to enforce the contrast between aesthetic beauty and hardscrabble living. It opens with a lush image of Munny in his farm yard chopping wood in front of a large tree, backlit by a gorgeous sunset. A scrolling description of the death of William Munny's wife by smallpox gives the barebones details that shape the viewers' first impressions of his character.

Almost before that impression settles in the viewer's consciousness, the narrative switches to a violent scene in the town of Big Whiskey where a cowboy whom a young whore has inadvertently mocked repeatedly slashes her face with a knife. The assault is horrific for its savagery, but the townspeople's reaction to it proves to be no less shocking. Little Bill Daggett (Gene Hackman), the sheriff of Big Whiskey, and the others view the "cut up whore" as simply "damaged property," and to resolve the situation Little Bill only fines the cowboys as punishment because they were not "given over to wickedness in a regular way."

Circumvention of the legal process is a familiar theme to anyone who has seen other Westerns, but rarely does the attitude motivating it find such a calculatingly cold-blooded representation. In this autocratic application of apprehension, judgment, and punishment, Little Bill is far more than simply a less varnished version of James Stewart's bounty hunter in *The Naked Spur*. He even goes beyond the despotic Judge Roy Bean (Walter Brennan) in *The Westerner*. Little Bill, in his chillingly dispassionate behavior, does not merely enforce the law. He generates it, adapts it, and applies it as he sees best, redefining a human being as chattel when it suits him to do so.

Almost every Western employs violence to move the narrative forward, and many take a careful look at its impact. A select subgroup, however, challenges assumptions about its efficacy within the genre. Films like *The Great Northfield Minnesota Raid* and *One-Eyed Jacks* strip away any mitigating misconceptions about it, and force viewers to see violence without any glamour or extenuating justification. *Unforgiven* not only does this, but it also presents detailed examinations of the corrosive impact of this approach to life's interactions.

Women often play a key part in outlining alternatives to the violent side of the nature of a Western's protagonist. Dallas begs the Ringo Kidd not to confront the killers of his father and brother. Amy Kane threatens to leave her husband (and almost does) if he does not eschew violence. And Claudia Munny, though deceased, continues to exert a strong inhibiting force on the behavior of her husband Will. At the same time, none has a lasting effect. Each man ultimately resists that influence and chooses instead to assert his manhood or to resolve his difficulties through a single violent act. What remains for the viewer to decide is whether that dismissal of a woman's pleas represents a liberating or a corrosive gesture.

Of course, *Unforgiven* also inverts the roles of that familiar dialectic. From the moment the cowboys are taken into custody, the whores demand the Little Bill administer a physical punishment to balance the violence against one of their own. When Little Bill decides only to fine the cowboys, Strawberry Alice (Frances Fisher) is outraged and they are not even going to be whipped. She convinces the other prostitutes to pool their money as a bounty they will offer for anyone killing the cowboys by declaring, "Just because we let them smelly fools ride us like horses don't mean we gotta let 'em brand us like horses. Maybe we ain't nothing but whores but we, by god, we ain't horses."

It is Will Munny, through his self-reflections, who engages the repercussions of violence and condemns it, despite his actions over the course of the film. Other characters in Westerns talk about the violence in their lives, but few examine it with the same unblinking discernment. Munny repeatedly speaks with great respect for the conventional moral values espoused by his now deceased wife, Claudia. He invokes her memory to shape the behavior of his children. He eschews any form of sexual gratification because of her spiritual presence. He no longer drinks and recalls with shame of his behavior when he was "a bad man." At the same time, when pressed by circumstances, he undertakes the cold-blooded task of killing two men in order to collect his share of a thousand dollar bounty. This is something, as noted by his partner Ned Logan (Morgan Freeman), that Will never would have done had Claudia been alive.

Unforgiven exemplifies the type of film that studies the legitimacy of the use of violence in Westerns not simply to enforce civic morality but because civic morality exists in name only. *Pat Garret and Billy the Kid*, *The Long Riders*, and *The Wild Bunch* are among the other motion pictures exploring the view that only violence can preserve order in the Western community. These films go on to show its application inevitably corrodes any ostensive system of values, whether it resides within an individual or a community.

Nowhere is this more evident than in *Unforgiven*. Little Bill is calculating, intelligent, and ruthless in his efforts to maintain civic order in Big Whiskey. Will Munny is equally calculating, intelligent, and ruthless in pursuit of the bounty money pledged because of the whores' discontent with Little Bill's pragmatic application of justice. The narrative captures their contrasting attitudes wonderfully, but it leaves their natures unexplained. In the end, the viewer remains hard-pressed to decide which man acts in a morally justifiable fashion. Indeed, one might argue that Will Munny and Little Bill Daggett are overwhelmed by the same pattern of behavior, a code informed by an instinctual animal savagery.

Unforgiven, however, takes its analysis beyond an exploration of individual morality. It suggests that brutality in itself destroys civic values, corrupting any tenet sustained by violence. Further, it shows the manner by which brutality begets further brutality. The animating feature of the narrative is the bounty that the whores put on the cowboys who have literally scarred one of their own. Because we are frustrated with the initial miscarriage of justice, we may feel sympathy for what they do. However, in short order we find that we have difficulty judging the ethical behavior of anyone in this movie because no social institution in the film has demonstrated its legitimacy to serve as a yardstick against which to measure individual actions.

Indeed, the film provides compelling evidence of the corrosiveness of communal life that will challenge any other interpretation of the movie. Civilization, represented by Big Whiskey, is violent, unpredictable, and unfeeling. Without much elaboration one can see an analogy between the scars on the whore's face, created by the cowboy's knife, and those on the landscape, created by the town. Eastwood as a director deftly plays upon this theme. He does not romanticize rural life, but he does capture its beauty in contrast to the ugliness of communal living. (Even Little Bill, the only visible embodiment of the civic institutions of Big Whiskey, chooses to build outside of the town so that he can stare at the beauty of the untouched countryside from his porch at sunset.)

The effects of civilization on Will Munny, at least as they have been valorized by his wife Claudia, have had no positive material impact. He lives a subsistence-level existence on a pig farm in the middle of the prairie. He is caught in an untenable position between two worlds, no longer possessing the brutal abilities of a gunfighter and unable to master the rudimentary skills of a farmer.

Because of his incipient sense of failure, Munny, with his former sidekick, Ned Logan, decides to join an aspiring gunfighter, the Schofield Kid, who is going to Big Whiskey, Wyoming, to collect the bounty put up by the whores. This improbable trio seems to signal the film's commitment to a typical coming-of-age plot—the young boy worshipping an aged gunfighter only to realize in the last reel the consequences of such a life. At every stage, the film rebuts this pattern. The Kid has no desire to learn anything from Ned and Will. He fails to see the disgust and shame that they feel when reminded of their past exploits. And he shows no awareness of the gravity of the task they have undertaken.

In the final analysis, it is savagery that remains consistent and unambiguous. The prostitutes of Big Whiskey are determined to exact revenge. An assault on one is seen as an assault on all, and their commitment to violence proves to be as formidable as that of the men who carry out their revenge. Unlike the Quakeress of *High Noon*, they make no effort to meliorate their response. The title of the film clearly shows that the savagery permeating its world crosses gender lines.

Unforgiven adopts a meta-narrative technique to tell the story of what life is like for a brutal man, and uses multiple perspectives that heighten

(Left to right) The Schofield Kid (Jaimz Woolvett), William Munny (Clint Eastwood) and Ned Logan (Morgan Freeman) in *Unforgiven* (1992).

the viewer's sense of the complexity of the topic while underscoring the pandemic quality of savagery. In campfire conversations, the Schofield Kid recounts to Will stories that the Kid's uncle had told of Will's violent behavior. Will Munny can only respond with efforts to deflect the Kid's enthusiasm, mumbling the excuse "I was drunk most of the time." Privately, he speaks to Ned of the shame he feels for such behavior. In contrast, English Bob (Richard Harris) has presented elaborate romantic accounts of his exploits as a gunman, and the journalist W.W Beauchamp has transformed these stories into Western novels. Revealingly, Little Bill, after beating English Bob senseless, recounts an alternative version of one of these stories to Beauchamp, stripping Bob's life of all grandeur and emphasizing the quixotic, sordid nature of violent death.

The telling and retelling of the assault on Delilah hyperbolically intensifies the savagery, while keeping consistent the tawdriness of its brutality. This becomes the paradigmatic pattern of narration for all accounts of violence in the film. As the Schofield Kid describes the incident to Will and then as Will describes it to Ned, the audience hears markedly different accounts from the event it has earlier observed. As with the accounts relating to English Bob, what comes across clearly is the investment that some characters put not in their acts but in the telling and retelling of them.

When Will, Ned, and the Kid finally succeed in murdering the men who disfigured the whore, the narrative's emphasis shifts from the bathetic to the horrific. The film shows the cowboys' deaths as slow and gruesome, disgusting even to the men who are responsible for them. Indeed, from the attack on the whore Delilah in the opening scenes, through Little Bill's beatings of English Bob and later of Will Munny, the sordid, clumsy, revolting nature of violence receives a great deal of attention. This critique of physical force goes even further when Ned is captured and beaten to death by Little Bill. Munny's single-handed, violent response to the murder, gunning down all of the men involved, concludes the action not so much with catharsis as exhaustion.

If stories of violence beget more violence, then only escape from his ethos can break the cycle. In sharp distinction to Little Bill and English Bob who cultivate a journalist seeking material about the Wild West, Will Munny does not want his deeds to be known or his life to be immortalized. Indeed, Will and Ned say little to the Kid about their pasts, and Will actively seeks to suppress information about himself: "Don't tell my kids none of the things I done." At the end of the film, when he simply disappears with his children, unlike so many Western heroes who are turning their backs on civilization, Will Munny is struggling to escape himself.

Some may feel tempted to see this representation as an anti–Western or at least as an effort to deconstruct the mythic concept of the Western. In fact, *Unforgiven* makes us more aware of the complexities in the best films in the genre. It employs all of the elements of a classic Western. It deals with the isolation of the hero. It highlights a single-minded determination to live by a code, no matter how those around the hero behave. And it embraces the idea that the West is a place in which the individual must impose a measure of order to give the world in which he exists some sort of stability.

Unforgiven differs from other Westerns only to the degree that it foregrounds the assumptions of the genre. This film follows all of the conventions of its type, but it makes the viewer self-consciously aware of the full implications of those assumptions. Antiseptic violence, unvoiced sexual appetites, and unacknowledged rapaciousness have no place in the film. Instead, *Unforgiven* represents the unvarnished world of the Western and leaves the viewer to decide on the acceptability of this genre.

Unforgiven analyzes the personalities of "bad men," and it presents viewers with an uneasy sense of the complexity of that term. By showing how a life of violence can so readily blur the distinctions between those who civilize this world and those who make it more savage, the film draws attention to the difficulties that we face in judging behavior in almost any Western with more than a rudimentary plotline and more than stereotypical roles. Other films exploring these ambivalences include *The Wild Bunch, Butch Cassidy and the Sundance Kid, The Great Northfield Minnesota Raid, Rancho Notorious, The Missouri Breaks, The Adventures of Frank and Jessie James, One-Eyed Jacks, The Long Riders, The Revenant, The Outlaw Josey Wales, The Westerner,* and *Bad Girls.*

Two

Angels with Dirty Faces
Gangster Films

A General Sense of the Genre

Gangster films have always been an American industry easily exported throughout the world through the popularity of individual features and the sheer volume of releases. In the process, Hollywood infused a uniquely American perspective, readily imitated by foreign filmmakers, on the way the criminal defines himself, his cohorts, and those upon whom he preys.[1] This included, from the start, a narrowly defined and highly stratified gendered perspective of society. As a result of this highly specialized cultural context, only the Western can claim greater uniqueness as an almost completely masculinized American film genre. (Films like *Gun Crazy* and *Bonnie and Clyde* stand as exceptions that prove the rule.)

Film scholars generally agree that D.W. Griffith's seventeen-minute film, *The Musketeers of Pig Alley*, appearing just nine years after Edison Studios' release of *The Great Train Robbery*, was the first Gangster movie produced in the United States. Sixteen years later, in 1928, Warner Brothers released the first Gangster film that incorporated sound into its narrative, *The Lights of New York*. However, it was a trio of motion pictures released in the early 1930s—*Little Caesar*, *The Public Enemy*, and *Scarface*—that gave Gangster films their distinctive stamp that continues to shape contemporary movies in this genre (and in the opinion of many led directly to a stricter enforcement of the Motion Picture Production Code).[2]

Gangster movies depict an urban underworld, alienated from the mainstream of society yet privy to many of the same ambitions for material and social success that motivate ordinary citizens. To achieve these goals, criminals ignore the restraints imposed by laws and advance their own

(Left to right) The Musician (Walter Miller), the Little Lady (Lilian Gish), the Bartender (Adolph Lestina), and Snapper Kid (Elmer Booth) in *The Musketeers of Pig Alley* (1912).

ends by any means available. In a perversion of Horatio Alger–style success, they celebrate concepts like Rugged Individualism and the Bootstrap Theory while dismissing ideas of a level playing field for all. It is important to note, however, that in these films gangsters do not seek to bring down the system in which they find themselves. Rather they seek to profit from it in a parasitic fashion.

With relatively few exceptions, Hollywood Gangster films take place in large urban areas, usually New York, Chicago, or Los Angeles. (*Badlands*, *Natural Born Killers*, *A Perfect World*, or *The Road to Perdition* are among the most prominent examples of non-urban gangster movies.) From the opening of *Little Caesar* when Rico Bandello (Edward G. Robinson) decides to go off to the big city to the arrival of Vito Corleone (Robert DeNiro) in New York in *The Godfather II* to the reign of Harlem drug lord Frank Lucas (Denzel Washington) in *American Gangster*, the attraction of urban life remains a constant. It is not simply the prospect of numerous opportunities for easy wealth but the tempo and energy of the metropolis that draw criminal, and filmmaker, to it.

The Bifurcated Worldview

When they arrive in cities, gangsters operate through cynicism and ruthlessness. They cannot accept the idea that truly canny individuals would ever believe in concepts like community pride and civic duty. Instead, they assume that the success of others comes from violating the rules and manipulating the system (*The Public Enemy*). In their view, only the timid and the socially obtuse—saps, suckers, and milquetoasts—insist on conforming to society's moral codes.

This juxtaposition of contradictory values inevitably produces tensions that neither the individual gangster nor the community can sustain for any prolonged period. Society, though slow to respond to the criminal's transgressions, ultimately recoils at his endeavors to throw off conventional social restraints and rebuffs his efforts to gain recognition as a legitimate entrepreneur. Eventually, in all but the most nihilistic films in this category, the community reacts to preserve the integrity of the legal system and social order by eliminating the threat posed by the gangster. This can take the form of legal efforts (*The Roaring Twenties*), quasi-legal endeavors (*The Untouchables*), or even a kind of vigilantism (*G Men*). However, in some instances, it is not the active efforts of society that topple the gangster but the simple fact that he cannot sustain himself in a world in which he is so alien to the dominant culture (*Clockers*).

Paradoxically, in most cases, the gangster's inability to survive comes about because he has a partial or imperfect understanding of the system whose rules he has learned to exploit. The movie gangster has a keen sense of individual human weaknesses, and this enables him to prey upon honest citizens and to dominate other criminals. He also has a sharp intuition regarding specific features of society. This allows him to take advantage of ambiguous laws, of public apathy towards certain crimes, and of racial, economic, and class fissures within the community for criminal profit. However, once success makes the Hollywood gangster less inclined toward felonious pursuits and more interested in enjoying what he has already attained, he finds himself unsure of the proper way to behave, particularly if he has removed himself from his criminal environment, even if only through inactivity.

Inevitably, motion picture gangsters aspire to a social acceptance that they associate with wealth and position, yet they lack the background to fit seamlessly into this setting. The brashness that propelled the criminal to the top of his profession now seems to reflect a gaucherie that proclaims him as out of place in proper society. Quite simply, these men do not know how to behave. Rico in *Little Caesar* admires a painting in the house of a wealthy man, and ascribes its high cost to the value of the picture's frame. (Movie buffs will see a great irony in the scene knowing that Robinson would become well-known as a prominent and discerning art collector particularly interested in Post-Impressionist painters.) Time and again, it is not simply a poor command of English but a weak grasp of the significance of words and the value of objects that lead to confusion and insecurity. Unsurprisingly, conspicuous consumption, often highlighted by poor taste, underscores the gangster's efforts to demonstrate his success and status (*Once Upon a Time in America*). More often than not the crushing tragedy of a criminal's life in the movies comes not with his death but with his realization that he will never achieve respectability.

The Triumph of Brutality

Despite the complexities of characterization and the intricacies of plot in many Gangster movies, its central characters can rarely tolerate ambiguity in their lives. The disorder that results from trying to sustain both law-abiding values and the criminal's code recurs in many of the films (*A Bronx Tale*). Inevitably, these movies show that one cannot accommodate both. Of course, an upright citizen may commit a crime or a criminal may perform an act of goodness, but the standards of the specific environments from which each emerges preclude any sustained duality.

GoodFellas—opening with Henry Hill stating, "As far back as I can remember, I always wanted to be a gangster"—underscores this mutual exclusion. Henry celebrates the difference between "wise guys" and the lives of the ordinary people who live in his neighborhood. "You know, we always called each other Good Fellas. Like you'd say to somebody: You're gonna like this guy; he's alright. He's a good fella. He's one of us. You understand? We were good fellas; wise guys." By the time that Henry enters a witness protection program at the end of the film, we understand the impossibility of a gangster becoming completely divorced from that world or ever successfully integrating into normal society.

Time and again, viewers see how criminal life cultivates attitudes and patterns of behavior that reflexively disrupt ordinary personal relationships. In a scene from *The Public Enemy* that set the tone for a gangster's relationship with his girlfriend for generations of future movies. Tom Powers (James Cagney) pushes a grapefruit in to the face of Kitty (Mae Clarke) as the only way he can imagine responding to her criticism. It was shocking

Two. Angels with Dirty Faces 59

(Left to right) Henry Hill (Ray Liota), James Conway (Robert DiNiro), Paul Cicero (Paul Sorvino), and (Joe Pesci) in *GoodFellas* (1990).

at the time, but it set a pattern for behavior that made it inevitable that twenty years later Vince Stone (Lee Marvin) would throw boiling hot coffee in the face of his girlfriend Debby Marsh (Gloria Grahame) in *The Big Heat*.

Few gangsters have the ability or even the inclination to maintain normal relationships. Tony Carmonte's incestuous desires for his sister influence much of what he does in *Scarface*. In *White Heat* the intensity of the bond between Cody Jarett (James Cagney) and his mother (Margaret Wycherly) stops just short of infantilization. In *Casino*, despite living a life of luxury and security, Ginger McKenna (Sharon Stone) systematically betrays her husband Ace Rothstein (Robert Di Nero) with her former pimp Lester Diamond (James Woods), tries to stage a kidnapping of Ace's daughter (Erika von Tagen), and then begins an affair with Nicky Santoro (Joe Pesci), supposedly Ace's best friend. Violence and betrayal

Kitty (Mae Clarke) and Tom Powers (James Cagney) in *The Public Enemy* (1931).

are as much a part of a gangster's domestic life as they are his professional one.

Despite all this, or perhaps because of it, gangsters often fascinate audiences as figures unwilling to submit to conformity and able to take advantage of situations to achieve success. A series of conflicting myths—rugged individualism versus concern for the underdog, the value of self-improvement versus the need to show concern for the society in which one lives—send contradictory messages about how viewers are invited to judge gangsters. Certainly, the attractiveness of the criminal comes from our admiration for his reckless determination to advance, just as an aversion to him comes from a sense of the ruthlessness that drives him.

Codes of Conduct

The most effective Gangster films do not simply highlight the differences between the gangster and society. They look carefully at the turmoil that arises when those on either side of the law who have adopted extreme positions in relation to the community attempt to move to its center. Gangsters first succeed by stepping outside the restraints on behavior that society imposes, but ultimately stumble when they seek to gain its esteem by adopting a life that accommodates those values (*American Gangster*).

Two. Angels with Dirty Faces

Frank Lucas (Denzel Washington, third from left, wearing a suit) with his crew in *American Gangster* (2007).

Police officers in gangster films begin their careers with an idealistic view of how to behave, yet eventually find that they cannot deal effectively with criminals unless they mimic at least some aspects of the lawbreaker's behavior (*Dirty Harry*). When one tries to do both, a kind of schizophrenia results as embodied by Johnny Depp's portrayal of the title character in *Donnie Brasco*.

Nonetheless, the impulse for inclusion remains strong, and so the struggle between contradictory values recurs throughout the Gangster film. The tantalizing question always remains whether the gangster is correct in depicting the honest life as a role for those who place unwarranted faith in the integrity of a system that in fact is eminently corruptible. This possibility gains biting force when the criminal encounters veniality in so-called pillars of the community (*The Untouchables*), suggesting that the concept of moral probity in the world is merely a sham that more canny individuals see through. The best gangster films take on this question and explore its complexities without seeking refuge in easy answers.

A viewer misses the point by wondering if one version glorifies crime while the other excoriates it. (In some films—*The Naked City*, for example—the criminal is brought to justice by representatives of the legal system. In others, his own kind dispatches him, as in *Road to Perdition*.) The Gangster film wrestles with a more complex concern. Rather than dealing in moral simplicities or reductive nihilism, it questions what means a man may use to achieve success and often struggles with the issue of whether the end justifies the means.

Specific Application

The elements outlined above are crucial factors for understanding how viewers broadly respond to motion pictures that fall into the Gangster genre. At the same time, as with Westerns and every other genre considered in this book, striking divergences within this group delineate clearly distinguishable subcategories. *Scarface* (the 1932 version), *The Godfather*, and *Reservoir Dogs* all conform to the broad features of the Gangster film outlined above. *Scarface* shows the consequences of the gangster who does not understand that no matter what he will always remain on the margins. *The Godfather* offers a view of a criminal organization that attempts to form its own society, only to show the same challenges arising over the ability to tolerate ambiguity. *Reservoir Dogs* goes to a nihilistic extreme, highlight the life of those who reject any connection with society. Nonetheless, the structure of each illustrates a particular area of the genre that demands special attention. The following pages will lay out the application of specific questions and particular topics through the examination of three films that exemplify the genre.

Scarface

This film was based on a novel by Armitage Trail, which in turn was based on the actual life of Al Capone. *Scarface* marks a shift in tone from the crime films of the 1920s that usually focused on the victims and the men (exclusively) who enforced the law, highlighting instead the violence and mayhem of gangster life. Indeed, after its initial release and subsequent public protests over its depictions of sex and violence, producers, sought to mollify critics. They changed the ending of *Scarface* and added material denouncing organized crime as a blight on the community. The print currently available has the added scenes with the chief of police and newspaper editor but not the contrived ending showing Tony's execution.

Scarface highlights a pattern that almost every subsequent Gangster movie will follow: the perverted Horatio Alger–like chronicle of a criminal's life. Tony Camonte (Paul Muni), the film's title character, rises to the top of the criminal world in Prohibition-era Chicago, outsmarting, intimidating, or simply eliminating anyone seeking to impede his progress. A single-minded ruthlessness serves as the key to Tony's success as a mobster. With the same savagery that one might encounter in a wild animal, Tony Camonte uses force without hesitation and without remorse. He practices it without emotion. It is simply a tool of the trade that he uses methodically to eliminate anyone who stands in his way.

Since the killings undertaken in *Scarface* consist of pitting gangster against gangster, viewers can become desensitized to their full effect, dismissing what happens as just retribution to men who "had it coming." That response, however, has a contradictory implication. Viewers who accept the inevitability and perhaps even the justifiability of violence in *Scarface* becomes more like Tony than they might care to admit. This makes judging Tony that much more difficult. By confronting viewers with the possibility of their own callous desensitization, the film humanizes Tony's characterization and that of other mobsters in other films. (In fact, the police are as quick to use violence as the criminals. When the police interrogate Tony, after the murder of Big Louis Costillo (Harry J. Vejar), one of the detectives casually asks his superior, "Shall I slap it out of him, Chief?")

Second only to his propensity for violence, an ambivalent attitude towards and volatile treatment of women characterizes Tony's nature. From the moment they meet, Tony pursues Poppy (Karen Morley), the girlfriend of his boss Johnny Lovo (Osgood Perkins). Tony and Poppy seem to have little in common. She frequently dismisses him, and he consistently misunderstands pejorative words that Poppy uses—like "effeminate" and "gaudy"—as compliments. Nonetheless, after murdering Johnny Lovo, Tony simply takes possession of Poppy. In a tone that suggests the attitude of a man who has done nothing more than assume a perquisite formerly enjoyed by an immediate superior, he arrives at her apartment and tells her: "Go pack your stuff." It remains an open question whether he feels any real attraction to Poppy or if she simply embodies the status and esteem that he is constantly seeking.

Tony's relations with the women in his family are even more dysfunctional. He behaves in a coarse and brutal fashion towards his mother, dismissing her fears and her moral concerns as irrelevant, and he evinces an unnatural attraction for his sister Cesca (Ann Dvorak). In the scene when Tony violently removes Cesca from a nightclub, he behaves more

(Left to right) Jim the Headwaiter (Maurice Black in an uncredited role), Johnny Lovo (Osgood Perkins), Tony Camonte (Paul Muni), and Poppy (Karen Morley) in *Scarface* (1932).

like a jealous lover than like a concerned brother. In a fit of rage he hits her and tears her dress, and the moment is filled with a palpable sexual tension. Later, when he finds Cesca in an apartment with Guino Renaldo (George Raft), Tony unhesitatingly shoots the man who has been his best friend. While this reflexive violence invites us to see Tony as little more than a mindless thug, it also underscores the imbalance of his emotions.

The consequences of this murder are more complex than the other killings that fill the movie because, although he seems self-sufficient, Tony relies on his friend and henchman Guino and his sister Cesca for emotional and moral support, and this gives his nature a small measure of humanity. After impulsively killing Rinaldo and being denounced by his sister, Tony loses his sense of place and moves about in a daze. It is only after Cesca forgives him that he revives. The essentiality of her support becomes clear when, in an ensuing gun battle with police Cesca is killed, and Tony completely loses his nerve.

The film underscores the brutishness that drives Tony's behavior by continually making ironic allusions to the idea of him as a tragic figure. When he murders Lovo, Tony whistles the same tune that he whistled when he killed Louis. ("Chi mi frena in tal momento," "Who curbs me at such a moment," is from Gaetano Donizetti's *Lucia di Lammermoor*. The three individuals who sing it—Lucia, her lover Edgardo, and her brother Enrico—bemoan their inability to escape fate.) Tony whistles it again shortly before he encounters Guino and Cesca together, but the narrative gives no evidence one way or the other of his comprehending the ironic implications of this gesture. In fact, far from achieving an operatic grandeur, Tony's absentminded whistling captures the behavior of a man who imperfectly understands the world around him even as he seeks to reshape it to suit himself.

What disrupts any tragic sense in these narratives is the way that gangsters die. It can be the self-pitying cry of Edward G. Robinson "Is this the end of Rico?" (*Little Caesar*); a mistress' dismissive summary of James Cagney's Eddie Bartlett, "He used to be a big shot" (*The Roaring Twenties*); or simply the ignominious execution on a dirt road of Joe Pesci's character Nicky Santoro (*Casino*). When cornered at the end of *Scarface*, Tony at first begs: "Gimme a break." Then he is shot trying to escape. In every case, whatever the details, a measure of shabbiness detracts from any drama of the end.

This conclusion seems particularly perplexing, for the loss of nerve appears to reflect a radical change in Tony's nature. Though it may be partially explained by the trauma caused by the death of Cesca, it seems more likely that the filmmakers felt the need to impose a moralizing ending on the picture to avoid charges of glorifying crime and violence. In either case, the ending may underscore the brittleness of Tony's nature, and show how unsuited it was to dealing with anything in the world that could not be dispatched with quick and direct violence.

Scarface is a film of aspiration, a morality tale that does not so much show the triumph of law and order as demonstrate the impermanence of a success built upon the methods that gangsters employ. It also highlights a certain fragility in this way of life. Despite a veneer of coarseness and brutality that seems to define his nature, Tony in fact resembles a hybrid plant, unable to survive for long outside the hothouse environment of his very special world. Indeed, Tony and his cronies, though they appear to be independent of the world around them, in fact depend upon a complex symbiotic relationship with it to exist. They do not so much prey upon society as take parasitical nourishment from it. Their survival is contingent upon remaining unobtrusive. When any criminal draws attention to himself, he becomes a threat to all his associates and an intolerable burden on society. His demise is inevitable. In this fashion, *Scarface* outlines a plotline that is repeated in similar films in this subgenre like *Little Caesar, Brother Orchid, Al Capone, Clockers, The Roaring Twenties, Boyz n the Hood,*

High Sierra, Mean Streets, Casino, Angels with Dirty Faces, A Bronx Tale, Prizzi's Honor, King of the Roaring 20s, GoodFellas, Once upon a Time in America, Miller's Crossing, The Usual Suspects, and *Road to Perdition.*

The Godfather

Unlike *Scarface*, a film depicting a mobster's rise and fall or *The Untouchables* which focuses on the overturning of a mob empire, *The Godfather* takes up the gangster culture from an evolutionary perspective, with a Darwinian-like sensibility informing its narrative. It first introduces the Corleone criminal empire as resembling an efficient and relatively benign business conglomerate. It goes on to chronicle the turbulent transition from one generation to another, defining it as a rite of passage for Michael Corleone (Al Pacino). And it ends with a (temporary) restoration of order. (Francis Ford Coppola would continue the saga of the evolution of the family in two sequels, *The Godfather: Part II* and *The Godfather: Part III.*)

In much the way that a motion picture about nineteenth-century industrial development would show the sociologic transformations wrought by the Industrial Revolution, *The Godfather* traces the cultural and communal forces, emphasized by a growing pressure to traffic in narcotics, that change the human elements in the Corleone enterprises. It depicts the complex relationships within a Mafia crime family with a seductive skill that shows their adherence to the most popular American myths: Rugged Individualism, the Bootstrap Theory, and the possibility of the continual reinvention of self. In a grand fashion the film depicts the paradigmatic shift in the nature of organized crime from the traditional and even honor-bound family institution of Vito Corleone (Marlon Brando) to the reconfiguration of the enterprise into a near-faceless corporate entity headed by his son Michael (Al Pacino).

The Godfather opens with the wedding of Vito Corleone's only daughter Connie (Talia Shire). Don Corleone gathers family and friends to celebrate an important event and demonstrate his generosity, for on such a day, as Michael tells his girlfriend Kay Adams (Diane Keaton), custom dictates that the Don will honor any appeal made to him. The festive atmosphere and the series of requests from supplicants gives the impression that benevolence informs the scope and tenor of the Godfather's empire. However, the film also indicates that any favor draws the supplicant into an inelastic system of reciprocity.

Two. Angels with Dirty Faces

When treated with the deference that he expects as leader of this community, he maintains a gentle demeanor manifest in his petting the cat while men ask favors of him. (The cat's addition to the scene was a serendipitous happenstance. It wandered onto the soundstage during filming, and Brando simply picked it up and continued the scene.) At the same time, he can be brutal to those who do not show respect.

One of the petitioners, Bonasera (Salvatore Corsitto) a previously aloof Italian-American undertaker, asks Don Corleone to kill two young men who assaulted his daughter and then escaped punishment from the courts. Don Corleone initially responds by refusing to have the young men killed and by chastising Bonasera for avoiding the Corleone family: "I can't remember the last time you invited me to your house for a cup of coffee, even though my wife is godmother to your only child." He then outlines the rules of the alternative social system that he has created, and he self-consciously, and with pride, contrasts it with the justice system of the United States. Dismissing the offer of money as recompense for this favor, Don Corleone instead demands obeisance: Bonasera must ask for Corleone's friendship, address him as Godfather, and kiss his hand. Only then does the Don order the boys beaten as Bonasera's daughter was.

(Left to right) Bonasera (Salvatore Corsitto), Sonny Corleone (James Caan), and Vito Carleone (Marlon Brando) in *The Godfather* (1972).

Given the complexity of Vito Corleone's worldview, understanding the ethical system of in which he operates is the key to understanding the movie, but that proves most challenging. When he turns down the proposal made by Sollozzo (Al Lettieri) to organize the illegal drug trade, for example, the Don clearly states that he does not have moral reservations but pragmatic ones, but can we believe him? He repeatedly shows himself to be a man who does not reveal his motives to others, and so it is quite possible that Don Corleone has chosen to dissemble and that other reasons propel his actions.

This is a key issue. A criminal who behaves in a purely pragmatic fashion, even if his actions seem less violent than those of others, is no different from any others. One who behaves according to a moral code, albeit one very different from the rest of society, introduces a new kind of criminal. The pragmatic leader feels motivations no different from those felt by Tony Carmonte in *Scarface*. The man of ideals, no matter how repugnant his values may seem to the rest of society, redefines the standards by which we should judge him. Any interpretation of *The Godfather* must turn on whether one sees its central figures as pragmatists or as idealists.

Of course, the world in which the Corleones exist emphasizes the need for violence, if only for self-protection. However, as in many other Gangster films, the conflicts take place between criminal families so that at some level the brutality will seem less significant to viewers, in much the same way that we excuse soldiers in war films who kill their enemies. Further, the film suggests that men who remain true to a code, like Michael and Vito, triumph over those like Sollozzo and Barzini (Richard Conte) who are simply pragmatists, but it could also be that they simply understand their business better than the others do.

A scene late in the film, when Michael travels to Las Vegas to negotiate the family's move there, illustrates the ambiguity that surrounds the motives of the central characters. As he talks to Moe Green (Alex Rocco) about the latter's public slapping of Michael's brother Fredo (John Cazale), Michael betrays no feeling. When Green angrily rebuffs Michael's offer to purchase Green's casino, Michael again shows no emotion. Throughout, he maintains complete control. Though he warns Fredo never to support an outsider rather than the family it remains unclear if this is because of the unwritten rules of the world he inhabits or because unity makes good business sense.

The behavior of other individuals heightens the sense of a new ethos emerging without resolving the pragmatist/idealist dichotomy. In contrast to both Vito and Michael, Sonny Corleone (James Caan) embodies the hotheaded man of action. One can find numerous counterparts to Sonny's character in the Gangster films of the 1930s, and the parallel is significant. Sonny represents a doomed figure from the start. Unlike Michael or Vito, Sonny has not evolved with the times, and his methods no longer guarantee the success that they might have enjoyed in an earlier era. Like his pursuit of women, Sonny's emotional recourse to violence emerges as a sign of weakness rather than as one of strength. It is interesting that the two Corleone sons, Sonny and Fredo, who in their own ways are shown to be unsuited to lead the family, are singled out as sexually promiscuous and publicly irrational.

Tom Hagen (Robert Duvall) stands as a unique representation amidst the conflicted attitudes that label various characters. Tom has been a family member since his childhood when Sonny brought him home. Don Corleone has treated Tom as if he were a son, but the distinction of blood and of his Irish heritage has always set him apart. Unlike each of the other sons, Tom is never disloyal. (Even Michael, the seeming paragon, joined the Marines and fought in World War II against his father's wishes.) At the same time, Tom can never attain full integration into the family, and that distinction remains important in outlining the social hierarchy of *The Godfather*.

What links Michael to his father are the very things that distinguish him from others in the crime family. He rarely raises his voice or shows emotion, yet he feels the significance of issues more keenly that many others. He behaves with decisiveness but never with rancor. The scene in the hospital when rival gangsters are coming to kill his father exemplifies all of this. Michael quick moves his father to another room, pretends he is armed as he stands at the hospital entrance, and endures a beating from a police captain, all to insure his father's safety. As the devoted and resourceful son, he acts with great initiative at a time when others in the crime family have been outsmarted and when the police show themselves as either compromised or corrupt.

Subsequently, it is Michael who comes up with a plan of action. In killing Solazzo and the police captain in his pay, Michael proves himself both decisive and pragmatic. A similar scene occurs in *The Godfather II* when the young Vito Corleone kills the local Mafioso, and the parallel strikingly underscores the similarities between the two men as they begin their roles as leaders of the family.

With the onset of gang warfare and Michael's exile to Italy, the film, though it has a great deal of running time remaining, moves towards its inevitable conclusion. Michael's courtship of Apollonia (Simonetta Stephanelli) in Italy and his subsequent treatment of Kay raise questions for the viewer about his nature. The physically declining powers of Don Corleone contrasted with his continuing mental acuity set the stage for his tutelage of Michael. The Don's participation in bringing his son into the same life that he has led leaves viewers having to decide whether to admire him or to see him as monstrous.

In the end, the film treats viewers to a summation of the meticulous planning that leads to the cataclysm that will right the fortunes of the Corleone family. Through deft cross-cutting, the final scene contrasts the Baptism of Michael Corleone's nephew (played by the infant Sofia Coppola) with the execution of the boy's father and of other enemies of the Corleone family. The murders begin as Michael recites the baptismal vows. These scenes juxtapose the rituals of the Church and of the crime family. Superficially, it might seem to indicate a parallel sacredness, but one can as easily read heavy irony into the contrast between the Sacrament that Catholics see as a spiritual rebirth and the violent extinction of life carried out by the Corleone henchmen.

The film seems to eschew the formulaic ending that would have the gangster brought down by the forces of justice. In the closing scene, Clemenza pays the same tribute, kissing the hand, to Michael that the undertaker did to Vito Corleone in the opening. By showing the mobster's obeisance to Michael, just as Cardinals would to a Pope, the film sets the Corleone crime family in ironic juxtaposition with the Catholic Church. While some parallels cannot be denied, including the hierarchical nature of both, the spiritual commitment which stands as the foundation of one institution would only be a source of bafflement to those committed to the other. In the end, the look of horror on the face of his wife Kay is more than revulsion over her husband's profession. It captures the shock of her realization that he has destroyed his soul.

The Godfather and other motion pictures in this category trace the erosion of distinctions between the gangster and those who pursue him. (The crooked police captain McCluskey, played by Sterling Hayden, stands in for a society that has come to accept and to some degree accommodate the criminal world.) They highlight the fact that the criminal world overlaps but also sharply delineates itself from the environment that the rest of us inhabit, but they also point out that the rules of behavior in society limit one's ability to meet the threat posed by criminals. The violence of *The Godfather* repeatedly reminds viewers that criminals enforce their values through behavior very different from our actions, yet it also sends the message that only similar brutality will have an effect upon criminals. Indeed, films in this category underscore the corrosive effect of gang violence on both criminals and law enforcers, and more often than not they highlight the similarities between the gangster and the law enforcement officer who seeks to apprehend him. In this manner it is like *Manhattan Melodrama, Bullets or Ballots, White Heat, The Amazing Dr. Clitterhouse, I Am the Law, The Naked City, The Detective, Q & A, Internal Affairs, Mulholland Falls, The Big Heat, The French Connection, G Men, 48 Hours, The Untouchables, Cop Land,* and *Training Day.*

Reservoir Dogs

In stark contrast to *The Godfather*, Quentin Tarrantino's 1992 film *Reservoir Dogs* shows the coarse, tawdry, violent, and bumbling side of mobsters, men who have no affiliation with community, in the traditional or non-traditional sense. These men are simply thugs, brought together to commit a specific crime. They come across as loners because each in his own way has no desire to be anything else.

The sense of alienation is compounded by the practice of Joe Cabot (Lawrence Tierney) by giving them colors for names to maintain anonymity in his various crews. The colors and the arbitrariness of their assignment says it all: These men are seen as anonymous and disposable.

With these designations, they only come to a gradual and imperfect knowledge of one another. Similarly, viewers only come to understand them in a gradual and fractured manner. By cutting episodically from one character to the other and jumping back and forth in the chronology of events that led up to the diamond dealer's robbery, Tarantino can represent each as unique while capturing the confusion and alienation that they all feel.

Nonetheless, Tarantino's character driven account never seems reductive. Even working within the relatively narrow paradigm of gangster characterization, the narrative plays upon flaws as a way of distinguishing each individual. Mr. Blonde (Michael Madsen) is a sadist who takes pleasure in inflicting pain. Mr. Pink is a sociopath driven by pragmatism. Mr. White (Harvey Keitel), who has killed police officers without flinching, defends the man who, he later learns, is a mole. Even Mr. Orange (Tim Roth), an undercover cop characterized by fellow officers as having "rocks in his head," becomes caught up in his role as a criminal and while trying to escape the botched robbery kills an innocent motorist.

Mr. Blonde (Michael Madsen), Mr. Brown (Quentin Tarantino), Mr. White (Harvey Kitel), Nice Guy Eddy (Chris Penn), Joe Cabot (Lawrence Tierney), Mr. Orange (Tim Roth), Mr. Pink (Steve Buscemi), and Mr. Blue (Edward Bunker) in *Reservoir Dogs* (1992).

Despite all the violence, the gangsters' lives are profoundly banal, as typified by their lengthy discussion of the meaning of the Madonna song "Like a Virgin." Even when Mr. Pink and Mr. White attempt a more serious conversation by debating the protocols for tipping waitresses, the arguments never rise above the level of precocious teenagers. As a way of underscoring their pedestrian world, Tarantino intersperses broadcasts from a radio station playing "K-Billy's Super Sounds of the 70s." Viewers hear the laconic voiceover of a bored and distracted disk jockey playing the songs of second rate bands from an earlier period punctuating everything from tedious rehearsals of the robbery to moments of extreme brutality.

By the time we hear the Stealers Wheel recording of "Stuck in the Middle with You" being played while Mr. Blonde cuts off the policeman-hostage's ear, we know that Mr. Blonde takes mindless pleasure in both. Like the bucolic landscape of *A Perfect World* or the edgy urban scene of hip L.A. in *Pulp Fiction*, the clash of sight and sound signals a similar imbalance in the lives of all of these men. *Reservoir Dogs* and the numerous other films in this subgroup highlight the psychopathic element to a greater degree than any other kind of Gangster film. Their central characters are completely unresponsive, even to the point of being oblivious, to the normal restraints of society.

Unlike the violent elimination of Michael Corleone's enemies that concludes *The Godfather*, the killings at the end of *Reservoir Dogs* produces no sense of purgation or even temporary closure. The deaths of Joe, Nice Guy Eddy, and Mr. White simply underscore the arrested development of each man, unable to find any sort of alternative to a self-destructive conflagration. Irony and confusion tinge everything. Even Mr. Orange's final revelation to Mr. White, who has just been shot defending him, is ambiguous. Does he confess to being a police officer to show Mr. White that his efforts were not simply fruitless but comical, or does he merely wish to clear his conscience of any deceit? Looking for resolution, however, is not the point. Quite the contrary, the arbitrariness of their savagery calls into question everything that they have done. By the end of the film these gun men, with all the mayhem that does nothing but produce chaos, have succeeded in trivializing their lives.

Indeed, the intense violence that runs throughout *Reservoir Dogs* does not celebrate the recklessness of the criminal lifestyle, nor does it posit the need to act in this fashion to survive in society at large. Rather, it is a film that highlights the complete alienation of the gangster from the rest of society, and shocks us into a confrontation with its deviance. Unlike films in the other two categories, gangsters in these movies are steeped in nihilism. There is never an inclination to find respectability or to become integrated into society. Though not always acknowledged, they embrace a sense of ostracism. In this way it is like *The Public Enemy, White Heat, Gun Crazy, The Asphalt Jungle, Bonnie and Clyde, Bloody Mama, Machine-Gun Kelly, Badlands, Dog Day Afternoon, Natural Born Killers, The Rise and Fall of Legs Diamond, New Jack City, Juice,* and *Pulp Fiction.*

Three

A Touch of Evil
Film Noir

In 1946, in what quickly became a highly influential essay, "A New Kind of Police Drama: the Criminal Adventure," the French film critic Nino Frank introduced the term Noir, applying it to four American motion pictures made during World War II—*The Maltese Falcon, Double Indemnity, Laura*, and *Murder, My Sweet*.[1] Frank classified these films as a variation on traditional crime dramas, unique in form and perspective from others made around the same time. Enthusiasts quickly expanded the use of Frank's term applying it to other cinematic representations of contemporary life that highlight personal alienation, moral ambiguity, and social deterioration.

Production Values and Ethos

More than any other genre, Film Noir draws our attention to the way that the self-consciousness of its formal style echoes the fixations of its thematic concerns. As one sees in *Murder, My Sweet*, starkly lit sets distort perception of the layout and place emphasis on darkness, isolation, and disorientation that threaten to overwhelm its protagonist. In *The Killers* many scenes set at night or in ill-lit rooms, affirm only a world other of menacing shadows and ambiguous boundaries.

The strong emphasis given to the contrasts of harsh light and dark shadows has fueled arguments by some critics that Film Noir exists only in motion pictures made from the mid–1940s to the late 1950s, when black and white was the film stock of choice. The assumption is that, with the dominance of color releases after that time, a vital element of the Noir atmosphere was lost. In fact, imaginative directors having been playing against such conventions for decades. Thus, when making *L.A. Confidential*, a film discussed below, the director, Curtis Hansen, set most of the scenes during the day or in bright light as a counterpoint to conventional Film Noir expectations.

This continuity of a Noir ethos over decades of cinematographic advancement underscores the complexity of the defining the material features of this genre. Camera angle is as important as lighting in the Noir world. Often directors eschew head-on, eye-level representations of characters or events. Instead, they frame shots from high or low angles. They offer oblique perspectives. They present the action from any point of view that disrupts ordinary perception. When combined with the play of light, dark, and shadows, these unnatural and unexpected perspectives do more than underscore contrast. They add to the viewer's distorted sense of the action (*Sin City*) calling into question our perceptions of almost everything we see.

Aural as well as visual materiality shapes the atmosphere of the Film Noir production. The soundtrack is an important feature of every film, but in the Noir film it takes on added implications. Whether with haunting jazz melodies of *Chinatown*, poignant blues heard in *Devil in a Blue Dress*, or melodies especially composed for the film, like the John Williams score

Easy Rawlins (Denzel Washington) in *Devil in a Blue Dress* (1995).

for *The Long Goodbye*, music accentuates the isolation, sorrow, and uniqueness felt by the Noir figures.

Intrusiveness plays against isolation throughout films in this category, and often a narrative voiceover, like the one used in *Sunset Boulevard*, brings the central character into proximity with the audience even as the noir lifestyle distances him or her from the film. Many of these interpolations give the audience privileged insights into the feelings of the character, and, as in *The Lady from Shanghai*. Other voiceovers provide a sense of the spiritual, emotional, or even physical environment of the film that is kept hidden from most of the individuals who inhabit those surroundings (*Out of the Past*). In every instance, this trait of speaking directly to the viewers creates empathy for an otherwise alienated figure, and clarifies how one understands an often opaque world.

The attitudes of Film Noir combine personal idealism, isolated from the more pragmatic and mundane views held by society, with a world-weary pessimism about one's ability to break free of the influence of the cynical majority (*Jackie Brown*). Consequently, the central figures in Film Noir continuously struggle to sustain their identities, even as they find

(Left to right) Mark Dargus (Michael Bowen), Jackie Brown (Pam Grier), and Ray Nicolette (Michael Keaton) in *Jackie Brown* (1997).

the boundaries of their worlds shifting. Many of these films begin with the central characters articulating doubts about their place in the world they inhabit or at the very least expressing worn-out resignation at the ambivalence they feel towards society. Despite the confidence the central character often shows, he or she cannot escape a sense of estrangement, and the narratives in this genre rarely if ever dispel the uncertainty that surrounds individuals.

Key Elements in Plot and Characterization

Film Noir involves a quest for comprehending an unsettled world in which accepted practices for understanding people, actions and institutions turn out to be based on nothing more than habit and hypocrisy. At the same time, viewers must take care in their interpretations of the central character. Narratives may seem to represent that figure as a rebel, but a close analysis shows that the opposite is true. The Noir protagonist has a near obsessive regard for social values, and what is most challenging to the Film Noir hero is the disparity between the rules and the way the world seems to function. In consequence, most often the central character works compulsively to unravel and understand the confused events that unfold around him (or, less often, around her as in *Mulholland Drive*[2]) and to restore conventional order. Often these efforts pessimistically reconfigure the elements of the traditional American success story, implying that every Horatio Alger–like triumph is really the product of corruption and double-dealing (*Touch of Evil*) but this does not mean that the Film Noir hero condemns the conventions. Rather, he or she is usually appalled by how they have been corroded.

Inherently deceptive relationships punctuate the narrative of Film Noir, and, because of a fundamental idealism, the central character often stands as a pawn manipulated by any number of different individuals (*Murder, My Sweet*). Few if any others seem to adhere to the values espoused by the central character. And, within a relatively short period after the opening of the film, duplicity and double dealing have made it next to impossible to judge the motives of any character based upon actions alone (*The Big Sleep*).

This is not always to say that the central character adheres to values more noble than those of the community. In some striking examples of this genre—*The Player* and *The Grifters*, for example—the opposite is true. The crucial point is that the central character operates according to a code of conduct generally given little more than lip service by the rest of society. To complicate the situation, men in this genre often have fatal involvements with women who prove to be as alienated and generally much more predatory than they are (*Basic Instinct*).

The central character can end up dead, disgraced, or at the very least broken in spirit. When he or she does survive more or less intact, it is because of a system of personal morality that sets this figure apart from almost everyone else. This code follows principles that fall outside and often above legal restraints (*The Maltese Falcon*). At the same time the central character cannot avoid judging the ineffectiveness of the system and resenting its failures to live up to the implicit social contract that it makes with the individuals in the community.

In an unstable and contradictory world, such a personal system of values stands out as an essential anchor. The central figures finds events continually reordering both the psychological and the physical landscape of the world he or she inhabits. Unpredictable acts overturn the order of

(Left to right) Sam Spade (Humphrey Bogart), Joel Cairo (Peter Lorie), Brigit O'Shaughnessy (Mary Astor), and Casper Gutman (Sidney Greenstreet) in *The Maltese Falcon* (1941).

things, and the narrative consistently frustrates conventional expectations. While this is often linked to excessive violence (*Blood Simple*), menace is even more prominent and often even more unsettling (*The Black Dahlia*). For all of the characters, dealing with the unexpected remains the great challenge, and in a hostile world it remains unclear how any situation will unfold or how any character will react.

Issues

Contradictions, misconceptions, and ambiguities punctuate the Film Noir narrative, and they do much more than create a brooding atmosphere. Disorientation dominates the atmosphere. In response, characters spend a great deal of time struggling, more often than not in vain, to order their perceptions to form a logical picture of the world around them.

In Robert Altman's *The Long Goodbye*, Philip Marlowe (Elliot Gould) must continually reorient his interpretation of what he is experiencing. Eileen Wade (Nina Van Pallandt), the woman who hires Marlowe to find her husband Roger Wade (Sterling Hayden), repeatedly gives different accounts of her background, of her experiences, and of her reasons for employing him. Additionally, Roger Wade, Dr. Veeringer (Henry Gibson), and others offer competing versions of events. Although Marlowe eventually refines the contradictory details into a single narrative, he is left with the sense of only partially comprehending the ethos of the world inhabited by these characters.

Viewers naturally turn to the central character of a Film Noir as a guide for assessing enigmatic people and ambiguous events. In a motion picture like *The Big Sleep*, the audience will make that commitment because Philip Marlowe (Humphrey Bogart) begins the movie conveying a sense of control of his surroundings. Nonetheless, in any Noir Film, whether quickly (*Blue Velvet*) or gradually (*Farewell, My Lovely*), this anchoring figure comes to realize how little impact any individual can have upon the events that shape one's life. This knowledge comes about through discoveries of systems that are far more complex than imagined and that operate according to rules heretofore unknown to the central character (*Dark City*). This increasing sense of a loss of control also puts interpretive pressure on the audience. It adds to the imperative to gain some level of comprehension of the events unfolding in the narrative.

Often, the difficulty in this situation comes from the clash between the integrity of the protagonist and the amorality or immorality inherent

(Left to right) Philip Marlowe (Humphrey Bogart), Vivian Rutledge (Lauren Bacall), and Joe Brody (Louis Gene Heydt) in *The Big Sleep* (1946).

in the surrounding world. This opposition is not always immediately apparent, for, in many of the Noir films, communities maintain the appearance of a conventionally ordered, if sometimes idiosyncratic, world (*Fargo*). Initial impressions never give a complete picture of the true state of things, and a hidden corruption exerts a pervasive, insistent threat to the integrity of society. Whether assailing institutions or individuals, corrosive degeneracy recurs throughout the action, undermining one's faith in the stability of anything (*Sin City*). No one knows whom to trust or indeed whether such an attitude is realistic in this world.

These disruptive impressions combine to create a high level of paranoia running through the movie (*Mullholland Falls*). This is not simply apprehension over a specific threat, and it goes beyond that to a feeling of being unable to put faith in others. It reflects a lack of assurance in the world at large and a lack of confidence in the perceptions of one's own senses (*Farewell, My Lovely*).

Marginalization compounds the difficulties. Whether as a punishment for having an independent nature, as a consequence of an inability to adapt, or simply as a capricious twist of fate, alienation marks the central character (*Miller's Crossing*). In Film Noir one is left to one's own resources to contest the world, and often the story of this struggle leads to a tragic outcome (*D.O.A.*). A perverse paradox often obtains. The individual craves integration into society, yet remains ostracized by being the only one who adheres to standards that should inform the behavior of the entire community.

This culminates in a feeling of complete disorientation (*Kiss Me Deadly*). In a society where the central figure is challenged to comprehend and contest forces of power, more often than not that character has at best an imperfect sense of whom or what he or she struggles against (*Kiss Kiss Bang Bang*). As familiar reference points prove unstable, the central character must struggle for definition without the benefit of the reinforcement of society (*Out of the Past*). As a further consequence, individuals have no larger communal reinforcement for their value system, and they often must contend with the sense that their views of the world and their patterns of behavior are completely distorted (*Memento*).

Consequently, an existential-like pessimism seems to dominate, yet one must apply that term carefully. A true commitment to this pessimistic view would inevitably result in paralysis. In the Film Noir, action, especially that which is linked to a quest for understanding events or redressing wrongs, characterizes the narrative. Events can often lead to a disastrous end, but in almost every instance the protagonist holds to the possibility of some form of redemption or at least affirmation.

Specific Application

As in other genres, one can find the same general traits in virtually all motion pictures that fall into the Film Noir category. At the same time, within this broad classification, one can identify distinct sub-groups that place different interpretive demands upon viewers. Among these categories, the differences turn upon the variance between the moral positions of the central character and the values of communal institutions. In the first instance, as shown by *Double Indemnity*, characters conduct their lives seemingly oblivious to the ethical system that prescribes behavior in the world around them. In the second category, exemplified by *Chinatown*, the central character naively assumes that his values coincide with those of the world in which he operates, and is profoundly shocked when he discovers that is not always the case. And in the final group, represented by *L.A. Confidential*, the community at large maintains a hypocritical position regarding values that proves to be far more cynical than the central character at first imagines. In all of these sub-groups, the action turns on the consequences of the limited and often flawed perceptions of individuals striving to understand the world around them, and in each instance moral ambiguity remains the dominant feature of the narrative.

Double Indemnity

Although Walter Neff (Fred MacMurray) the scheming insurance agent of *Double Indemnity*, is antithetical to the protagonists of most Noir films, he does have a world view strikingly similar to that of Sam Spade (Humphrey Bogart), the principled private detective of *The Maltese Falcon*. Each begins thinking of himself as worldly-wise and ends the action struggling to understand the forces that have caused the cataclysmic events around him. Each is captivated by a woman who proves to be more ruthless and coldblooded than he is. And, each inhabits a world in which the social institutions meant to preserve order can do little more than attempt to restore equilibrium after every disruptive upheaval of ordinary life. Nonetheless, as dark as the ending of *The Maltese Falcon* may seem—with the supposedly gold statuette of the bird proving to be counterfeit, Brigid O'Shaughnessy (Mary Astor) coming forward as a murderess, and Spade standing alone and disillusioned—its conclusion seems positively upbeat in comparison to the desolation at the end of *Double Indemnity*.

We come to know Neff through a voiceover delivered in the confessional mode. Speaking into a Dictaphone, he lays out events after the fact, and explains in precise detail how he and Phyllis Dietrichson (Barbara Stanwyck) planned and carried out the murder of her husband (Tom Powers) to collect on an insurance policy. Even as he begins the narration, Neff cannot drop the wise guy/tough guy attitude: "I killed him for money and for a woman. And I didn't get the money, and I didn't get the woman."

Neff's portrayal illustrates with particular precision how our impressions of the central character shape our understanding. Through Neff's presence in so many scenes, his perspective serves as a gloss for the world that we see on the screen. Like Joe Gillis (William Holden) in *Sunset Boulevard* or Leonard (Guy Pierce) in *Memento*, Neff introduces us to a society existing parallel to but generally unperceived by the community of the film.

From the opening scene, despite Neff's wise guy banter, a shallowness imbedded in his every observation undermines the credibility of many of the conclusions that he reaches. As Neff describes the Dietrichson home, he adds a cynical commentary on both the décor and the inhabitants. When he speaks with Phyllis, he mixes business and flirtation. For Neff nothing is straightforward or simple, so he can never take seriously Barton Keyes (Edward G. Robinson) and the Pacific All Risk Insurance Company, yet in the end he returns to both for a measure of absolution.

Walter Neff (Fred MacMurray, left) and Barton Keyes (Edward G. Robinson) in *Double Indemnity* (1944).

Because of the persona he has adopted, the film itself is too smart to leave interpretation of characters and events solely to Walter Neff. While the voiceover gives his unfiltered impressions, *Double Indemnity* allows the viewer to judge whether or not he really is as smart as he thinks he is. This approach neither exalts nor degrades Neff. It presents an intimate view without forcing a specific reading of the significance of those impressions.

The balance here is crucial. *Double Indemnity* turns on the idea that we see everything from the point of view of a man who thinks he is clever and who nonetheless finds himself caught up in events that he neither fully controls nor understands. In this way the film gives viewers room to question Neff's conclusions and to reassess his situation.

Of course, the narrative cannot allow the central character to slip into a mere caricature. Its effectiveness rests on the narrative's ability to project Neff's humanity, which means not simply showing his flaws but highlighting his complexity as well. This comes across most vividly through scenes that develop Neff's relationship with Barton Keyes, his supervisor and in a sense his conscience. Time and again, Neff demonstrates a keen affection for his boss while making it clear that they operate according to drastically different value systems. In particular, when Keyes explains to Neff what it means to be a claims man, trying to get Neff to become his assistant, Neff can only think of the tedium of the job and the loss in salary that a change would entail. The way that each man approaches his job at the insurance company gives viewers a clear sense of their similarities and differences. In particular, Keyes underscores the contrast between himself and his subordinate with a sharp summation that captures Neff's overconfident nature: "You're not smarter, Walter. You're just a little taller."

Keyes' acerbic comment underscores an important feature of this sub-category, one generally at variance with other types of Noir films. The world that Neff disparages is neither as corrupt nor as indifferent as he believes it to be. Indeed, here and in other films in this category, it represents a viable alternative that the central character chooses to accept or reject.

Phyllis Dietrichson's character also takes on an important dual role, albeit one tied closer to exposition than to theme. Like Cora Smith, Lana Turner's hard-edged adulteress in *The Postman Always Rings Twice*, her sexuality provides Neff with motivation for committing murder and fraud. In addition, Barbara Stanwyck's portrayal of Phyllis suggests a psychopathic nature that goes well beyond the animal appetites that motivate

Neff. After the murder of her husband, she shows a self-possession that contrasts sharply with the desperation that she articulates earlier in the film, and these conflicting moods leave the viewer to decide if she is completely manipulative or a desperate woman torn by incompatible attitudes.

As is the case in so many films of this genre, the actual crime precipitates rather than resolves a crisis. The murder unfolds as a cleverly planned and smoothly executed scheme with both Neff and Phyllis showing remarkable composure under pressure. Nonetheless, almost as soon as they have committed the crime, Neff begins to experience apprehension over what he has done. "I could feel my nerves pulling me to pieces." Here Neff's sense of alienation intensifies. It comes not simply through adherence to an alternative ethical code but from the conflicted nature that seeks to reject conventional values yet cannot fully escape them.

Though Fred MacMurray's Neff serves as the model for this type of character, countless Noir films reproduce a similarly conflicted figure. For example, William H. Macy's performance in *Fargo* as Jerry Lundegaard, the man so desperate for money that he arranges his wife's kidnapping, projects similar dichotomies, though, despite the movie's graphic violence, he does so in a more muted form. Like Walter, Jerry's solipsistic outlook distorts his sense of the world around him. Further, as did Barton Keyes in *Double Indemnity*, police officer Marge Gunderson (Frances McDormand) offers viewers a principled alternative to Jerry's cynical and desperate conception of the world.

When Keyes proves as formidable as Neff had feared, the scheme begins to fall apart. Once Keyes, as the embodiment of society, expresses suspicion over the cause of Dietrichson's death, Neff and Phyllis begin to trust each other less. Concurrently, like the bumblers in so many other films in this sub-genre, Neff begins to feel that he is embroiled in a situation more complicated and devious than he understands: "You planned the whole thing. I only wanted him dead." This leads to the unraveling of the tough, cynical persona that Neff has projected for most of the film. Neff desperately wants to pull out of the arrangement, but, when he attempts to break free, Phyllis coolly browbeats him back into line, showing a ruthless streak heretofore concealed.

From this point, the accelerating collapse of their enterprise begins. With no sense of how little control he has over events, Neff decides to eliminate Phyllis, but does not realize that she is more ruthless than he is. Like the best Noir films, however, their final confrontation raises more questions than it resolves. Phyllis shoots Neff once, and then tells him she loves him. The scene has a wonderful ambivalence, for it balances the possibility that she has had a change of heart with the very real alternative that she is continuing to toy with him. Neff, with none of the subtlety that characterizes Phyllis, shows no such hesitation, and kills her the moment he gets the chance.

Had the narrative concluded at this point, audiences would have had an unambiguous sense of Neff as a bungling thug. However, Neff cannot forget his ties to Keyes, and so goes back to his office to record a full account of what has transpired. The film ends as it had begun, at the Pacific All Risk Insurance Company, with Keyes standing unobserved by Neff and hearing his confession (though early in his dictation Neff has rejected that label to describe the account he is giving). However, it gives no clear indication of whether Neff has earned the absolution that he seems unconsciously to seek.

This attitude underscores an important distinction between the individuals in Film Noir and those who populate Gangster films. While criminals take advantage of upright citizens who live by the rules, they never question the value of society. Indeed, the ultimate aim of many criminals is to gain acceptance in the world of those upon which they prey. Characters in this sub-genre like Neff clash with people like Keyes because they cannot accept the fact that others might sincerely subscribe to the tenets that they so easily dismiss. They always seek another explanation for conformity. Other such films include *The Postman Always Rings Twice, Body Heat, Fargo, Night of the Hunter, The Player, The Maltese Falcon, The Force of Evil, Blood Simple, Harper, Sunset Boulevard, Cape Fear, Memento, The Grifters, The Third Man, Get Shorty, Basic Instinct,* and *Out of the Past.*

Chinatown

Though *Chinatown* quickly establishes clear links to the Noir films made in the 1940s—opening with stylized titles and jazz background music presented in the opening credits evoke pre–World War II Los Angeles—it is not simply an act of homage or a gesture of imitation. Director Roman Polanski, in his reverence for that type of movie, demonstrates in his own motion picture how the most successful Film Noir efforts function. He builds audience awareness of the plot slowly and carefully. He situates his central character in an environment that is both more baffling and more hostile than he initially realizes. And, most significantly, Polanski recreates the period in which Film Noir came to prominence without becoming self-conscious or slipping into parody. Indeed, the movie's exploration of incest and sexual abuse acknowledges how the genre's evolution now allows explicit representations of the dark impulses only hinted at in earlier films like *The Big Sleep*.

For all these reasons, *Chinatown* represents an important Film Noir sub-group: that in which the isolated individual copes with an amoral or at least indifferent society. To do so, the motion picture takes the signature features of the genre as the parameters within which its narrative must unfold. From there, it structures the character development to suit the sensibilities of an audience well-versed in Noir tendencies.

At the same time, the film cleverly critiques well-worn assumptions to give viewers already acquainted with the genre both a feeling of familiarity and a sensation of newness. In the opening scene, for example, Jake Gittes exudes callous indifference when he brags to a distraught client whose wife has been caught *in flagrante* about his proficiency at documenting marital infidelity, so viewers are hard pressed to rank him in the same light as prototypical figures of the genre like Philip Marlowe. This deft gesture adds a layer of cynicism to the narrative by stripping from the detective the one standard that in earlier films set him apart from the sordid world around him. Unlike countless predecessors, Jake would never think of uttering the signature self-righteous phrase "I don't do divorce work." For Jake, divorce work is "my métier."

Despite this self-aggrandizing statement, Jake's apparent aptness for even this line of work is called into question by a series of events that show Jake's limited abilities and circumscribed awareness of his environment. In the first instance, he is easily duped

Jake Gittes (Jack Nicholson) in *Chinatown* (1974).

into conducting a fraudulent investigation by Ida Sessions (Diane Ladd), a woman who calls herself Evelyn Mulwray and claiming to suspect her husband of being unfaithful. Then, after the evidence that Gittes has collected leads to a sensationalized account in the local newspapers of Hollis Mulwray's (Darrell Zwerling) alleged affair, Jake shows that he is anything but prototypical the hardboiled detective, proving instead to be extremely thin-skinned when a stranger in a barbershop chastises him over his part in the scandal. Finally, the previously glib Gittes is speechless when the real Evelyn Mulwray (Faye Dunaway) comes to his office, tells him she did not hire him, and threatens him with a law suit.

To recover from the embarrassment he feels over being so easily fooled, Jake pursues an investigation of Mulwray that propels the action of the film. He finds that Mulwray is a public official troubled over the clandestine diversion of water, but for most of the movie Jake has no idea what is behind this concern. (The effort is at the heart of a complex scheme to buy farmland at depressed prices and convert it into residential and commercial real estate, though Jake and the viewers will not learn this until near the end of the film.) As in other films in this category—like *Criss Cross*—the narrative is driven by the central character's gradual realization of his minimal understanding of his surroundings and his lack of control over events.

Indeed, though the movie plays with expectations about a Film Noir environment, it never falls into a prescriptive representation of what that world entails. When Jake encounters Lou Escobar (Perry Lopez), a former colleague from the Los Angeles Police Department, most viewers, alert to conventions, will see it as noteworthy that Jake and Lou worked the Chinatown beat together. Later, Jake will tell Evelyn Mulwray that he got into trouble in Chinatown over his failed effort to protect someone, introducing expectations of some sort of redemptive encounter that will expunge guilt for previous failures. Despite these suggestions, however, the narrative never resolves the ambiguities surrounding Jake's time in Chinatown and certainly does not provide catharsis at the film's conclusion.

Any assumptions viewers' may make based on types are also mutable. Jake is not the tough guy that one expects. As noted above, he often exudes bravado, yet usually behaves more like an aggrieved businessman than a hardboiled detective. When an associate asks Jake what he plans to do when he finds out who attacked him with a knife, Jake replies that he will "sue the shit out of him."

Most significantly, *Chinatown* puts Jake in a realistic context. He is baffled by the extent of the conspiracy because he has no experience with something of this magnitude. He keeps seeing it in terms of the tawdry domestic work that he usually does for a living. Nonetheless, as someone with a code of values in spite of himself, he shows a consistent determination to get to the bottom of the mess that surrounds him, and ultimately understands the scope of the fraud being perpetrated.

In fairness, Jake's success at discovering how the multimillionaire Noah Cross is engineering fraudulent land purchases shows that he has the persistence and an adequate level of skill for the narrowly focused work that he has chosen to do. However, despite a world-weary façade, Jake is at heart an innocent. When he finds himself enmeshed in a far more complex and ruthless environment, he spends much of his time groping for a way to comprehend that world. After finally coming to some sense of the intricacies of Cross' plan to acquire large amounts of land in Los Angeles County, Jake confronts Cross and asks him bluntly, "Why are you doing it?" While Cross' answer is as ambiguous as the rest of the narrative, the overall discussion about Cross' motives—centering on power—gives a clear indication of how different their worlds are.

The most shocking exposure of all, and the one that underscores Jake's relative innocence, is the incestuous relationship between Nora Cross and his daughter Evelyn. Although it is not directly related to the criminal plot to garner land for commercial development, its revelation explains much of the neurotic behavior that drives Evelyn, and gives an unambiguous picture of Cross who feels neither remorse nor guilt over it all. More than anything, it is emblematic of the corruption just beneath the surface of the narrative that Jake and many others are, for much of the film, simply too innocent to grasp.

The film ends by underscoring the nihilism that has run throughout its narrative with a scene that suggests a replication of the trouble that Jake earlier had in Chinatown. Evelyn Mulwray is shot as she tries to escape police custody with her daughter (Belinda Palmer). Her death and the apparent triumph of Noah Cross who, as a result of Evelyn's death, will presumably now have guardianship of his daughter/granddaughter and most definitely will continue his scheme to obtain land, make all of Jake's efforts seem fruitless. His associate can only comfort him with the fatalistic phrase: "Forget it, Jake. It's Chinatown." This does not simply reflect a sense of hopelessness. It reminds both Jake and the audience of the indifference felt by the world of the film to everything that has had a profound impact on Jake's life.

Films in this group often foreground men with a rather touching naiveté. In *Chinatown*, the charm of Jake Gittes rests on the genuine innocence that gradually emerges from beneath his worldly-wise exterior. In contrast, the Evelyn Mulwray figure reinforces the image of the strong woman, though in her case also one who is highly disturbed, with few illusions about the world that she inhabits. Other films in this sub-group include *D.O.A., Criss Cross, The Killers, Farewell, My Lovely, The Naked City, Murder, My Sweet, Lady in the Lake, Insomnia, The Lady from Shanghai*, and *Jackie Brown*.

L.A. Confidential

As does *Chinatown*, *L.A. Confidential* repeatedly demonstrates a keen sense of the central elements of the original Noir films of the 1940s. However, each movie reflects very different choices on how to incorporate those features effectively into a motion picture appealing to contemporary audiences. While *Chinatown* chooses to push expectations to the limit by presenting an atypical Film Noir hero in Jake Gittes dealing with a typical Noir themes of individual corruption, *L.A. Confidential* follows the programmatic approach to characterization but presents a profoundly nihilistic view of social institutions surrounding its characters. It is grounded in an environment much harsher than the one Jake Gittes encountered, that of a pervasively vicious and self-gratifying world immersed in materialism and contemptuous of higher values. In *Chinatown* men like Noah Cross can take advantage of corrupt, timid, or naïve individuals to circumvent social restraints. In *L.A. Confidential* the system itself breeds corruption. From *The Big Sleep* to *Mulholland Drive*, films of this sub-group have produced the most pessimistic representations of the Film Noir world.

L.A. Confidential begins with a brash voiceover commentary by tabloid journalist Sid Hudgens (Danny DeVito). In a sardonic tone, he offers an intimate, cynical overview of the world that the film will explore, and introduces key narrative themes: the contrast between innocent appearances and ingrained corruption, the glamour of the Hollywood scene that in fact rests on shabbiness, and the pervasive impact of organized crime existing only slightly beneath the surface of suburban respectability. Sid's opening monologue is evocative of a similar introduction, delivered with harsh indifference, by Joe Gillis (William Holden) in *Sunset Boulevard*, but it presents a world filled with people far more mean, ruthless, and grasping than the character that William Holden portrays.

Nonetheless, it follows a familiar cinematic pattern. *Blue Velvet*, *The Big Sleep*, and *Touch of Evil*—to name just three examples—all portray the same desolate world existing beneath a seemingly benign landscape that is in fact corroded by greed and cynicism.

A quick succession of scenes presents most of the central figures of the movie, all members of the Los Angeles Police Department. Detective Bud White (Russell Crowe) is first seen beating up a spousal abuser, establishing him as a man who sees violence as a way to uphold the law. Fellow detective Jack Vincennes (Kevin Spacey) is shown serving as technical adviser for *Badge of Honor*—a television show, presented in a manner that self-consciously mimics the popular 1950s series *Dragnet*, celebrating the virtues of the LAPD. Jack also works with Sid Hudgen to supply copy for *Hush Hush* scandal magazine, often by the entrapment of naïve individuals working on the fringe of the movie industry. Finally, Sgt. Edmund Exley (Guy Pearce), in contrast to Bud's thuggishness and Jack's venality, exudes a priggish sense of self-righteous integrity, though in fact he is driven as much by ambition as by his self-righteousness.

Despite these initial representations, at one point or another each of

(Left to right) Dudley Smith (James Cromwell), Bud White (Russell Crowe), Edward Exley (Guy Pearce), and Jack Vincennes (Kevin Spacey) in *L.A. Confidential* (1997).

these men demonstrates his willingness to accommodate alternative or conflicting attitudes to those apparently dominating traits. This does not indicate a vacillation within their characters, but rather highlights a number of ambivalent attitudes inherent in their natures. In short, again seemingly like Philip Marlowe or Sam Spade, they acknowledge the duplicity of many of those around them without feeling completely comfortable adopting the same attitude.

At the same time, and in a much broader fashion than Jake Gittes, these men all operate under the illusion that they understand their environment and that it is laid out in fairly simple terms. Even those who feel that they have a sophisticated sense of the world around them see good and evil in a fairly straightforward fashion. They all categorize individuals as being in one group of the other, and all operate accordingly.

Only two characters show a sense of the full complexity and ambiguity of their environment. Lynn Bracken (Kim Basinger) works as a call girl with a group of women, many of whom have undergone plastic surgery, who cater to men's fantasies about having sex with movie stars. Lynn makes clear over the course of the film, it is not simply cosmetic changes that shape her profession. Rather its is a willingness to manipulate the tenuous awareness that many have of individual identity.

Captain Dudley Smith (James Cromwell), the police officer supervising White, Exley, and Vincennes, shows a sinister, coldblooded, and calculating understanding of the perspectives held by these men, and ultimately proves to have a sociopathic willingness to manipulate them. Early on he singles out Bud as a police officer who is must useful brutalizing criminals. He disparages Exley's ambitions to become a detective because Exley refuses to work outside the law. And he dismisses Jack Vincennes as a nonentity, content with small payoffs from Sid and the associative glamor that he derives from his television connections.

Captain Smith well understands that appetites and desires act as a measure of corruption rather than as normal motivations for human behavior. From the start, the impact of sexual cravings on ordinary lives is a prominent theme, but, as the story unfolds, its significance becomes increasingly distanced from physical gratification and tied instead to a desire for dominance. (The violent rescue in the middle of the movie of the young woman who had been abducted and gang raped reflects the kind of behavior that White and Exley believe justifies their approach to policing. It is only at the end of the film that they come to realize that their actions unwittingly provided a smokescreen that obscured a more complex web of crime.) The same sort of complications appear in *Touch of Evil* and *Mulholland*

Drive, and in each instance sex and sexuality come to represent artificiality and alienation rather than reconciliation or intimacy.

L.A. Confidential plays on these conventions when Bud falls in love with Lynn, despite, or perhaps because of, her role as a whore whose looks mimic the Film Noir star Veronica Lake. However, Exley's own obsession with Lynn and her coerced complicity bring to a head the animosity that he and White already feel for each other. Bud's predictably violent reaction only stops when he comprehends that all of them are being manipulated by Dudley Smith. That revelation moves the film towards its conclusion.

That new sense of purpose, however, also reflects the isolation experienced by individuals with moral principle rather than demonstrating a broad move toward reformation according to societal values. In fact, they come to see that to achieve any change they must adopt the methods of the corrupt society they oppose. Thus during the interrogation of District Attorney Ellis Loew (Ron Rifkin), White and Exley hold Lowe by his ankles out an open window high above the sidewalk until he gives them the information that they seek. Having come to see themselves as morally isolated within a system grounded on corruption, they respond with brutality as the only counter to this force.

The climatic shoot-out at a deserted motel court seems to vindicate Exley and White and to expunge dishonesty from the Los Angeles police force by killing so many of the officers involved in the corruption. However, the final scene rebuts such an upbeat interpretation. The film concludes with the battered Bud retiring with Lynn to Arizona, Dudley Smith being hypocritically honored as a fallen hero, and Exley, who shot Smith to prevent the latter from escaping justice, receiving an award for valor. Rather than setting things right, the conclusion shows an institutional willingness to paper over corruption, and leaves open the question whether Exley has been corrupted or at least co-opted.

Individuals in this subgroup, at least those with whom viewers are likely to identify—like Edmund Exley, Bud White, and Jack Vincennes—exude a cynicism that in fact masks at least a measure of idealism, though they have a capacity for viciousness that would have shocked even Walter Neff. These figures generally pride themselves in their worldliness, but they are generally shocked by the extent of corruption within the institutions that they encounter. Curiously, they do not come away with the despairing view that nothing can be done. Rather, they display a muted hope that, through accommodation, they can achieve some good. Other films in this subgroup include *Mulholland Drive, The Long Goodbye, Blue Velvet, The Big Sleep, Touch of Evil, Kiss Me Deadly, Pulp Fiction,* and *The Conversation.*

Four

Die, Monster, Die
Horror Films

Don't Be Afraid

To a degree that surpasses even Westerns and Gangster movies, violence animates Horror films. It disrupts normal life, allows for no conventional explanation for its presence, and isolates ordinary individuals from their community. It can be the sudden appearance of zombies walking through a rural cemetery (*Night of the Living Dead*). It may be the ferocious

metamorphosis of a man into a beast (*The Wolf Man*). Or it can be the abrupt transformation of a seemingly benign object into a vengeful spirit (*Child's Play*).[1]

However, the best motion pictures in this category go beyond physical suffering to present probing representations of the emotional and psychological upheavals that result when normal expectations are disrupted (*The Shining*). These films follow the intellectual, emotional, and at times even spiritual growth of their protagonists (*1408*). The most fortuitous endings have and their central characters arrive at clearer understandings of themselves and of how their natures fit into their world (*Rosemary's Baby*). Others simply underscore the false security they had felt because of a seemingly normal existence (*Jeepers Creepers*).

A General Sense of the Genre

At their core, Horror films all conform to a simple and straightforward formula. They narrate the cathartic struggle between individuals and forces with unnatural powers. This conflict can be all the more unnerving when it involves seemingly human antagonists. Michael Meyers from the *Halloween* movies, Jason from the *Friday the 13th* sequels, and Freddy Kruger from the *Nightmare on Elm Street* series, all have abilities far beyond those of normal human beings. Even Billy Loomis and Stuart Macher from *Scream* possess a preternatural durability, showing superhuman strength and dexterity, and, in the

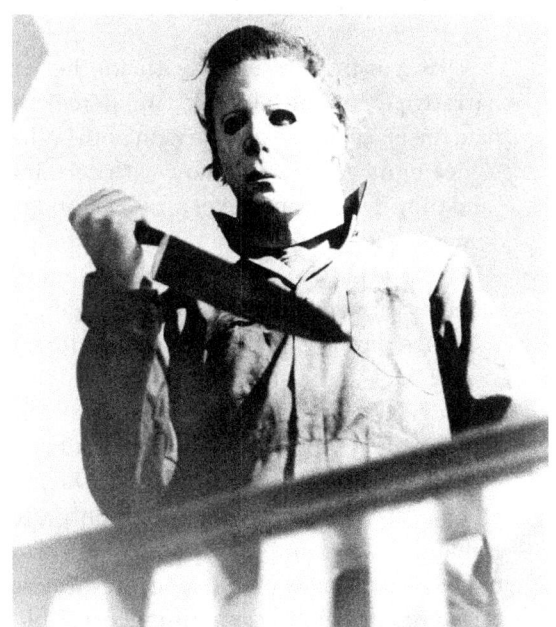

Above: **Michael Myers (Tony Moran) in *Halloween* (1978).**
Opposite: **The Undead seeking prey in *Night of the Living Dead* (1968).**

final scenes, surviving a series of what should be fatal wounds to return relentlessly to assault their victims. Nonetheless, it is not so much their deeds that terrify us, as the sense that we cannot rely upon the conventional methods used to cope with threats to our wellbeing. As a result, the greatest terror produced by Horror film antagonists comes from their abilities to call into question our assumptions about the natural order of things (*The Evil Dead*).

Characters must deal with a world in which the familiar boundaries have shifted. The individual fights for survival, in a world suddenly different from that in which the character thought he or she had existed. Often a moral imperative overlays the action, and equates the source of horror with evil. By confronting this horror the hero not only proves his or her abilities but also comes to a clearer sense of the integrity of self. As Laurie Strode (Jamie Leigh Curtis) discovers in *Halloween*, this individual experience stands as a rite of passage or maturation, though survival comes with a loss of innocence and a weakening of faith in the efficacy of social institutions to preserve order and promote individual good.[2]

Psychological Landscape

Horror films resonate with another familiar and highly prescriptive narrative form, the fairy tale, and perceiving that analogy helps to illuminate the fascination we have with both. Whenever we see a story beginning "Once upon a time," we know with certainty that it will end with the line "and they lived happily ever after." Although we cannot be sure how handsome princes, fairy godmothers, evil stepparents, and oppressed heroines will behave in the interim, we know that eventually the characters designated by the genre as "good" will triumph. This same predictability informs narrative development within most Horror films.

However, the parallel does not end there. Fairy tales and Horror films both deal with the fantastic.[3] Both focus on isolated individuals threatened by forces with powers beyond the limits experienced by normal humans. And both achieve resolutions when the individual overcomes the threatening preternatural forces, usually only after the protagonist reconfigures fundamental assumptions about the world in which he or she exists. In consequence, many of the same interpretive patterns that we apply to fairy tales prove useful in examining Horror films.

As is the case in fairy tales, the programmatic quality of the Horror genre pushes one to re-establish a sense of personal security that has been temporarily threatened by some fantastic power. It is as much a metaphysical as a physical effort. The central narrative traces a quest for understanding events, forces, or individuals falling outside the normal limits of human experience. Finding an efficacious model for behavior becomes the key to survival.

The affinity between fairy tales and Horror films becomes even more evident when we see the parallel contexts that structure the development of their narratives: they both challenge their protagonists with creatures whose behavior operates outside the normal limits of the story's environment. They often highlight alienation in examining the way an individual functions or fails to function in the conventional world. Paradoxically, this position of an outlier can make some characters more adept at dealing with preternatural threats, for their marginalization has already made them less likely to trust the efficacy of ordinary methods than individuals who are not estranged (Mina Harker in any of the film versions of *Dracula*).

A further parallel exists in terms of interpretation. Just as critics like Bruno Bettelheim have seen fairy tales as cathartic exercises for repressed feelings, some cinema scholars—Barry Keith Grant is one example—find Horror films performing the same function. For some viewers, belief in this emotionally cleansing function encourages psychoanalytic based readings of these motion pictures.[4] Others find this approach too restrictive. There is, however, a general agreement that the Horror genre plays upon our emotions to a degree not found in other film categories.

Perhaps more than any category, Horror movies seek to provoke extravagant emotional and visceral reactions in their audiences. From the early films like F.W. Murnau's *Nosferatu* made in 1922 to Drew Goddard's 2012 *The Cabin in the Woods* brutality has always acted as an undercurrent. At the same time, an audience can feel more comfortable with these extremes and more tolerant of their representations because it knows the genre. No matter how gruesome, the violence likely will not eliminate the central characters. (A film like *The Sixth Sense*, dealing as it does with a dead hero, provides a good example of how a clever director enhances the movie's effect by playing upon and against this familiar premise.)

In addition, no matter how erotic the atmosphere, the audience knows that the central characters will not abandon themselves to hedonism and thus ignore the moral limits on behavior imposed by their commitment to conventional moral codes. As Randy Meeks, the cineaste in *Scream*, makes clear in a scene late in the movie when he outlines his "rules" of Horror films, standards plays a key role in determining the char-

Nosferatu/Graf Orlok (Max Schreck) in *Nosferatu* (1922).

acter's fate. However, while in the most simplistic versions, this condition becomes simply a matter of good surviving and bad perishing, especially if bad means being sexually active, the best films take a much more sophisticated view. In times of chaos, moral values become crucial guides for behavior. Although individuals may feel ambivalent about their true worth (*Christine*), openly resentful of their restrictiveness (*Stigmata*), or simply unsure of their applicability (*Fallen*), following them gives much needed direction at times when characters feel unsure how to proceed. In the end, a truly sophisticated Horror film devotes as much attention to interrogating the dominant value system of the movie as to finding ways to defeat the preternatural threat.

    The character's affection for the status quo stands as a consistent feature in Horror films, but, paradoxically, it is a willingness to deviate from conventional societal expectations that enables characters to survive. Consequently, individuals progress towards a kind of enlightenment through a state of physical, emotional, and psychological flux. When, characters achieve a unified or balanced position it brings closure to the film. At the same time, over the course of the movie, attitudes, ranging from idealism to irony, can reflect the diverse perceptions of the individual's nature.

Characters overtly and covertly debate the merits of their way of living, and resolution in these films rests as much on their endorsement of the identity that defines them as it does on the destruction of the source of horror (*Altered States*).

Finally, given the Horror film's interest in the nature of the individual, isolation inevitably emerges as an important concern, generally for the protagonist but occasionally for the antagonist as well. As noted earlier, in some cases the individual may begin the film in an already marginalized position (*Willard*). However, within a genre that so quickly reveals its characters' inability to find a means to cope with threats that defy the logic of their environment, even well-integrated figures can quickly find themselves isolated from all of the social institutions that gave their lives stability and security (*Hereditary*).

Either physical or psychological elements may introduce the threat of isolation, but the results are the same. The central character often faces conflict because of a nature that cannot, initially at least, find solace in its environment. The characters whose natures reflect preternatural traits are equally alienated from the world around them, often with the implication that he or she has become aberrant through some kind of sickness or injury (*Wolf*). When personality traits or simply when the atmosphere surrounding his or her existence seem aberrant, emphasis turns on the human struggle to reach maturity or a full identity (*Carrie*).

Of course, by the end of a horror film, protagonists have experienced too much to retain intact the naïve worldview they held at its beginning, but the parameters of the genre insure that their refinement over the course of action result from a relatively narrow range of choices. They must decide whether to reform their natures to deal with a very different world than they had imagined existed, or they must adapt their views to accommodate a much more complex but essentially similar world to the one defined in the opening scenes. In most cases the film will celebrate the individual's ability to cope with difference and still recover or restore the status quo. Only rarely does it advocate the need for a radical change in perspective.

Key Elements in Plot and Characterization

In oppositions more clearly defined than in any other genre, Horror films pit good versus evil, stability versus anarchy, normalcy versus perversion. Horror movies generally feature characters striving to lead ordinary lives, albeit not always with complete success, who find themselves in positions that threaten their sense of stability, and then are forced to take action to remedy the situation. In the process, these individuals come to grips with the fundamental features that give meaning to their lives and very often validate or solidify their place in the world.

To highlight the challenge, the narrative always forces the protagonists to struggle against larger-than-life creatures or forces. These preternatural figures are almost always inherently more powerful than the humans whom they oppose (*Frankenstein*). Often they possess a ruthlessness (*Nightmare on Elm Street*) or an awareness of the complexity of human nature that far surpasses that of the individuals whom they challenge (*It*). In consequence, the struggle between these two forces is resolved in favor of the humans only when they come to a clearer sense of themselves and their world than they held at the beginning of the film.

Characters achieve this understanding of self after going through the difficult process of comprehending their antagonists' abilities to function outside the ordinary parameters of human action. The preternatural powers these creatures possess are doubly disturbing because they appear as intrinsic, if generally unnoticed, to the world they inhabit. Like most others, the central characters move about unaware of these forces until an accident or bad luck brings about the confrontation. Often, it is simply a matter of being in the wrong place at the wrong time. On other occasions, hubris can precipitate the struggle. A character can defy warnings (*The Blair Witch Project*) or naively engage in ritualistic acts that bring forth the evil preternatural figure (*The Mummy*). In every instance the struggle takes place on the individual level, and as often as not a subversive impulse rather than a direct assault poses the greatest threat.

Here characterization plays a key role. The protagonists may exude innocence (*Halloween*). They may have an imperfect or shallow sense of themselves (*Christine*). Or, they may depend upon a social sophistication that they naively believe suffices to deal with the world (*The Wicker Man*). In every case, no real change can occur, and consequently no success in the struggle can come about, without the character overcoming these illusions to reach a clearer sense of self.

For the Horror film protagonist, such a realization comes only through a climactic confrontation. Although not every encounter turns upon an explicitly moral conflict, as will be noted in the discussion of the second sub-group of Horror films, a number of these movies explicitly or implicitly privilege the struggle as the conflict of good versus evil. They go beyond the preternatural (*The Haunting*), and deal with supernaturally

Heather Donohue (Heather Donohue) in *The Blair Witch Project* (1999).

evil powers, often specifically identified as the devil (*The Omen*). In these instances the goal of the contest becomes more overtly spiritual. The opponent covets the independence of the central character's soul, and seeks to enthrall it.

Whether the antagonists are seemingly indestructible sociopaths, disembodied spirits, or fiends from hell, the essential feature in any Horror films—relentlessness—remains constant. However it may be constituted, ordinary individuals are suddenly confronted with an unrelenting force or forces that directly threaten their physical well-being and the integrity of their natures. These individuals cannot ignore that threat, but rather they must engage it in a contest for survival. Furthermore, even when a group of people is involved, they usually must undertake this struggle without help from the larger community. The result of that confrontation generally favors the ordinary individual, but, whatever the specific outcome, in the end it either affirms or overturns the adequacy of individual identity.

Issues

Knowing oneself features prominently in the structure of any Horror film, though the way that the narrative introduces that attribute can vary greatly. Characters can begin films with a solid sense of who they are in relation to the world, only to have that self-assurance eroded over the course of the action (*Get Out*). Individuals can find themselves easy prey for preternatural forces because their own sense of self remains ambiguous and even conflicted (*Carrie*). Or figures feel keenly their separateness from others, and struggle to exist in an environment which few others perceive as they do (*The Cat People*).

In a genre in which seemingly inexplicable events regularly challenge one's concept of the world, conviction functions as a crucial mitigating factor for understanding what is occurring. In many instances, belief may not go beyond an affirmation of the status quo, often with disastrous results (*Children of the Corn*). It can also, however, serve as an anchor for individuals when they are confronted with terrifying conditions (*Dracula*). Or it can produce a single-minded mania that has self-destructive implications (*Frankenstein*). Whatever their specific manifestation, issues of belief serve to define the ethos of the Horror film and to give the audience a clearer sense of the psychological and spiritual resources of the individuals under attack.

Of course, resolution inevitably comes through trauma. The narratives of Horror films engage our attention by presenting fundamental threats to putative certainties about our being. Preternatural characters intrude upon ordinary lives, and individuals affected by them come to the realization that the world is far more complex and unpredictable than they had imagined (*Poltergeist*). The central question to be resolved hinges on the character's ability to cope: Can he or she, with a nature shaped by a stable and predictable world, rely upon conventional methods to deal with these very different circumstances, or do new experiences require new ways of conceiving the world?

Any number of patterns of behavior lend themselves to the confrontations that are the focal points of the genre. However, because of its power to unsettle ordinary relations, sexual activity, whether sublimated or overt, is often the catalyst for introducing disruptive forces into the environment (*Bride of Frankenstein*). Sex not only embodies a primal drive within all humans, but the overwhelming power of sexual desire underscores the tenuous control that individuals exert over their natures. When sexual appetites take hold of our consciousness and override the societal restraints that keep our impulses in check, we become different people, in some cases to a monstrous degree (*Hellraiser*).

However, despite the power of sexuality in the Horror genre, it is a serious interpretive mistake to assign it an exclusively perverse role. Time and again, these films affirm the view that sexual attraction has the ability to ennoble characters as well as to debase them, and as often as not physical desire provokes characters to assume roles as defenders and protectors as inciting them to become predators (*Dracula*). In its own right, sexuality stands as a morally neutral, if powerful, source of energy. The context in which one exercises it provides the standard for determining its harmonious or corrosive function.

Violence, while having less potential than sexuality for wide-ranging interpretations, takes on a similar role as a powerful catalyst within the narrative structure. As an inherently destabilizing force, violence disrupts the individual's ability to exist with equanimity in the world that he or she inhabits. No matter what the source, its application inevitably foregrounds threats and dangers that had heretofore gone unnoticed, and, because of the destructiveness that naturally accrues from it, violence highlights the seriousness of the struggle. This explains the role of graphic representation in establishing the ethos of the genre. The ferocious engagements with the preternatural forces and the devastation that results from them underscore for both the central characters and the viewers the consequences of defeat.

While sex and violence highlight specific questions implicit in the narrative structure of many Horror films, the dominant concern around which all others revolve is the privileged position afforded to a genuinely conservative view of the world. This genre makes a concerted commitment to argue for the preservation of the traditional mores and attitudes that had surrounded its audiences from an early age. Certainly, in almost every instance, the complacent view of the world held by the central characters at the opening of the movie faces a ferocious challenge embodied by the forces that assault those characters. Nonetheless, despite the jarring revelations of a force outside of the conventional world, the foundations of that world rarely come under stress, and the end of the film generally presents the re-affirmation of communal values and assumptions.

Specific Application

Horror films deal with the struggle of individuals to maintain the integrity of their natures and their concept of their places in the world, as well as to preserve their physical and mental well-being in the face of preternatural antagonists. At the same time, these films also fall into clear-cut sub-groups reflecting different aspects of the challenges that present themselves to the protagonists. *Dracula* embodies the sub-category defined by the contrasting attitudes or identities that precipitate a struggle for physical, intellectual, and emotional dominance: how our minds and imaginations interact with the world around us becomes a measure of our power to control that environment. The sub-group exemplified by *The Exorcist* self-consciously presents very straightforward struggles between conventional conceptions of good and evil. In the final sub-group, *Scream* emphasizes the physical rather than the metaphysical make-up of the world surrounding the characters. More than just an archetypal slasher film, it offers a stark example of the transformative power of evil, creating monsters motivated by revenge and boredom, but most significantly never operating above the bestial level.

Dracula

Tod Browning's 1931 film *Dracula* might strike contemporary viewers as both a grandiose and dated example of the Horror genre. In fact, such a response is not a reflection of flaws in the motion picture itself, but rather it comes about as an unintended consequence of the success of the original and the proliferation of its often inferior imitators. Familiarity has bred contempt, and, in consequence, what in 1931 stood as innovative techniques in a genre seeking to make the transition from silent to talking motion pictures now may seem wooden, dated, and predictable.

A bit of film history reinforces this view. *Dracula* emerges out of a tradition of powerful movies featuring preternatural themes and monomaniacal villains. German Expressionist films, highlighted by *The Cabinet of Dr. Caligari*, directed in 1919 by Robert Wiene, F.M. Murnau's *Nosferatu*, released in 1922, and Fritz Lang's 1931 film *M* (admittedly more Noir than Horror though an influence nonetheless) are particularly strong influences. Indeed, throughout *Dracula* one can detect resonant echoes of the production values, narrative pacing, and staging techniques of the first two works in particular. Nonetheless, as with *The Cabinet of Dr. Caligari* and *Nosferatu*, Browning's film establishes its unique character by making the central figure's eccentricities stand out and through an understated representation of the terrifying conditions surrounding that individual.

Like its critically important cinematic antecedents, *Dracula* inverts the conventional emphasis of Horror films. The personality of its title character, rather than that of any of the men or women who attempt to oppose him, dominates the narrative. This in turn highlights the unequal struggles between ordinary individuals and single-minded, preternatural forces whose very presence calls into question the convictions by which the protagonists guide their lives (*The Fog*). The most effective of such films rivet our attention on the force that is disrupting these lives, and they make that character as attractive, in his way, as any of the other figures in the movie. This is the whole premise behind *Interview with the Vampire*. However, this film (and indeed the Anne Rice novel upon which that motion picture is based) succeeds, to whatever degree that it does, because it evokes associations with the earlier movies that had established viewer expectations for the genre.

Count Dracula (Bela Lugosi) in *Dracula* (1931).

Even by 1931 these traits had become familiar, but, of course, Browning takes his film well beyond stylistic evocations of his predecessors, playing with convention and thus alternating certitude and ambiguity, as it lays out the complex features of the narrative about to unfold. The film grounds its narrative on the violent clash of cultural perspectives, and it makes this point by repeatedly juxtaposing an exotic and disorienting environment that challenges the certitude of the perceptions of protagonists and viewers alike with the mundane world to which both the protagonists and the viewers have accustomed themselves. Like all films in this genre, formulaic tendencies move the action forward. Nonetheless, salient details within the narrative repeatedly raise subtle interpretive issues that engage our attention and force us to reconsider hasty generalizations.

The motion picture's initial scenes are perhaps the most challenging for contemporary viewers. So many subsequent films have imitated them that, atavistically, Browning's original representations can now seem clichéd. Nonetheless, they remain powerful examples of the genre and hold up well under close scrutiny.

The film's opening quickly introduces the clash of conventional Western beliefs with an environment that refuses to grant validity to such assumptions. Near dusk in a remote Transylvanian village, apprehensive natives attempt to discourage a brash Englishman, Renfield (Dwight Frye), from keeping a midnight rendezvous with a coach from the castle of Count Dracula. The innkeeper emphasizes the danger by making the blunt revelation that Dracula and his wives are vampires who "feed on the blood of the living." (This statement leads to one of several incongruities in the film. Although a trio of unidentified women are seen shortly in several of the sequences in the castle, Count Dracula makes no mention of his wives, nor do any of these women accompany him to England. One can only speculate, based on Dracula's behavior towards young women in England, on the nature of the association.)

Typical of the pattern of characters in this genre, Renfield not only will not be dissuaded, but he smugly dismisses such concerns as ridiculous. When a local woman insists on giving Renfield a crucifix for protection, his condescending response evokes contemporary attitudes that equate religion to folk beliefs and he implies that both reflect little more than superstitious ignorance. (The relation of religion and superstition in Horror films will be discussed at greater length in the next section.)

Admittedly, the scene comes dangerously close to self-parody, but that tone reflects the risky pattern of exposition that the director has chosen to follow. The narrative self-consciously invites viewers to feel the same disdain for the villagers' concern that Renfield expressed. However, in causing viewers to identify with Renfield at this point, the film puts itself in a position to challenge audience skepticism later when Dracula has enthralled the young man.

As if in response to Renfield's skepticism, the scene quickly shifts to the bowels of Dracula's castle where he and a group of unidentified women sinuously emerge from their coffins. At first glance this "revival of the monster" scene may seem all too familiar and completely predictable, but a hasty dismissal misses the point. This episode does not aim to shock or to even startle us. Rather, it frames the parameters of a dialectic the dialectic that will be repeated time and again for the remainder of the movie, implicitly asking which point of view, Renfield's materialism, with its faith in cause and effect logic, or the villagers' mysticism, which embraces the extraordinary, will prove the more efficacious response to Dracula.

In fact, judging any scene in *Dracula* by its ability to frighten us takes the same naïve perspective that Renfield shows early in the movie. Suspense is not the point of a motion picture like this. Horror films announce their aims early on, and they expect anyone familiar with the genre to anticipate the action of the motion picture from beginning to end. From the opening scenes of *The Mummy*, we can gauge fairly accurately who will become Ardeth Bey's victims. As soon as Larry Talbot is bitten in *The Wolf Man*, we can anticipate the change announced by the film's title that will overtake him. In *House on Haunted Hill*, we understand all too well what will happen to those who ignore the implicit warnings of a notorious past and enter the desolate building. Narrative characterization, not suspense, makes *Dracula* and other films of this type entertaining. It is not what Dracula or other characters do that matters. Rather, it is why they behave as they do and what that says about the central characters that engage our attention.

The really unnerving element in any successful Horror film proceeds from the ability of the antagonist to exist within the bounds of ordinary society and indeed to manipulate events to his or her advantage. The ease with which the preternatural creature accommodates to this environment stands as an unvoiced testament of our vulnerability. (Indeed, it is the exception, as in a contemporaneous film like *Frankenstein*, for one of these creatures to be so clumsy and ill-informed as to call immediate attention to his or her presence within the community.)

Of course, Horror genre antagonists are not self-effacing. The tension of these films comes from the dexterous maneuvers of the preternatural figures within society, often announcing their conditions and yet never completely acknowledging them. Thus, when Renfield meets Dracula, the Englishman is rightly disconcerted by the count's stylized behavior and assertive affinity with marginal presences. "Listen to them. Children of the night. What music they make." At the same time, Renfield remains at a loss as to how to respond. When in plain sight the count walks through a large spider web without disturbing it, he implicitly and smugly invites Renfield to question how it such thing could occur.

These gestures make important statements about the title character. Dracula is much more at ease with his nature than are figures in other movies in this category (*An American Werewolf in London*). Dracula shows no remorse, does not feel afflicted, and has no lingering self-doubts. He does not wish for integration. Rather, he flaunts his ability to survive in the ordinary world while living according to his own conditions, going so far as to draw attention to his uniqueness as a way of cowing and then controlling the ordinary human beings whom he encounters.[5]

Foremost, one should not allow dialogue to become a distraction from the key feature of *Dracula* and other films in this sub-group. As in the contemporaneous motion picture *The Mummy*, psychological control, not the persuasiveness of discourse or even the dominance of physical force, stands as the films' antagonists' most powerful weapon. After Dracula leaves their initial interview in the castle bedroom, Renfield simply collapses in a faint when he sees a bat at the window. The three women from the crypt then enter the room, but are sent back by Dracula's dismissive gesture as he silently walks in through the open window. The scene ends with Dracula bending over Renfield.[6]

This recurring cinematic signature, cutting away from the action shortly before depicting the assault but clearly implying what is to come, becomes an emblematic feature of the film. Browning consistently shows Dracula on the point of violence, but generally stops short of showing the attack. This is not simple squeamishness. Rather, the artful editing centers our attention on the psychological force behind Dracula's character. His power comes out of his dominant personality, emphasized by the great many close-ups of Lugosi that Browning gives the viewers. The strength of his will makes him an even more terrifying prospect than someone simply able to overcome individuals through brute force.

That is not to say that Browning eschews evoking images of violence. On board the ship, *Vesta*, bound for England, the narrative shows Renfield, now a much changed, degraded creature, calling Dracula master and facilitating the Count's methodical slaughter of the crew. While we actually see nothing more ghastly than the shadow of the dead captain tied to the ship's wheel, the implication of what has transpired cannot be missed. However, even that carnage has significance beyond merely emphasizing the brutality of Dracula. It highlights his implacable determination. He appears as an inevitable force against which resistance seems to be futile.

Despite the repeated suggestions of Dracula's sating himself on the blood of his victims, violence does not propel the narrative. As in many films in this category (*The Howling*), sex and sexual desire play much more important roles in the action of the film than do images of physical force. These appetites have attractions equally powerful for protagonists and antagonists. Indeed, when viewed through the prism of their attitudes toward sexuality, the distinctions between the principal characters become blurred, and consequently the basis for our judgments becomes less assured.

Beyond that, sexuality itself represents a much more complex feature of the human condition than merely the desire for sensual gratification.

While physical attraction remains an inherent part of sexuality in these films, control informs all of the relationships. This proves to be particularly the case among men, and, as a result, whether the male is a hero or a villain, his relations with women follow much the same pattern: The struggle for dominance is the defining force for men in their relations with women. Sexual or emotional gratifications are at best secondary considerations.

This practice of using females as markers of power becomes most evident once Dracula arrives in England, where his interest seems exclusively fixed on women. Almost as soon as Dracula leaves the ship, he assaults a flower girl, presumably to slake his blood lust, and then goes to Covent Garden to hear Wagner's opera *Tannhäuser*. By hypnotizing a maid, he manages to engineer an introduction to Dr. Seward (Herbert Bunston), his daughter Mina (Helen Chandler), Lucy Weston (Frances Dade), and Mina's fiancé John Harker (David Manners). Though there is no immediate explanation for his behavior, it seems clear that Dracula is eager to gain a measure of control over the group and that he intends to assert it through the women.

Just as Renfield voices the viewers' skepticism about the existence of vampires only to have his authority undermined, Mina does the same for Dracula. She ridicules the awkward formality of his speech. However, as with Renfield, in a very short time we see her enthralled by Dracula's power in scenes where he need not say anything, but only fix her with a resolute stare.

Dracula's impulse towards dominance is evident in every episode in which he appears. He continually seeks to manipulate conditions and direct the way that events unfold. In the Seward drawing room, through gestures, glances, and casual comments, Dracula suavely flaunts his power over Mina. However, Dracula's control, even over his own emotions, remains limited. When Van Helsing, the vampire slayer who has come to investigate Renfield's strange cravings for blood, confronts Dracula with a mirror, which does not reflect the vampire's image, Dracula loses his composure and stalks out of the house.

Power and control are not simply Dracula's obsession. John Harker cannot trust anyone else to care for Mina, and continually endeavors to dominate her. When, for example, she tells him that their life together is finished even though she still loves him, his reaction is to attempt to seize control. He rebukes Van Helsing, and threatens to call the police if Mina is not allowed to go with him to London. Equally intent on maintaining control, Van Helsing and Dr. Seward insist that she will be safe in her bedroom, now covered in wolfsbane.

This is not simply a matter of male egos struggling for dominance, though that certainly plays a role in the confrontation. The narrative is illustrating the real threat posed in the film: a stubborn adherence to conventional thinking. Harker represents another skeptical substitute for viewer reaction, and the fact that we can see the danger of the position he occupies works subtly to undermine our own disbeliefs.

In keeping with the ethos established earlier, women remain the weak link in opposition to Dracula. What this says about the narrative structure of the film raises interesting interpretive issues, not the least of which relate to the ability of contemporary viewers to feel sympathy for what they see. In any case, the count's attraction to women and theirs to him remains undeniable. Both Mina and her maid conspire to give the count access to the house. Mina brings John onto the patio away from the wolfsbane (placed over doors and windows in the house to repel vampires) and attempts to attack him, but Van Helsing confronts her with a crucifix. The nurse, apparently also under Dracula's spell, removes the wolfsbane from Mina's room, and opens the patio doors to admit Dracula.

The scene shifts to the final confrontation at the ruined Carfax Abbey, where Dracula has taken Mina. Van Helsing and John find Dracula's coffins filled with Transylvanian earth, and, as Van Helsing prepares to drive a stake through Dracula's heart (though as with all other violence it takes place off-screen), John finds Mina. When Van Helsing joins the couple, he tells them that Dracula is dead, and he sends them away saying that he has some further business to which he must attend. The film then ends without explaining Van Helsing's task or making clear to viewers what will happen to Mina or how Lucy has been dealt with.[7]

The protagonists in this sub-genre clash with preternatural forces that not only have greater physical powers but also, and more significantly, see the world from a radically different, often alienated, and usually solipsistic perspective. That point of view is not simply indifferent to the dominant social values, but it preys upon those who conform to them. (In some ways this is an attitude similar to that of the gangster, explored in Chapter Two.) The antagonists in this subgroup consider society only in terms of personal satisfaction. The central characters in these films do not find their values threatened but simply disregarded by their antagonists as inadequate. The struggles depicted measure the efficacy of the dominant value system when tested by a formidable opponent, utterly uninfluenced by the mores of the protagonist's world. Other examples include *The Mummy* (all versions), *Frankenstein*, *Night of the Living Dead*, *Poltergeist*, *The Sixth Sense*, *The Fog*, *House on Haunted Hill*,

The Howling, The Others, Nosferatu, The Reptile, Curse of the Zombies, and *Bride of Frankenstein.*

The Exorcist

William Friedkin's *The Exorcist*, made in 1973, amply illustrates the defining elements of the value-laden second sub-genre of Horror films. Films in this category move from the conflict of individual personalities to that of broader moral positions. Specifically, they delineate a struggle between good and evil to define the character of human identity.[8]

Like all motion pictures of this group, complex contemporary attitudes toward religion raise crucial credibility problems for viewers of *The Exorcist*. The film finesses that difficulty by making religion the skeptical refuge of its two principal characters. Chris MacNeil (Ellen Burstyn) is an atheistic actress who turns to the Church in a desperate effort to save her daughter, but she feels no real belief in its dogma. Father Damien Karras (Jason Miller) is a Jesuit psychiatrist who fears that he has lost his own faith and is appalled by the idea of being involved in what he sees as an atavistic ritual from a superstitious age. In the end, it remains for viewers to decide the role of goodness and spirituality in the film's resolution, and the concepts of innocence and evil stands as equally difficult propositions to resolve.

This sort of ambivalence and disorientation does not simply inform the development of characterization. These traits permeate the very structure of the narrative to anchor the framework of the film. The opening scenes, for example, offer a quick shot of the Georgetown home where most of the subsequent action will occur before shifting to a lingering presentation of an archeological dig in northern Iraq. This juxtaposition of twentieth-century Washington, D.C., and a Middle Eastern setting with an ethos evocative of the Old Testament subtly introduces alternative perspectives on the nature of material and metaphysical worlds. The narrative heightens this disparity when the archeologist in charge of the dig, a Jesuit priest named Lankester Merrin (Max van Sydow), is greatly disconcerted by the discovery of what seems to be a small pagan sculpture along with a Christian religious medal.

Very little dialogue punctuates the scenes in Iraq, and, when characters do speak, they do little to dispel ambiguity. Quite the contrary, while the action in the desert uses cryptic images from the distant past (crude idols) and ominous figures in the present (armed guards) to invoke menace, it presents no clear sense of the source of anxiety. Like the remainder of the film, causes and motivations are left to the viewer to establish.

This pattern of introducing alternative points of view without providing a clear sense of underlying facts becomes a way of building the tension of the narrative. These representations also invoke, and even play upon, viewers' expectations based on their experiences watching similar movies. Since Horror film conventions of eschew logical explanations for what occurs, those familiar with the genre will understand that certain events lie outside the bounds of conventional reasoning. Even Regan's possession, while it seems unambiguously to be the work of the Devil, takes place with seemingly no motivation or aim. The viewer can reference other films in the sub-genre—*The Omen, Damien: Omen II, Carrie*—to get a sense of possibilities, but interpretation remains a matter of individual conjecture.

Indeed, *The Exorcist* shows a masterful sense of character and plot development without dispelling any of the ambiguity that the narrative has so carefully cultivated. Early scenes outline the warm mother-daughter relationship between Chris McNeil and her daughter Regan (Linda Blair) in the secure confines of their Georgetown home. At the same time, the narrative deftly suggests just a hint of menace with the discovery of a Ouija board and Regan's reference to an invisible friend, Captain Howdy. When such seemingly offhanded references are made, experienced filmgoers presume a sort of foreshadowing of the events to occur and expect the main characters to be oblivious to such warnings. Even though these articles are red herrings, never developed further, they nonetheless set the tone of the film and create a sense of tension and anticipation in viewers.

The Exorcist purposely delays introducing the real antagonist, first foregrounding the normal elements of the environment of the film and inviting the audience to accept the perceptions that central characters have of the world around them. Simultaneously, without dismissing these attitudes, it suggests, in time-honored fashion, that the world is more complex and more threatening than characters perceive (*In the Mouth of Madness*). Much of this is done through innuendo, like the recurring and unexplained interpolation of grotesque faces in early scenes, which underscores impending menace.

Typical of this group, characterization of all of the central figures develops in a predictable fashion. The point of this sub-genre is to show the normalcy of the beliefs (secular and religious) of the central characters, and then to test how their attitudes enable them to stand up against supernatural powers, as one also sees in *Fallen*. In *The Exorcist* characterizations are developed through individuals' family ties. Complementing Chris' strong domestic bond with her daughter is Father Damien's loving, if distant, relationship with his mother in New York City. What is evident in the representation of the two familial situations is the contrasting emotional atmosphere. Chris, though a single parent, seems quite happy and content and able to cope with her life. Damien, though devoted to his mother, cannot escape feeling guilty for his inability to do more to help her.

Once Friedkin has established the fundamental ordinariness of the MacNeil home and of Father Damien's life, he calls into question the presumed stability of their worlds. From the start, Chris, though sweet to her daughter, has a fractious relationship, consistently dismissive, and at times abusive, with those whom she employs and cast members with whom she works on the motion picture she is making in D.C. Father Damien, although he is a respected psychiatrist, worries that he is unfit for his job, fears that he has lost his faith, and feels unable to give his mother the care that she needs.

Ordinary domestic stress is gradually displaced by more serious threats. Disturbances that began with the noise in Chris' attic escalate to Regan's bed shaking. A local church has a statue of the Blessed Virgin Mary desecrated. Father Damien has an unsettling visit with his mother, who is now in a mental hospital. The narrative shows no connections between these initial disruptions. Instead, they introduce a disturbing, disjointed atmosphere into the film.

Then, with precipitous violence, bizarre behavior accelerates the pace of the film. Over the next few scenes Regan's strange demeanor increases and becomes even more uncharacteristic. The ambiguity of the situation is underscored when doctors can find no satisfactory diagnosis for Regan's condition. At home Regan has another violent attack. Combining crudeness and brutality, the voice of the demon is now heard for the first time, first declaring its possession of Regan and then demanding in coarse terms sexual congress: "Keep away. The sow is mine. Fuck me. Fuck me." While the impotence of the physicians creates unease, what shocks the audience more than anything is Regan's profound transformation.

The intensity of the action increases exponentially, showing just how little authority the characters have over the world around them (*Stigmata*) and underscoring the need for the audience to impose its own order on the events that unfold. Chris returns to an empty house, and discovers that Burke (Jack MacGowran), the film director who was supposed to be watching Regan, has died in an accident. A psychiatrist visits Regan and asks her about the person inside her, only to be violently attacked by the girl who now appears to be fully under the control of the demon. The insistent undertone is that ordinary social institutions prove incapable of dealing with Regan and with all that afflicts her.

At this point, the narrative introduces a wonderful surrogate for the audience. Lt. Kinderman (Lee J. Cobb), a police detective, comes on the scene to conduct an investigation of the murder of Burke. He is a figure who is neither skeptical nor gullible but one open to experience, albeit not someone able to resolve the mystery that brings him on the scene.

As religious images begin to accrue, the conditions of the struggle become clearer. While examining the murder scene, Lt. Kinderman finds an image like the one discovered at the archeological dig shown at the film's opening. Chris, who had cheerfully declared her atheism earlier, seeks a religious solution. Father Damien, who had earlier proclaimed his fear that he had lost his faith, shows a pronounced reluctance to participate in what he sees as a superstitious mockery of Catholicism.

Father Merrin (Max von Sydow) in *The Exorcist* (1973).

Paradoxically, Chris and Father Damien serve as important features in lending credibility to the exorcism. Friedkin has foregrounded two characters who wish to believe—Chris to see that her child is made well and Father Damien to find confirmation for his faith—even as they find the premise for belief ridiculous. They assume attitudes with which many viewers will identify, and consequently the erosion of their disbelief can draw the audience into more readily accepting events on the screen.

Permission for a priest to perform the exorcism comes a bit more quickly than Father Damien has suggested was possible, but that is a minor weakness in the narrative. The remaining action follows the predictable ending for Horror films, even if it leaves to the viewer the responsibility of forging a unified interpretation. In fact, the conclusion occurs when both Chris and Father Damien accept the possibility of exorcism.

Of course, for the narrative to sustain credibility, Friedkin must maintain a balanced attitude towards the religious ceremony that takes place. It can be represented neither as a simple triumph of the forces of goodness nor as an artificial resolution. Consequently, the exorcism has a fatal effect upon both priests. When, during the exorcism, Father Merrin dies of an apparent heart attack, Father Damien attacks Regan. During the struggle the priest throws himself out the window, and, as his life expires, he is given the Last Rites of the Catholic Church by his friend Father Dyer (played by a Jesuit priest, the Rev. William O'Malley, S.J.).

The ending is fitting, for, in this second group, values overtly shape the development of the narrative. As often as not, the clash between protagonist and antagonist turns upon matters of faith, though not always theology. More than any of the other sub-groups, belief defines the individuals in these films, and they affirm their identities through the struggles to establish the pre-eminence of their creeds. Other motion pictures in the subgroup include *Children of the Corn, Carrie, Audrey Rose, Rosemary's Baby, The Omen, Fallen, Stigmata, In the Mouth of Madness, The Evil Dead*, and *Damien: Omen II*.

Scream

The final sub-category I wish to take up maintains the Horror film imperative to use violent confrontations to challenge the efficacy of the way individuals cope with the world around them. Its defining feature, however, radically alters the depiction of the nature of the antagonists that assault the central characters. Rather than holding the alternative moral position of some tortured creature with a perspective in conflict with the surrounding world or the frankly immoral perspective of satanic creatures, the antagonists in this category eschew any sort of principled commitment. Instead, these figures see the world in an amoral, situational fashion that provides no rational explanation for their behavior other than a desire to exercise impulses of innate viciousness and/or the imperative to carry on personal vendettas with the sole aim of injuring others.

Unfortunately, the predominance of violence and the commercial success of a number of youth-oriented movies in this category in the 1980s have led some to apply the dismissive and reductive label "slasher movies" to films in this sub-genre. That term misleadingly privileges the action of the film and gives too little attention to the motivations behind that behavior. And just as Film Noir is often mistakenly relegated to movies of the 1940s, exclusively associating this group with films of the 1980s suppresses the fact that a number of motion pictures in this category spring from a much earlier period and continues into the present.

While one cannot and should not deny that graphic violence serves as a distinguishing element in these films, over-emphasis has led to a distorted view of its significance. The intensity of the violence becomes a way to measure the more chilling feature of this sub-genre. Unlike the preternatural figures in the first group, whose perceptions of the world clash with those of the central characters, or the supernatural embodiments of evil in the second group, the antagonists in this category are no more than ordinary individuals. Indeed, they are complete materialists. They demonstrate no metaphysical grounding. They operate in the moment with a machine-like frenzy. And their motivation for mayhem goes little beyond inordinate blood lust. Protagonists find themselves confronted not with opponents moved by a different code of behavior but rather by creatures who see no point in any value system.

As early as Spencer Tracy in *Dr. Jekyll and Mr. Hyde* or Claude Rains in *The Invisible Man*, both films from the 1930s, antagonists in this category of Horror film have shown a sociopathic disregard for any moral restraints. Unlike Ardeth Bey in *The Mummy* or the unseen figures of *The Haunting*, these characters do not affirm an alternative world-view. They simply use often enhanced physical powers and an inordinately high tolerance for pain to engage in assaults on ordinary human beings. The real Horror of this category comes not from the violence but rather from the callous randomness and the relentless determination with which it is perpetrated.

The 1996 film *Scream* provides a rich representation of this subgroup and a thoughtful look at the expectations that define it. The genius of the film lies in its ability to highlight its conventions and assumptions without going so far as to turn its presentation into self-parody. To that end, *Scream* takes a formulaic narrative structure and overlays it with a clever line of self-criticism. Indeed, it works so hard to fulfill expectations for the genre that in several scenes it takes on an overt meta-textual quality, as characters, events, and settings provoke viewer reflections on its qualities as a Horror film.

To further these connections, the dialogue repeatedly and self-consciously plays with cinematic terms and conventions. Throughout the film, characters and scenes reference a dozen different Horror films from *Frankenstein* to *Psycho* to *Friday the 13th*. All of this goes beyond simple cleverness to remind viewers insistently of the conventions of the motion picture that they are watching.

At the same time, *Scream* does not pretend to hold itself aloof from the genre. Rather, it self-consciously and unabashedly celebrates the form. The film opens with a prototypical Horror film scene that establishes the elements of menace, power, ubiquity, and anonymity that characterize the killer. It also cleverly insinuates the meta-textual awareness of the genre that permeates the motion picture. The series of anonymous calls to Casey (Drew Barrymore), alone in her parents' house in the country, highlights the isolation and vulnerability that victims feel. In each successive conversation, the caller becomes increasingly aggressive and threatening, building the tension of the scene. He quizzes Casey on her knowledge of the Horror film genre, making correct answers the condition for survival, temporarily at least. Though more overt here than elsewhere, this kind of toying with the victim is common in this sub-genre (most notably in Freddy Krueger's invasion of characters' dreams in *Nightmare on Elm Street*).

When the killer actually attacks Casey, the graphic violence of the action sets the tone for the entire movie. Casey, like other women assaulted in the film, and paradoxically unlike any of the male victims, vigorously defends herself. This proves to be a recurring attribute in films of this category. (*Halloween* serves as the paradigmatic instance.) The superficial explanation for this condition is that in a genre that mixes sex and violence, there is a greater appeal to see women in situations of peril. However, that response elides a more significant issue. Men in these films passively accept their fate, as if they lack not simply the physical stamina but the psychic will to resist. Women, on the other hand, struggle mightily against the annihilation of self, though more often than not any particular confrontation can be won only when she adopts and sustains the same single-mindedness determination as her attacker.

With this in mind, one sees the cleverness of *Scream* in its manipulation of Horror conventions. While it may be more self-conscious in this gesture than other films in the category, its effectiveness comes from following models made familiar by its predecessors. The film announces its intentions in the opening sequence referenced above. Drew Barrymore, who plays Casey, would have been the actor best known to audiences at the time of the movie's release. Viewer expectations would lead to the presumption that Casey would survive the first attack to become the central character of the motion picture. When she does not, it alerts filmgoers to the fact that traditional patterns will not necessarily shape the narrative.

For further complication, immediately after the opening attack, Billy Loomis (Skeet Ulrich) sneaks into Sidney Prescott's (Neve Campbell) bedroom, creating subtle parallels to what has happened at Casey's house. Throughout the action, the film wonderfully shifts our perceptions of circumstances between views alternately implicating and exonerating Billy. The intrusion into Sidney's room also foregrounds the proximity of sexual desire to violence in the movie. (One sees this conjunction in the category as early as *Dr. Jekyll and Mr. Hyde*.) Billy and Sidney playfully spar over sexuality, with Billy hoping to move their relationship from an R rating to NR-17. Sidney rebuffs Billy's overtures, for a time at least conforming to the taboo against sexual activity in the heroine of a horror film, by asking if he "would settle for a PG-13 relationship."

As the film establishes characterization, it creates a paradoxical view of Sidney that also challenges viewer expectations. While it shows her as someone popular with her classmates, it also presents Sidney as different from other students (*Like Me*). The story of her mother's murder to underscore that separation, and her vacillating suspicion of Billy neatly adds to her general sense of isolation.

From isolation, characters quickly develop paranoia, a feeling common in Horror films that comes from a sense that events or individuals are not what they seem, and that one has little control over one's environment (*The Others*). Over the course of the film, the narrative makes very skillful use of technology to forward that impression. The telephone calls, first to Casey and then to Sidney, add to the tension of each scene, and the possession and use of cell phones make otherwise trusted characters objects of suspicion. Technology gives the killer mobility not available in earlier movies of this type, and devices like a fiber optic camera do as much to create fear as they do to create security.

In addition to showing technology as a disruptive, even threatening, condition, the film also engages in a running critique of the media. The Gale Weathers character (Courteney Cox) serves to satirize tabloid journalism by lampooning how a sensationalist style of reporting engages the popular imagination, and slyly pointing up the same titillation that draws some viewers to films in this group. Gale's celebrity status continually rivals whatever story she reports, and this aura of notoriety underscores a sense of the populace's susceptibility to suggestion and lack of critical resources. While Gale is not the equivalent of the murderer, she exerts greater control over situations than do most other participants.

Additional evidence of media control of perception and interpretation comes through references that characters continually make to films, often going well beyond the range of the Horror genre. As noted above, individuals make analogies to situations in their lives and to incidents in movies that they have seen. Indeed, scenes in popular films become the benchmarks by which the teenagers of the movie attempt to understand conditions in their world. In this way Randy Meeks (Jamie Kennedy), the film geek, provides not simply a running commentary of the Horror film genre but a model of the new character whose nature is shaped by media. (In many films in this subgroup, adults are absent or occupy minimal roles in a macabre imitation of the structure of the *Peanuts* or *Muppet* movies.)

As *Scream* draws to a conclusion, it underscores its traits as a Horror film and steps back to critique them. The scene in which Randy explains "the rules" governing horror films, for example, sets up expectations that are immediately challenged by Billy and Sidney engaging in sex in the bedroom, breaking one of the most significant Horror film taboos for characters seeking to survive. Further, as the violence escalates near the end of the film, it takes on a near slapstick quality threatening to undercut its impact. At the same time, the relentless determination of the murderers, Billy and Stu (Matthew Lillard), reestablish the menace of the narrative. In describing their plans, they have a calculated self-assurance that produces a chilling effect, and in carrying out those plans they take a tremendous amount of physical abuse that reinforces the preternatural tone of the Horror genre.

The film ends with a duality. In a melodramatic fashion, Billy confesses his motive. A desire for revenge has maddened him, so he wants to kill Sidney on the one year anniversary of the death of her mother. At the same time, Stu seems to act out of a kind of juvenile sadism and a willingness to follow Billy's lead. In essence, while *Scream* nods towards the established horror motive of revenge as in most films in this category, it

(Left to right) Stuart Macher (Matthew Lillard), Billy Loomis (Skeet Ulrich), and Sydney Prescott (Neve Campbell) in *Scream* (1996).

quickly spirals into ominous, pointless violence. In many such gestures, *Scream* pays tribute to the genre by heightening our sense of the elements that make it up.

The films that emphasize implacable violence and the killer's superhuman ability to withstand pain and injury, typified by *Scream*, offer the most common illustration of this approach. Though it would seem that implacable violence of the killer stands as the most distinguishing feature of such films, it is in fact the reflexiveness of the acts that distinguishes them. Although, in some instances, the killers claim a desire for revenge or some sort of retribution as the motivating factor, in fact they represent a near mindless commitment to brutality that the protagonists cannot explain or outwit but can only overcome. Other films include *The Cat People, Halloween, Dr. Jekyll and Mr. Hyde, Like Me, Friday the 13th, The Wolfman, Nightmare on Elm Street, Child's Play, The Others*, and *An American Werewolf in London*.

FIVE

It Came from Outer Space
Science Fiction Films

A General Sense of the Genre

One of the earliest feature-length films made (at least what at the time was considered feature length) was a Science Fiction narrative. In 1902 Georges Melies produced, directed, and played the lead role in a fourteen-minute French motion picture, *Le Voyage dans le lune* (*A Trip to the Moon*). Loosely based on the works of Jules Verne and H.G. Wells, it depicts a group of individuals who travel to the Moon in a projectile fired from a large cannon, encounter Selenites there, and return by tipping their projectile off the edge of a cliff and falling to Earth.

Despite this initial effort and some interesting follow-ups, a half-century elapsed before the genre rose to prominence. Although when Fritz Lang's *Metropolis* appeared in America in 1927 the reviewer in *The New York Times* called it a "technical marvel with feet of clay," it proved to be a¹classic and Saturday matinee serials chronicling the adventures of Buck Rogers and Flash Gordon (with Buster Crabbe as the title character in both) were staples at cinemas in the 1930s, it was not until the 1950s that Science Fiction films appeared with any regularity. Since then, however, their appeal has never diminished, with each succeeding decade producing a steady stream of pictures with at least one stunning representation of the genre. *2001: A Space Odyssey, Star Wars, Blade Runner, The Matrix, 28 Days Later*, and *The Last Jedi* are just a handful of examples.

Whether because of or in spite of this popularity, defining the genre can be a bit tricky. In a number of instances, apparent thematic similarities and analogous narrative patterns make distinguishing between Science Fiction and Horror films quite challenging for some viewers. Nonetheless, while many of the issues touched upon in Science Fiction movies may

Lunar inhabitants in *La Voyage dans la lune* (1902). Pheobe, goddess of the moon (Bluette Berron), and other Selenites (dancers from the Folies Bergère).

seem to echo those featured in Horror Films, a significant difference in scale and content obtains. Before proceeding with a discussion of the makeup of Science Fiction films, I propose to clarify these distinctions.

As a start, I should elaborate on a further distinction implicit in my definition of the genre. I have consciously not included Fantasy films in either the Horror or Science Fiction group because I have found, more often than not, the tendency of Fantasy films to fall into mixed-genre categories. *Harry Potter and the Sorcerer's Stone* could qualify as a Horror film since it reflects the struggles of an individual to overcome attacks by preternatural forces on his identity. *The Lord of the Rings* seems like Science Fiction since it chronicles the assault by alien forces upon an entire civilization. *It's a Wonderful Life* appears similar to melodrama, and *The Wizard of Oz* has elements that resemble those of a Slapstick Comedy. While Fantasy remains an important classification, its amalgamation of diverse generic traits has led me to put it outside the scope of the current study.

Distinctions between Horror and Science Fiction genres, as I define each, are easier to make, relying as much on the scale of their perceptions as on anything. The Horror genre examines life on the microcosmic level. It places the focus of attention on the individual, presenting an examination of how a character, generally of average intelligence and ability, copes with surroundings that, as he or she abruptly realizes, have become radically different from normal expectations. This recognition comes out of an unexpected conflict with preternatural forces. The isolated struggle of the individual to reconcile this new awareness with previous conceptions and to cope with the attendant threat to his or her welfare takes place without any acknowledgment from the broader community. Consequently, the narrative turns the audience's attention to the complexities of the individual's nature while all but ignoring the traits of the larger world that contextualizes the movie.

In Science Fiction, on the other hand, the narrative focuses attention on the community as a whole, and it highlights the conflicts that emerge when the representatives of a contrasting culture threaten that entity (*The War of the Worlds*).[2] That is not to say that the narrative erases individuality, but, typically, it delineates characters in terms of traits that define their roles in society. This is true even in a film like *Blade Runner* that

Rick Deckard (Harrison Ford) *in Blade Runner* **(1982).**

seems to privilege the marginal. Both the central character, Rick Deckard (Harrison Ford), and the cyborg whom he pursues, Roy Batty (Rutger Hauer), seem to be on the margins of society at best. In the climactic scene, however, in when Roy challenges the nature of humanity, Deckard clearly emerges as representative of society rather than just as a rugged individualist and the cyborg shows how desperately he wants to be part of that society.

Thus, although one finds any number of colorful figures in Science Fiction films, the genre places its emphasis on a world's ability to survive extraordinary physical challenges to its integrity. Of course, the narrative foregrounds individuals and highlights their efforts in such struggles, but it defines them in terms of their cooperation within the community when faced with a crisis that threatens its existence (*Lost in Space*). Even when a film like *Independence Day* offers background information on several of the characters, the central concern remains the invasion of the Earth by alien forces and the broad efforts of citizens to combat that threat. Civilization rather than personal identity always stands as the endangered element.

Consequently, physical challenges also typically confront characters in this genre, and little time is spent examining the structure of the world they inhabit. The Science Fiction film chronicles a clash between two cultures, or at the very least their representatives. In *Them* characters find themselves facing unreflective brutes with uncanny instincts for physical survival. In *The Day the Earth Stood Still* they must deal with a life-form operating according to a very different world view. In *The Terminator* characters must confront the hybrid or mutant results of their own scientific blunders. In these struggle efforts for material dominance make sweeping cultural critiques.

Technical Considerations

To a degree that surpasses the concerns of any other category of film, including Horror, the impact of special and visual effects upon the viewer's interpretation of a particular motion picture stands as a prominent concern in the study of Science Fiction films.[3] (Although the two components overlap in the narrative, they represent distinctly different technical representations that a sophisticated viewer must take into consideration. Special effects can be accomplished on the set, like the use of bursting blood packs to convey the idea of a wound. Visual effects are added in editing,

Five. It Came from Outer Space

Terminator (Arnold Schwarzenegger) in *The Terminator* (1984).

like the use of computer enhancement to simulate a jump into hyperspace. See the glossary for more detailed descriptions of these and related terms.)

Science Fiction films anchor their narratives on examinations of the impact of developments in science and technology, and viewers rightly expect these advances to be reflected on the screen. Moviegoers will long remember some of the fantastic interstellar panoramas in *2001*. They will marvel at the panoramas of *Metropolis*. And they will be transfixed by the slow-motion choreography of projectiles in the gunfight in *The Matrix*.

However, as the examples taken up here will demonstrate, these effects should contribute to the success of the movie rather than determine it. Just as stunning cinematography cannot redeem a bad movie, a powerful narrative and clever production techniques can make any technical limitations superfluous. For instance, Fritz Lang's *Metropolis*, though made over nine decades ago, employs imaginative lighting, striking sets, and innovative filming techniques that can still engage our imaginations, while sophisticated computer enhancement cannot save films like *Star Wars: The Phantom Menace*. Thus, while special effects doubtless highlight the pleasure that we derive from certain aspects of viewing these films, giving them undue prominence is akin to making fireworks all there is to celebrating July 4th.

Indeed, two of the films studied in this chapter as exemplary of the genre—*Invasion of the Body Snatchers* and *Alien*—display a minimal

Cityscape in *Metropolis* (1927).

reliance upon visual and special effects, and instead draw their narrative power from an ability to foreground the central concerns of the genre in a manner both familiar and surprising. The third film studied here—*The Matrix*—has already generated a cult following based on its special effects, its cyber-punk aura, and its evocation of Hong Kong action films, but, as I will show in the section devoted to it, these elements merely enhance rather than establish the importance of the film.

Cultural and Aesthetic Context

Generally, Science Fiction films assume the dual task of both critiquing specific features of the society that they present while endorsing and even in some instances legitimizing the broad cultural assumptions that define its essence. In consequence, motion pictures in this category tend to offer a more conservative (in the traditional sense of the word) perspective than do those in any other genre. In particular, in no other category examined in this study do we find such an intense concern for the preservation of contemporary society.

In consequence, broad aspects of the culture stand as the central concern of any Science Fiction film. At times it becomes a celebration of the values that inform our way of life (*The Fifth Element*). At times it represents a warning of what might occur if aberrant tendencies, antipathetic to fundamental values, go unchecked (*Fahrenheit 451*). At times, it even takes the form of a critique of the flaws and blind spots in our society (*Minority Report*), though this is generally the exception that proves the rule.

Science Fiction films affirm the societies in which the characters live or with which they identify. When institutions prove corrupt, like the heartless corporation that puts human lives at risk in the *Alien* series, they represent values antipathetic to the rest of society. Or, when society becomes dystopian, there is still an ideal form against which characters measure it (*Elysium*). Thus, while the narrative may make viewers intensely aware of the strengths and weaknesses of the world of the film, it still affirms the unspoken assumption of its fundamental value.

Key Elements in Plot and Characterization

As already noted in the Technical Considerations section, engagement with the environment stands as a key interpretive factor in this genre. This goes well beyond the impressions derived from individual perceptions of the world that shape the narrative in Horror films. It highlights the broadly accepted mores, the social institutions, and the objective composition of the world of the film so that viewers clearly understand that the civilization itself stands under threat.

Science Fiction films take pains to describe at length either the existing culture or, when that is already familiar to the audience, the nature of the culture that seeks to displace the current order of things. *Invasion of the Body Snatchers*, for example, graphically dissects American society while giving no real attention to the world of the forces that threaten that society. In contrast, *Invaders from Mars* takes a knowledge of modern America for granted and goes into some detail to explain the world of the invaders. In either case, concern for community remains the prominent force driving the narrative.

Given that emphasis, it is logical that characters in Science Fiction have identities much less complex—sometimes little more than archetypes—than those of individuals in other genres. As reflections of a larger culture, they have representative natures and display a near-unshakeable sense of the rightness of their beliefs (*Earth Vs. the Flying Saucers*). These attitudes govern the way that they perceive and respond to the larger forces that assault their world (*Silent Running*). The narratives use such characters to highlight the sweeping concerns of the genre, either in their buoyant faith in the structure of the world as they know it (*Close Encounters of the Third Kind*) or in their dark resentment of the conditions that surround them (*Elysium*). In every case, individuals define themselves exclusively in terms of the society in which they exist. Even apparent loners—like Han Solo in *Star Wars*—ultimately affirm their identities a through a particular society.

Plotlines are no less programmatic than characterizations. Typically, the action turns on the efforts of the central characters to preserve something (*The Time Machine*), or at the very least to recover it or to understand how it came to be lost (*Planet of the Apes*). As a result, conflict nearly always manifests itself as an often chaotic and always disruptive force (*Strange Invaders*), sometimes working from within (*Total Recall*) and sometimes from outside the community (*Alien*). It always, however, challenges the way of life privileged by the narrative, and the action unfolds as characters endeavor to defend and preserve that way of life. Consequently, individuals may experience some doubt about a specific course of action, but they rarely, if ever, feel unsure of the core values upon which they base their decisions on how to act.

Because of the emphasis on social structure and on the preservation of cultural values, societal integration and communal cooperation are privileged traits. The scientist who feels he knows better than society and acts independently often puts everyone else at risk (*Jurassic Park*). This works conversely as well. The lone figure who perceives the danger to the com-

Han Solo (Harrison Ford) in *Star Wars* (1977).

munity feels loyalty to the group, but will often experience difficulties in getting its members to accept and act upon this perception (*RoboCop*) before the peril threatening the annihilation of society becomes overwhelming. Often the threat to societal stability comes from within, from characters unwilling or unable to function as members of the community. In particular, the same blinding individuality that will draw characters into compacts with aliens will also drive them towards a hubristic exploration of the limits of technology. When the technology proves too powerful and complex for the human intellectual to control, disaster, or at least the threat of it, emerges (*The Omega Man*).

At times the perspective comes as an inversion, often in the form of a dystopia. The narrative often unfolds against the backdrop of a sterile world ravaged by the ignorance, stubbornness, or carelessness of its inhabitants (*Mad Max*). It highlights the ominous possibilities of life in the future, and it sends a grim message: either the world that the viewers know must recognize the danger of becoming this desolate environment, or else that world will suffered terrible changes (*I, Robot*). As a result, these films vacillate between Pollyanna-like optimism in the way our world runs and a crushing pessimism regarding our future.

Perhaps some of the most interesting Science Fiction films engage our imagination by their satiric evocation of elements in our own lives. A film like *The Running Man*, for example, takes a basic dystopian plot and enhances its impact through topical references. Playing off contemporary interest in daytime quiz shows, professional wrestling extravaganzas, and reality TV, *The Running Man* can present a sardonic commentary on the foibles of the world of the viewer without stepping over the boundary into self-parody. *Mars Attacks!* and the two *Men in Black* films do much the same thing. While they may seem parodic to some viewers, others will find, as with the *Scream* films in the Horror genre, that they offer an invaluable meta-fictional commentary.

Issues

Despite the numerous variations on the theme, the dominant, fundamental issue in all Science Fiction remains the examination of social values. Time and again, films question the adequacy of the institutions and mores of the worlds in which the characters find themselves. However, that proceeds along a variety of lines. The nature of technology and its impact on individual lives has become a dominant concern in many films.

A machine's ability for relentlessly consistent iteration and an unquestioning commitment to a prescribed pattern provide stark contrasts to the phlegmatic and at times irrational behavior of humans.

Nonetheless, while the contrasts are clear, the conclusions that we might draw are not. Technology stands as emblematic of larger issues, often represented in the form of questions that the narrative leaves to the audience to resolve. Does the civilization that has achieved striking scientific advances also possess the wisdom to use their discoveries properly (*Planet of the Apes*)? Is there a correlation between practical knowledge and cultural development, or are they antipathetic (*Star Trek*)? Are there secrets in the make-up of the universe that are better left undiscovered (*Forbidden Planet*)?

The limitations of human beings and the ability of particular cultures or civilizations to compensate for those limitations also come under examination in many Science Fiction movies. If technology stands as a force that one must control or else risk extinction, then one's culture becomes the primary resource for coping with a world changed by mechanical advances (*Fahrenheit 451*). The ability of a culture to respond to the challenges becomes as central a concern in these films as is the challenge itself (*2001: A Space Odyssey*). Even more to the point, one must ask whether particular cultures, with their frailties and contradictions, are worth preserving at the expense of the efficiency produced by technology (*Brazil*).

Perhaps the most insistent feature in Science Fiction movies is its exploration of the uneasy relationship between pragmatism and idealism within our own society. When films examine the behavior of futuristic civilizations, they inevitably turn the mind of the viewer back to contemporary life. We can hardly see films in *The Hunger Games* series without wondering to what degree we have deadened ourselves to the structure of our society in return for a narcotic-like recreational euphoria.

Specific Application

As in all of the other genres studied here, a number of subcategories exist within Science Fiction films. They all depict assaults upon a civilization. However, from category to category the emphasis changes, and consequently so do the protocols for interpretation.

Invasion of the Body Snatchers exemplifies the first subgroup: films that foreground the struggle of a society familiar to the audiences—contemporary Western civilization. It offers an analysis of a community under duress, or, at the very least, scrutiny of it from alternative world perspectives. In a Darwin-like fashion the opposing cultures generally struggle for hegemony and survival, and the employment by at least one of the protagonists of an advanced technology, often to gain dominance, underscores the fragility of any culture.

Alien represents another group, one that sets the action in the future and focuses on the way that an evolving society attempts to define itself. This temporal displacement allows viewers a clearer sense of the dominant elements of their own world through narratives that feature contrasting representations of two or more civilizations. The rapaciousness of the creature in *Alien* remains striking, but its greater significance lies in its representative function as it forces viewers to see uncomfortable parallels.

Finally, *The Matrix* represents the subgroup that sees the future as a dystopia, a consequence of the degeneration of our society. In this film degradation comes about because machines have simply outstripped the humans and now compete for control. In other examples in this category, the society itself has failed to adapt to social changes and in consequence has corroded, but no matter what the agency, the central concern remains a critique of a society that has proven to be slow to adapt to the changing problems that confront it.

Invasion of the Body Snatchers

Many filmgoers have seen this 1956 film, directed by Don Siegel (whose other films include *Madigan, Dirty Harry, Two Mules for Sister Sara*, and *The Shootist*) as both a commentary on the Cold War mentality that dominated the consciousness of Americans in the 1950s and a condemnation of the homogeneity and conformity of the suburban life-style that came to popularity in that same decade. While these observations may well prove accurate, they do not address the singular significance of this work. *Invasion of the Body Snatchers* very deftly sums up the protocols of the Science Fiction category in dealing with the clash of contemporary American culture and an alien force antipathetic to that way of life. This older version of the film offers a significantly important reminder of what suspense can achieve. At a time when the form of a Science Fiction film can overshadow its content, *Invasion of the Body Snatchers* shows how effectively a Science Fiction film can present a chilling narrative without elaborate special or visual effects.

The narrative of *Invasion of the Body Snatchers* is set over a three day

Becky Driscoll (Dana Wynter) and Miles Binnell (Kevin McCarthy) flee San Mira in *Invasion of the Body Snatchers* (1956).

period from Thursday morning to Saturday night and is framed by scenes in the present (that Saturday evening) signaling to viewers that all else that occurs is an account of recent past events. It opens at the emergency room of the hospital with Dr. Miles Bennell (Kevin McCarthy) frantically claiming that he is not insane. As viewers will learn by the end of the film, the police have brought Miles to the hospital because his erratic behavior has made them think him a lunatic. Like many Science Fiction characters in this category, he possesses knowledge that others do not find credible (*E.T. the Extra-Terrestrial*). He begins to tell his story to a psychiatrist in an attempt to prove his sanity and to warn his listeners of the danger that they face. As is often the case in Science Fiction films, those listening serve as surrogates for the audience. The ability of Miles to get the people in the emergency room to accept his story reflects directly on the credibility of the film's narrative.

Miles is the local doctor in the small town of Santa Mira, California.

Siegel carefully establishes the ethos of normalcy and promotes a familiarity with the setting by alternating many wide-angle shots of the town with a number of scenes featuring mundane activities like mowing the lawn. At the same time, Siegel introduces a slightly discordant note. Miles has hastily returned from a trip to deal with several patients clamoring to see him, only to have each cancel the appointment before coming in for an exam.

What stands out in this film in contrast to others in the genre is its deliberate pacing. The title of the motion picture makes very clear what to expect in the plot. At the same time, unlike other films in this category (*Independence Day*), the narrative takes great pains to defer confrontation with the force that menaces society. When Miles, accompanied by an old girlfriend Becky (Dana Wynter), visits Becky's cousin, Wilma, who thinks that her Uncle Ira is not her Uncle Ira, the tone is low key and the behavior quite predictable. Miles responds to hearing those symptoms with the same kind of skepticism that he will meet in others at the end of the movie, He recommends that Wilma see a psychiatrist, and puts aside any further thoughts about her problem.

After these establishing scenes, the pace of the film accelerates. As is the case in many films of this sort (*Signs*), evidence begins to accrue to give significance to the concerns that Miles had earlier dismissed. A local psychiatrist, Dr. Danny Kauffman (Larry Gates) tells Miles that for the past two weeks a number of people have been claiming that relatives are not themselves. He is called to a friend's house, where Jack Belicec (King Donovan) shows him a body resembling Jack but not fully formed. A puzzled Miles can only advise Jack to watch the body's development. When, in the middle of the night, the body at Jack's opens its eyes and has a cut duplicating one on Jack's hand, viewers begin to feel a real sense of the danger that the town faces.

At this point, a conspiratorial tone begins to cloud the narrative. Miles, like many other characters in this category, to starts feel unsure of those around him and of the environment in which he exists. He finds a replica of Becky in the basement of her father's home. As Miles' fear builds, those who had initially aroused it now seek to allay his concern. Wilma tells him that she believes that everything is all right. At Miles' office, Jimmy Grimaldi (Bobby Clark), a child who had feared his mother, has become affectionate towards her. As Miles comes to the point of doubting his own conclusions, he finds seed pods in his greenhouse that seem to be forming bodies. He realizes that the change is finalized when people fall asleep.

The narrative masterfully plays upon a concept that has become a staple of this category. Even as the world seems to go on in a normal fashion, a tremendous threat to its safety and integrity looms (*Men in Black*). Miles and Becky now find themselves struggling to survive as the environment that they had thought stable and inviolate erodes around them. They realize that the invasion is widespread and that the town is already infected. Contact with the outside world is cut off, and the remainder of the film turns on efforts to escape.

As is the case in many Science Fiction films (*The Thing*), close friends undermine the efforts of the central characters. Indeed, by building paranoia and by providing perfectly credible reasons for such a feeling, Siegel deftly increases the tension of the film. It becomes obvious that the invading pods have now taken possession of everyone in town, and are spreading like an infectious disease. In short order, Jack and Teddy Belicec (Carolyn Jones) and then Becky are also co-opted. Near the end of the film, as Miles runs along a crowded highway trying to get someone in the passing cars to stop to help him, there is a real sense of futility and defeat in the film.

It at this point that viewers encounter an interesting narrative decision. The scene returns to the hospital and to the men listening to Miles' story. Their skepticism disappears when a man who was driving a truck full of pods comes in as an accident victim. The film ends with people beginning to take measures to cope with the threat.

Originally, the 1956 version did not have the bracketing scenes in the hospital, but began with Miles' return to Santa Mira and ended with him alone on a crowded highway. The directors included the change to give a more upbeat conclusion. It is a shift as abrupt as the sudden demise of the aliens in *War of the Worlds*, a conclusion parodied in *Mars Attacks*. However, the ending of Siegel's film is far less important than its narrative thrust. Like all movies in this category, *Invasion of the Body Snatchers* presents a clear critique of our current way of life and offers no assurances that it can sustain itself.

The Invasion of the Body Snatchers, like many of the films in this group, was made at the height of the Cold War. (That is not to relegate this sub-group to a single period, however, for the theme of contemporary society being tested by one completely devoid of its assumptions and aspirations has long been and remains a popular subject.) While it may not have been a conscious decision on the part of filmmakers, clearly the narrative in the film, showing a threat from an alien force, echoes the fears of a country concerned with the threat posed by the Soviet Union. It also highlights the homogeneity of suburban American culture. Other examples include: *The Thing, Close Encounters of the Third Kind, Alien versus Predator, It Came from Outer Space, Invaders from Mars, Predator, The War of the Worlds* (both versions), *Independence Day, Jurassic Park, Timecop, Mars Attacks, Signs, E.T. the Extra-Terrestrial,* and *Men in Black.*

Alien

Films like *Invasion of the Body Snatchers* explore the vulnerability of a society to aggression from creatures from another world—positing a straightforward them-versus-us dichotomy. However, as that movie's title subtly affirms, films in its subgroup rarely, if ever, question the desirability of preserving the status quo that outsiders challenge. In marked contrast, motion pictures like *Alien*, released in 1979 and directed by Ridley Scott, fall into a category of Science Fiction films that express at the very least ambivalent feelings towards specific features of a particular society, and assert an interest in offering a more complex critique of the status quo.

Their narratives, generally set in the future, continue the pattern of testing a civilization's ability to withstand external assaults (*Starship Troopers*), but they also examine what they portray as increasingly problematic relationships between humanity and technology (*Timecop*). In this fashion, movies in this group assume a transitional analytic position between films that simply reinforce the need for a familiar world to survive in a struggle against a foreign one and those that examine the consequences of a dystopian society that has become a threat to itself. In all of these categories, the narratives rarely if ever question the ideals upon which societies are built, but in the latter two subgroups there is a stronger sense of imperfections in the ways societies implement those standards.

The title of the motion picture *Alien* attests to the narrative's awareness of the expectations that viewers bring to Science Fiction movies. Its terseness announces the plot as a confrontation between representatives of an established culture and an outsider. What the movie goes on to do so brilliantly is play upon the inherent subjectivity of the application of the term alien. Despite the clear cut, either/or distinctions that the word makes, over the course of the film, viewers are asked to consider the arbitrariness of its use. *Alien* reinforces that concept through a narrative that gradually establishes the crew of the ship and the creature whom they battle as microcosmic representations of their respective worlds, a trait common to many films in this category. By the conclusion, events have come to suggest that every individual in the film—as well as the predator who stalks them—could qualify for the role of title character.

As in any Science Fiction motion picture, ethos plays an important interpretive role. Like the opening of *Silent Running*, *Alien* very carefully establishes the environment in which the action will unfold. In a gesture that asserts the important role of technology within the film, and in a subtle evocation of the issues of *2001: A Space Odyssey*—a film in the third category—machines and not humans are the first images to be presented.

The initial scenes inside the spacecraft reflect a calm, almost serene tone devoid of movement. Before any character appears, the camera takes viewers on a visual tour of the ship, the *Nostromo*, presenting it as a self-sustaining entity.[4] Indeed, when the computer springs to life and revives the dormant crew, one gets the clear suggestion of a world where humans have fallen under the direction of machines. The crew reinforces this image of a dependent relationship when they call the computer that controls the ship Mother.

A very interesting aspect of this film underscores the role of this group as a bridge between the first and third subcategories of the genre. Films in the middle category willingly show as flawed the society that Science Fiction conventions would normally privilege—the one under assault. They are not dismissing the value of the society, but they do call upon viewers to accept its imperfections.

As members of the crew appear, they quickly establish the bonds holding together the community within the ship as a frayed, at best, with interactions often punctuated by bickering and rivalry. At several points, the narrative suggests that conflict resides inherent within the social structure (*The Dark Planet*) rather than from simple friction between individual personalities. The first sign of discord comes from a disagreement over how shares of the profits of the ship are divided. The hierarchically ordered divisions emerge from discussions of variances in compensation. The operating crew—Dallas (Tom Skerritt), Kane (John Hurt), Ripley (Sigourney Weaver), and Lambert (Veronica Cartwright)—receive full shares. The lowly maintenance men, Brett (Harry Dean Stanton) and Parker (Yaphet Kotto), are awarded half shares. In a subtly prescient gesture, the science officer, Ash (Ian Holm), stands apart from all.

As the debate over the equity of share distribution unfolds, it becomes clear that not simply the salaries but the various tasks performed by the crew produce sharp delineations in standing. It short order, however, the audience sees even these distinctions as relative. For the *Nostromo* is a salvage ship, a scavenger vessel with attendant low status anywhere in the space hierarchy.

Five. It Came from Outer Space   137

After the communal ties among the crew have been called into question, the narrative goes on to cast doubts on individual professional abilities. Although the ship consists of little more than a collection of foragers, successive scenes show that even performing this job may be beyond their abilities. The damage they do to their craft in an effort to land suggests that the crew is barely in control of the machines that they attempt to use. This means that even a slight knowledge of technology gives characters a marked advantage, and it only heightens the social friction. The two crewmen who can repair the ship, Brett and Parker, show themselves in their own rights to be sullen and maladjusted. They respond to the dependence of others by a passive-aggressive work slowdown that manipulates the situation without achieving anything more than demonstrating their power to do so.

The narrative of *Alien* painstakingly sets up the atmosphere of the film: a group of ordinary people, marginally competent, who are asked to enter a world that they are not equipped to face, and then they are confronted with a situation well beyond their capabilities for response. The hostile environment of the planet visited by the *Nostromo* exacerbates the helplessness of these individuals. All space explorers have a dependence upon their equipment for their survival. Few, however, are shown to be as ill at ease as this group in using technology to insure their safety and comfort.

When the crew begins to look for the source of the distress beacon in the remains of a ship wrecked on the planet's surface, the action accelerates. When they discover the alien ship and the enormous skeleton of its pilot, many viewers will assume that this is the protagonist suggested by the title. The crewmen who come upon the scene are dwarfed by the creature's magnitude, and it gives viewers a false sense of where the hazard lies. In the scenes on board the strange craft, the narrative plays with what we presume will next occur, and it makes effective use of images and pacing to create an atmosphere of danger and tension.

Paradoxically, the danger in fact comes from a rather diminutive source. As Kane examines a series of pods found in the hold, a creature from one quickly attaches itself to his face. Its sudden appearance and dexterous assault set the tone for the remainder of the film. Nearly forty minutes of running time have elapsed before the real adversary has appeared, and then it attacks with startling speed and ferocity. From that point until the conclusion, the crew members struggle to show resourcefulness sufficient to cope with the new threat to their well-being.

A real impediment to any success is the conflicted roles that divide the crew. Although their human frailties are all too clear, the film also makes a stronger case for the flawed structure of the world they inhabit. (In this fashion it neatly inverts the premise of films like those in the *Star Trek* series.) A sign of the difficulty that they will have coordinating their efforts arises almost immediately. Although ordered by the ship's commander, Dallas, to open the outer door of the ship, Ripley, the third in command after Dallas and Kane, follows the accepted procedure, and refuses to allow the party back on board. In response, the science officer, Ash, defies her by releasing the entry hatch.

As the narrative quickly makes clear, any decision on what to do in an emergency is compounded by an uncomfortable division of the authority on the ship. Dallas is the captain, but he must follow the direction of machines—Mother and Ash—in matters that are outside the running of the ship. Conflicted aims and dependence upon mechanical guidance lead to paralysis, and the human community has a great deal of difficulty determining a clear course of action when faced with the threat of a hostile life form.

Indeed, once inside the *Nostromo*, the invader determines how events unfold, and in the process it raises further questions about the competence of the crew and the ability of their world to withstand external challenges. As the crew combs the bowels of the ship, the various tubes and other

The predator that stalks the crew of the *Nostromo* in *Alien* (1979).

pieces of equipment all seem ominous and underscore how alienated these men and women are from their environment. The creature they are pursuing, on the other hand, shows itself both at ease and adaptable within the complex structure of the craft. It quickly evolves to fit the demands of this new world in which it finds itself, shedding its skin and growing to an enormous size.

Furthermore, the alien also demonstrates a fiercer desire for survival than do most of the humans whom it faces. The creature shows decisiveness and ingenuity. In contrast, the crew remains unsure of the best way to defend themselves and unable to make technology work in their favor. Dallas, reflecting the group's continuing dependence on machinery, turns to Mother for advice on how to deal with the alien. In a perverse response, the computer sidesteps the role as protector and refuses to act, saying that there is insufficient data to make an assessment. As the crew tries to track the alien, their instruments for detection prove ineffectual and their weapons for defense are inadequate. The crisis intensifies, and the technology upon which they depend and that defines their world proves increasingly useless. When the alien kills Dallas and takes his body away without a trace behind, it creates a disquieting impression of invulnerability. This increases the paranoia of the crew, whose loyalty to one another is already questionable.

The turning point in the plot occurs when Ripley gains a way into Mother's database, overriding the command that blocked access and inverting the pattern of machines controlling humans. From information in the computer, Ripley discovers that the ship's mission has been altered to collect the alien as a specimen for scientific study and that the instructions consider the crew expendable. Ash reveals his complicity in this plan, calling the alien "a perfect organism" and saying that "I admire its purity," as he discloses his identity as a robot. From the start of the voyage, the unnamed and faceless company that owns the ship, with chilling and calculated cunning, has made the apprehension of the alien its primary aim, and executives have used the crew with the same callous disregard that they have displayed in their use of technology.

This is also a moment of readjustment for the audience. The social constructions within the ship, so carefully outlined over the course of the narrative, now seem misleading and artificial. Rather than serving as representative figures of a specific civilization, the crew appears to be its disposable tools. However, the narrative again inverts expectations by giving at least one individual the opportunity to challenge both the hegemony of the company and the power of the creature attacking them.

After the creature has killed all of the other crewmembers, Ripley rebels against both technology and the world defined by the faceless corporation that employs her. She sets in motion the system to destroy the ship. Once again machines become a threat, although it is the paradoxical condition that this threat is Ripley's only chance for salvation. When Ripley escapes in the shuttle, there is a false sense of relief. The narrative quickly reveals that the alien, in stowing aboard the shuttle, has proven as adept as Ripley at surviving.

In the final struggle, neither technology nor community is of any use. Ripley relies on ingenuity and daring to save herself. This proves sufficient. The film ends in a moment of tranquility that re-establishes both humanity and a sense of community. Ripley sits peacefully stroking Jonesy the cat in her lap, and records the disturbing events that have preceded her escape from the *Nostromo*. As she sets about to wait for rescue, she affirms her faith in the larger community even over the narrow, self-serving attitudes of the corporation.

An alien culture—a term one can be applied to either of the groups in the film—shows absolutely no regard for the alternative society that confronts it. Animosity is instant and relentless. It is the conflict between two societies with complete incompatibility of material needs and cultural values. Other examples include: the *Star Wars* series, other films in the *Alien* series, *Forbidden Planet, The Dark Planet, Silent Running, Starship Troopers*, and *Star Trek*.

The Matrix

The third category of Science Fiction films combines features of the first two. These movies are set in a post-apocalyptic future, and they generally hearken back to a period of tranquility in our civilization that has been destroyed by human hubris, ignorance, or simply bad luck. They examine the consequences of the loss, and explore the requirements and the sacrifices necessary to restore the world to its former condition.

The Matrix is representative of a long line of such films, all offering variations on the same general theme. In some cases human ingenuity has undermined itself by unwittingly creating a force in technology that competes for power and control (*Terminator*). In others technology has not so much been a rival as a dangerous and improperly understood instrument (*Planet of the Apes*). No matter what the starting point, however, every instance presents an indictment of human behavior for its inability to control forces that its curiosity set in motion.

Alienation and menace (like that found in *Blade Runner*) stand as key elements of the atmosphere of films in this category. Both come to the forefront in the opening scene of *The Matrix* with police cornering Trinity (Carrie-Anne Moss) in a deserted hotel room. This scene very neatly establishes both the abilities and the limitations of the marginalized group that Trinity represents. In quick order she dispatches the police, but the real struggle begins when Agent Smith (Hugo Weaving) arrives. (Viewers will subsequently learn that agents are machines, operating unobtrusively within the Matrix with the mission of capturing rebel humans and maintaining order within the programs.) Smith clearly intimidates Trinity, and, after a pursuit ensues across the city rooftops, she only barely escapes.

Having opened the film with a representation of the prototypical rebel struggling against the system, the narrative next presents a paradoxical alternative in the person of the computer geek Neo, a.k.a. Thomas A. Anderson (Keanu Reeves). In the era of cyber naiveté that produced *The Matrix*, Neo's character could be seen as an edgy iconoclast. Even here, however, innocence is a fragile quality. Neo's hacking has given him a vague sense of a system called the Matrix, and the narrative introduces Neo as someone aware that things are not as they seem, yet not sure what to make of it all. What is certain is that some force is enticing Neo to continue his efforts to understand what the Matrix is. (From the beginning the narrative self-consciously makes reference to Lewis Carroll's *Alice's Adventures in Wonderland*. It provides handy metaphors for the bafflement that Neo feels, and it also underscores the proximity of Science Fiction to Fantasy.) This image of questing for a solution to a question that the central character cannot even clearly formulate recurs throughout films in this category (*Soylent Green*). Through the individual's efforts to comprehend his or her environment, the narrative can, in the best films of this type, offer a full explanation of that world without falling into tedious exposition.

The early scenes underscore the impossibility of neutrality for Neo. In short order, Neo finds himself caught between the threats of Agent Smith and the blandishments of Morpheus (Laurence Fishburne), also the name of the Greek god of dreams. Like other central characters in this subcategory (the Arnold Schwarzenegger character in *The Running Man*, Ben Richards, is another example of this sort of figure), Neo is caught in a system that he does not understand. Morpheus offers a resolution by giving Neo the chance to gain full understanding of the Matrix, which, of course, Neo accepts: "You stay in Wonderland and I show you how deep the rabbit hole goes."

A series of scenes tracing Neo's liberation from the enormous storage area where his energy is being harvested graphically illustrates the material world outside the virtual Matrix. Neo is subsequently brought to the *Nebuchadnezzar*, a hovercraft made in the USA in 2069. He begins his re-education through the Construct, a computer program used to counter the Matrix.[5]

The initiation portion of the film enables exposition without excessive pedantry, as Morpheus shows Neo the desolated world that is the result of the war between humanity and the Artificial Intelligence that they created. Like the adversaries in the other two categories, little is revealed about the nature of this machine community, for the primary concern remains the restoration of human society. The key elements in the constitution of the machine world are its parasitic dependence upon humans

(Left to right) Cypher (Joe Pantoliano), Morpheus (Laurence Fishburne), Neo (Keanu Reeves), and Trinity (Carrie-Anne Moss) in *The Matrix* (1999).

as a source of energy and its determination to control its environment. Little additional information is forthcoming, but this is very much in keeping with the atmosphere of a dystopian world. These films presume the viewers' the sweeping assumptions of its corrosive nature. That makes it unnecessary, in the view of most scriptwriters, to articulate a more detailed description of it.

To a degree, that same approach guides the way the audience is given a sense of the society that Morpheus seeks to restore. Shifting into a messianic tone, Morpheus expounds on the idea that Neo is the one destined to free the human race, a resurrected figure of the man who first freed people from the Matrix. This is the closest the film comes to a metaphysical explanation of human life and probably as much as filmgoers can expect from most movies in this category.

Balancing Neo's gradual integration into the society on the Nebuchadnezzar is the growing disaffection of one of the crew, Cypher (Joe Pantoliano), with the life of physical hardship that they all lead. In a scene in which he is eating steak and drinking wine in an elegant restaurant, Cypher acknowledges that it is all a product of a computer program but also decides he prefers the illusion of physical gratification over real life drudgery on the *Nebuchadnezzar*. He colludes with Smith to betray Morpheus and return to the Matrix. The narrative does not go any further in exploring ontological concepts, but it certainly raises issues for the audience to resolve in the interpretive process.

In particular, Cypher's behavior implicitly calls into question both the nature of reality and the force of free will. It asks viewers to consider the possible validity of Cypher's claim, that living in a comfortable world, one whose material aspects are present only in his mind, is preferable to the misery of palpable existence. If one grants that premise, then it challenges the validity of Morpheus' entire undertaking. Further, if, as Agent Smith later says, humans cannot survive in a Matrix engineered to give them perfect contentment, then presumably they need the opportunity to make choices, or exercise free will, that the modified Matrix now provides. Viewers may accept or reject the validity of Cypher's argument as they choose, but they must confront it if only to understand the behavior of Morpheus, including the killing of other humans, which he justifies as a necessary act to achieve a greater good. (At one point Morpheus explains experiencing death virtually causes individuals in the energy farm to expire.)

As in many such films (*Total Recall* or *RoboCop* are good examples), once the environment and the source of conflict have been described, action scenes and special/visual effects take over the narrative. Cypher's betrayal of the group leads to the capture of Morpheus. This, in turn, provokes the decision by Neo and Trinity to confront the agents and rescue their leader.

Although the subsequent action takes place over a number of scenes, it can be summarized rather briefly. Over the course of combat with the agents, Neo is first defeated and then, through a questionable romantic device, reanimated as someone now capable of fighting on the level of agents. The film ends with Neo's defeat of Agent Smith, his rescue of Morpheus, and his issuing a challenge to the machines from a phone booth inside the Matrix.

The most significant achievement of *The Matrix* is that, while following the predictable pattern of films of this genre, it has given viewers a range of provocative interpretive alternatives. Other examples include *The Terminator, Planet of the Apes, The Hunger Games, The Running Man, Blade Runner, Total Recall, 2001: A Space Odyssey, The Handmaid's Tale, Planet of the Apes, The Time Machine, 1984, Soylent Green, RoboCop,* and *A Clockwork Orange.*

Six

Monkey Business
Slapstick Comedies

Let Me Get This Straight

Of all the types of films considered in this study, Comedy stands as the most complex and amorphous. The diverse strategies that film directors apply to provoke laughter make it possible to divide it into any number of subgroups, each equally useful for understanding responses to a particular group of films. To keep the discussion manageable, however, I have focused on two categories that highlight the major comedic impulses: disruption and reconciliation. In this chapter, I will discuss the disruptive types, Slapstick Comedies, and in the next the ones with reconciling impulses, Screwball Comedies, alternately often called Romantic Comedies.

Before going further, however, I want to note an important feature distinguishing both from several other types of movies examined in this book: the function of women in these films. In Westerns, Gangster movies, and Film Noir women typically have at best strong supporting roles, and at worst near or complete invisibility. In some Horror movies like *Scream*, analyzed in Chapter Four, and certain Science Fiction movies, like *Alien* discussed in Chapter Five, strong female roles are becoming more common.

However, Slapstick and Screwball Comedies have always put talented female actors (though not necessarily female directors) on an equal level with their male counterparts. It is not my intention to make this book a study of women in film, an number of fine analyses are already in print.[1] At the same time, no commentator can speak with authority about Slapstick and Screwball comedies without acknowledging the profound screen impact of women on the development of both genres.

A General Sense of the Genre

Slapstick Comedies draw their name from the chief prop of a chaotic, ad hoc type of entertainment popular in Italy from the 16th to the 18th centuries, the Commedia dell' Arte. In many of the improvisational scenes, actors struck other characters with a paddle-like device, a slapstick, which on contact makes a loud noise but inflicts little pain. The history of that implement neatly conveys the pace and structure of this type of motion picture. They generally affect a great deal of movement and an enormous expenditure of energy, but in the end Slapstick Comedies tend to produce little real change in the status quo.

Through the frenetic action of the Mack Sennett Studios during the silent film era, Charlie Chaplin, Mabel Normand Harold Lloyd, Maria Dressler, Buster Keaton, Anita Garvin, and others set the tone for what to expect in Slapstick Comedies that continues through the present era. At the same time, Slapstick is more than pratfalls, free-for-alls, and other assorted mayhem. From Groucho Marx and W.C. Fields on to Eddie Murphy and Melissa McCarthy, rapid fire, anarchic dialogues prove every bit as effective at generating laughs as do the disruptive physical performances of other comics in this genre. Both madcap monologues and anarchic gyrations rely on the same techniques to produce humor: frenetic action, an exaggerated response to one's environment, and a penchant for non-sequiturs.

At the same time, more than simple eccentricity shapes identities in these films. The impulse for radical individualism informs characterizations throughout the genre. The action underscores the struggle of rebellious individuals striving to retain their independence within a world that insistently pressures them to conform. Broad physical humor and acerbic dialogue challenge the primacy of societal rules. Communal values serve as both a foil for the comedy and an anchor for the narrative. In the end, resolution comes either through society's taming the Slapstick hero's resistance to authority or by the community finding a way to live with his or her eccentric personality.

Cultural and Aesthetic Context

As noted above, the impact of Slapstick Comedy comes from physical humor. That is not to say, however, that the genre is devoid of wit. Beyond simply the clever manipulation of language, the best slapstick shows a keen sense of playing to and against the expectations that viewers bring to the cinema. Indeed, some of the funniest bits in Slapstick Comedy come out of projects founded on parodic associations with other genres (*Young Frankenstein, This Is Spinal Tap, Blazing Saddles, Airplane!, The Naked Gun*). Lampooning other well-known movie forms highlights the farcical perspectives that dominates tone of the genre. However, Slapstick goes well beyond simply burlesquing other types of films. In its most effect practice, it strains against orthodox constraints while simultaneously underscoring the need for such conventions to provide a measure of stability.

Slapstick films offer a sharply defined characters given perspective by their contrast with the mores of the world around them (*Bringing Up Baby*). While these individuals generally do not openly reject society's values, they show a contrasting inclination to strain against the limits imposed by them. In this way, a symbiotic relationship obtains. An element of mockery may season the action in Slapstick Comedies, but the key revelation in the narrative comes when the audience sees the main character's ultimate dependence upon acceptance by society (*Uncle Buck*). It is through understanding the nature of that individual's relationship with

(Left to right) Derek Smalls (Harry Shearer), Nigel Tufnel (Christopher Guest), and David St. Hubins (Michael McKean) in *This Is Spinal Tap* (1984).

Buck (John Candy) in *Uncle Buck* (1989).

the community that the audience comes to understand the dynamics of the film. Often this reflects not a rebellion against social norms as much as it shows the central character's complete lack of awareness of his or her deviance from them.

Throughout the *Pink Panther* series, for instance, Inspector Clouseau (Peter Sellars) steadfastly remains blissfully ignorant of the degree to which his behavior is at odds with that of others. On the contrary, he has the impression that his every action is sanctioned, even lauded by society. Miraculously, he survives and even prospers in that context, giving those films the opportunity to comment on the mores of the world that they depict.

Nowhere is the reciprocal relationship between the Slapstick comic and the community more evident than in the seemingly anti-social films of the Marx Brothers. In movie after movie, Groucho, Chico, and Harpo (and occasionally Zeppo), in their behavior, their language, and their characterizations, insistently resist pressures to conform to the dictates of society while determinedly existing within the community.[2] As a counterbalance, Margaret Dumont, appearing in most of their films as a representative of the dominant culture, establishes the standard against which they rebel. She survives, despite all the turmoil, because in all the movies the Marx Brothers balance their reckless insistence on the right to disordered single-minded behavior with an astute sense of just how far to go without provoking the community to ostracize them.

For example, in *A Night at the Opera*, perhaps the most chaotic of their films, the boys (a term often applied to them and redolent of the childish/childlike natures that govern their behavior) attempt to trick a prominent opera singer into a constricting contract. As is often the case in such Slapstick films, they completely misperceive the situation and end up signing an unknown tenor who sings in the chorus (Allan Jones) and who is in love with the lead soprano (Kitty Carlisle). Groucho, Chico, and Harpo respond to the confusion that results by engineering a happy ending that restores order to the opera and insures that the young lovers (the tenor and his girlfriend) are united. Despite all of their raucous rebelliousness here and in their other films, the Marx Brothers are among the most socially self-conscious of Slapstick comedians. Rebellion is always individualized and tends to be short lived. In the end reconciliation with society, albeit usually on their own terms, becomes a way of finding peace and satisfaction in their lives.

While not all Slapstick Comedies work so hard to preserve conventional order, the best in this category move viewers to accept the genre's dual role. On the one hand, the audience must allow for the raucous, even coarse, humor that fuels the action of these motion pictures. At the same time, we are asked to engage the way each film critiques society in order to judge its accuracy and assess its worth.

Key Elements in Plot and Characterization

Some critics have labeled Slapstick Comedians as clowns, and within limits that serves as a useful term. However, the disruptive associations adhering to that image belie the central impulse of the Slapstick Comedy:

acceptance. Society puts clowns on the periphery, gaudy figures instantly recognizable as the other and almost always ostracized from most social institutions. (When clowns reproduce these institutions in their own world, the grotesqueness of their imitations underscores the inherent flaws and weaknesses of the form that they mimic.) It might be more useful to see the central figures in Slapstick Comedies as rebellious children, operating more or less single-handedly, who seek to maintain their position at all costs (*Bridesmaids*).

Unlike the solipsistic and clannish clown culture, the Slapstick figure rejects isolation. He or she wants to be part of society, albeit on his or her own terms. One sees the difference very clearly in the so-called "Little Tramp," Charlie Chaplin, who portrayed characters almost always desperate to be part of the world that they inhabited. Indeed, the pioneers of slapstick—mentioned earlier in the chapter—repeatedly took the tack of legitimizing their behavior by manipulating social conventions rather than overtly rejecting them.

In a paradoxical manner, the disruptive behavior of the Slapstick character reinforces the viewers' sense of the comedian's longing for acceptance. Although anarchy seems to be the hallmark of Slapstick Comedies,

(Left to right) Megan (Melissa McCarthy), Rita (Wendy McLendon-Covey), Becca (Elie Kemper), Anne (Kristen Wiig), Lillian (Maya Rudolph), and Helen (Rosie Bern) in *Bridesmaids* (2011).

as often as not their characters act out of an ignorance of proper decorum. In the end, most will believe that they have deferred to the dictates of society. Of course, more often than not, they do not change their patterns of behavior but rather, consciously or not, they learn sufficient control to live within the world around them. Indeed, an acceptance of restraint, not a concession to reconfiguration, characterizes the development of most figures in this genre.

In much the same way animals can be domesticated while retaining their basic natures, so then people in Slapstick Comedies are generally tamed rather than changed by the world around them. The transition is never easy, for they struggle instinctively to sustain their attitudes and their approaches to life in a society that demands more self-control and cooperation. Ultimately, individuals in these comedies negotiate a position that allows them to retain many of their behavioral quirks while conceding a certain level of conformity to the demands of society.

Affinity and empathy are key traits that insure the social acceptability of the Slapstick Comedian who never fully relinquishes loyalty to the conventions of the world in which he or she exists (*Trainwreck*). To underscore this condition, Slapstick narratives have their heroes confronting renegade elements of the culture, figures who openly live outside the mores of the world (*Identity Thief*) or who hypocritically manipulate social values with no real loyalty to those institutions (*Trading Places*). Initially, at least, it may well seem that these renegades and the Slapstick hero share an antipathy for the restraints of the conventional world. To a degree that remains the case, but a fundamentally positive attitude toward society sets the Slapstick comedian apart

Amy (Amy Schumer) and Aaron (Bill Hader) in *Trainwreck* (2015).

from the malevolence of the others. Furthermore, a basic loyalty to the community grounds the character, and provides a guide for the limits of outrageous behavior. Ultimately, an affinity, even though attenuated at times, with conventional value systems sustains the Slapstick comedian and sets him or her apart from the anti-social antagonists who serve as foils.

Even when no clear antagonist emerges, the Slapstick comedian has to have someone to highlight his or her behavior, for the Slapstick character cannot act without a foil. He or she needs a partner (Abbott and Costello, Laurel and Hardy, Martin and Lewis), a steady rival (W.C. Fields and Mae West, Groucho Marx and Margaret Dumont), or even frustrated interactions with society itself (Richard Pryor, Melissa McCarty, Eddie Murphy, Amy Schumer, Jim Carrey) to throw his or her acts into relief. In this relationship, there is an element of the vaudeville straight man who sets up the jokes (though as already noted Margaret Dumont made the gendered aspect of the term anachronistic by the 1930s). Nonetheless, the partnership is more than a throwback, for the so-called straight man does more than facilitate situational humor. He or she often serves as emblem-

Mae West and W.C. Fields in *My Little Chickadee* (1940).

atic of the world against whom the slapstick comic struggles, even while seeking a form of integration.

While a storyline exists for these films, the narration more often than not turns on episodic confrontations. Through a character or characters who resist the status quo, Slapstick Comedies challenge many of the assumptions of the social institutions that shape our lives. In doing so, these comedies walk a narrow line between good-natured criticism and unbridled ridicule, and the distinction remains crucial.

Negotiation stands as the key element in these movies. Slapstick characters seek acceptance without reformation. Society relentlessly strives to assimilate them. In most cases, a synthetic resolution occurs. Society develops a measure of tolerance, and characters find themselves domesticated without completely losing their identities (*The Nutty Professor*). In a few instances, the film culminates in the triumph of the individual through achieving social status or control without sacrificing his or her independence (*The Blues Brothers*), but more often than not resolution comes about through compromise or at least accommodation.

Issues

When a character in a Slapstick film challenges authority, what ensues is generally represented as a fairly straightforward struggle. The individual seeks independence, and society endeavors to compel conformity. The best movies of this genre, however, do not present these attitudes as strict polarities. Rather, their narratives offer multiple perspectives which in turn creates varying degrees of sympathy for either position. (*Barbershop* gently lays out the parameters of this sort of contest.) In any case, the result is a clash of the values, attitudes, and behaviors of the individual (*Ferris Bueller's Day Off*) or small group against those of society as a whole (*M*A*S*H*) with the viewers left to decide upon the validity of these attitudes.

Whatever the emphasis, the terms of the struggle configure our sense of the characters. Much of the discourse in a Slapstick film will revolve around the issue of who can legitimately define the behavior of a particular character: the self or society. Films like *The Distinguished Gentleman* juxtapose familiar institutions with a rebellious figure to underscore the differences, but they also show each side of the dichotomy capable of at least some measure of adjustment. Further, although the conventions of the genre favor individualism, some of the most effective Slapstick comedies

Thomas Jefferson Johnson (Eddie Murphy) in *The Distinguished Gentleman* (1992).

play against the type and invert these expectations to endorse the mores of society, though even here the status quo general undergoes a degree of alteration (*Beetlejuice*).

In either case, Slapstick narratives almost always ask viewers to assess the validity of specific social structures and the general legitimacy of society. Because of the attention given to the nature of the character who rebels, the constitution of the institutions that demand conformity becomes an equally important question. (This is one reason that assaults on the status quo are so popular in this genre. The viewers, presumably, are already familiar with its institutions and so extended exposition is not necessary.) The sympathy or antipathy that the audience feels for the social environment surrounding characters tips the interpretive balance.

All of these features point towards the pivotal concern of motion pictures in this genre: the question of how much one must compromise to survive and what will be the impact of conformity on the individual. Resolving this issue without upsetting the narrative's equilibrium requires great skill, for, if either the Slapstick character is crushed or improbably survives without change in defiance of society, the credibility of a form that relies on verisimilitude would be greatly blunted. Only when the genre is taken to an extreme form in parody does the narrative countenance the clear-cut victory of one extreme over the other. It is generally more palatable to find a middle ground that leaves the character substantially intact while defusing his or her threat to the order of society.

The Particular Influence of Women

This most dynamic issue often finds its resolution tied to the way a film accommodates the impact of women on the plotline. As noted at the opening of the chapter, women always played integral roles in films in this genre, but mutability has characterized their status, particularly when compared to the stability afforded by the archetypal roles assigned to their male counterparts. One sees this in the brilliantly understated assertions of female status that began with Margaret Dumont. Although, as noted earlier in the chapter, she generally served as a foil for Groucho's comic lines in the Marx Brothers films, the effectiveness of the repartee rested on Dumont's characters projecting an unshakeable determination to be taken seriously on their own terms. (Albeit, this was usually made easier by a solid social standing that cushioned her from most shocks.)

In contrast, Mae West's libidinous portrayals gave both a narrower scope to her characters and a much more emphatic sense of their natures. Her roles were defined by sharp one-liners that were always grounded in sexual innuendo, and they were delivered with a bravado that defied anyone to challenge her proclivities. While these extreme characterization, for both Dumont and West, might seem to some as bordering on stereotypes, in fact they enforce an antithetical view. Whether withstanding the onslaughts of the Marx Brothers or emphatically demanding championing physical gratification, their roles, legitimizing a character's strength through traits related almost exclusively to gender, enhanced the comic effect of the Slapstick farces in which they appeared and gave support to a range of subsequent representations adopted by other female leads.

Over the course of the 1930s, a series of determined actors in comic leads—like Jean Harlow, Claudette Colbert, Myrna Loy, Rosalind Russell, and Kathryn Hepburn—took advantage of that achievement and began to assert themselves as more complex figures. As conventional Hollywood thinking responded to the success of their portrayals, subsequent actors from Jane Russell and Marilyn Monroe to Myra Randolph and Kristen

Wiig were able to refine and expand their roles, making them independent of male leads.[3]

Specific Application

All Slapstick characters operate on the margins of society, but some find themselves more comfortably situated in that position than do others. This first group—with *His Girl Friday* as a representative example—shows the ability of these marginalized characters not only to survive outside of society's restrictions but also to outline an alternative that still found acceptance in the dominant attitudes of the world in which they find themselves. This occurs because, although one might consider individuals like Walter, the ethically challenged the editor of a metropolitan newspaper, and Hildy, the star reporter ambivalent about her career, misfits in terms of the way that they interact with society, they and other such characters are far too clever and successful to be labeled as outsiders.

Animal House represents the most anarchic category of the three considered here, but its parodic perspective, and not its hectic action, best defines it. Films in this group, like the best in farce, ridicule the status quo even as they show the flaws in the characters who seek to set themselves apart. (And *Animal House* makes the ridicule self-reflexive during the final credits when it shows that the most rebellious characters, with the exception of D-Day, eventually integrate into the world against which they rebelled.) The audience is then faced with deciding the value of such achievements in a world already shown as hypocritical and valueless.

Clerks embodies a category that sets itself in stark contrast to the previous two. Films in this group foreground the bleakest elements of Slapstick comedy. They enforce an abiding sense of despair that replaces the buoyant defiance of films like *His Girl Friday* and the optimistic assumption of ultimate acceptance found in *Animal House*. Schadenfreude best describes our response to movies in this last category, though some might say if we did not respond with laughter we would end up crying.

His Girl Friday

Because *His Girl Friday* involves a formerly married couple, Hildy Johnson (Rosalind Russell) and Walter Burns (Cary Grant), critics often label the film as a Romantic or, in the nomenclature of this text, a Screwball

Comedy. However, the fact that the motion picture ends in, or at least points toward, their remarriage does not qualify it for such a label. (*Gentlemen Prefer Blondes* illustrates the point as well.) The movie's central problem does not deal with marriage, a crucial characteristic of the reconciliation impulse that animates Screwball Comedies, but rather it turns on a clash between eccentric personalities and conventional lifestyles.

His Girl Friday is not driving toward the romantic reconciliation of Hildy and Walter. Rather, it turns on the gradual admission by Hildy that the chaotic world of a reporter suits her more than would a place the tranquil, domestic environment that Bruce Baldwin (Ralph Bellamy) offers her. Indeed, Hildy repeatedly identifies herself as "a newspaperman," not because of any gender insecurity but rather through a total identification with her chosen, male-dominated profession. (Of course, to a degree this tendency can be attributed to the fact that *His Girl Friday* is a remake of *The Front Page*, first a popular stage play and then a successful film released in 1931, in which the Hildy Johnson character was a man played by Pat O'Brien. Though some may dispute it, this is a strong indication to me that the disputative relationship between Hildy and Walter does not grow out of sexual tension but of professional ambition.)

In the opening scene, with Hildy's grand entrance, the film emphatically foregrounds her as the central figure of the action. By sweeping into the newsroom, greeting colleagues, and offering rapid fire wisecracks, Hildy makes it clear, despite her announced intention to resign, that she is very much in her element. On the other hand, she tells Bruce, her fiancé, to remain behind, on the edge of the general office area, relegated to the role of the odd man out and implying the irrelevance of the world that he represents.

When Hildy goes on to apprise her ex-husband, Walter, of her plans to leave journalism and to berate him for the disinterest that caused their marriage to fall apart, it might seem that a Screwball Comedy is about to begin. However, in short order the narrative clarifies the terms of their struggle: their arguing over Hildy's decision to abandon her career alerts us that their bickering is far less about differing perceptions on domestic tranquility than about professional ambition.

It hardly can be surprising that both Hildy and Walter ignore Bruce for most of the movie because *His Girl Friday* emphatically is not about Walter's efforts to win back the love of his ex-wife. (Bruce is so nondescript that at one point Walter describes him, in an inside joke, as "the guy who looks like Ralph Bellamy [the actor who plays the role of Bruce].") On the contrary, the struggle of the movie turns on Hildy's efforts to deny her

Walter Burns (Cary Grant) and Hildy Johnson (Rosalind Russell) in *His Girl Friday* (1940).

ties to reporting and Walter's attempts to make her see it as her true vocation.

Even the choice of the title, a term used to identify a woman who assists an executive in a range of subsidiary tasks, suggests that Walter's concern centers on regaining and controlling a valuable employee and not on recovering a former wife. Walter sees the world only in the context of the newspaper business, and he admires Hildy as someone who shares that same tenacious devotion. In fact, the danger that Hildy might accept employment with another paper seems of far greater concern to Walter than the chance that she will become a housewife and live in Albany.

Of course, although he is completely committed to the newspaper business, the narrative makes it very clear from the start that Walter has no concern for noble sentiments or professional standards. He cons and connives anyone from whom he wants something because he holds himself outside the restraints of society. When trying to influence public events by offering to make a political endorsement that he has no intention of actually issuing, he blithely says, "It's the first time I ever double-crossed a governor." Walter has grown accustomed to manipulating people and events, and indeed he relishes the opportunity to do so. He is quick to size up a situation, has an unerring sense of another's foibles and weaknesses, and is ruthless in his determination to exploit those flaws. This cold-bloodedness is an important feature of his nature, for the narrative uses it to establish a crucial difference between him and Hildy, alike in so many other ways.

At the same time, their similarities prevent viewers from judging Walter as completely odious. We see the appealing elements in Walter's nature, albeit juxtaposed with the venal ones, early in the film when he and Hildy re-establish a rapport based on their abilities to be more than a match for one another in intelligence and verbal dexterity. The archness in both never permits a scene to become cloying. When Walter, dripping with insincerity, tries to sweet-talk Hildy by telling her "There's been a lamp burning in the window ever since you left," she caustically replies, "I jumped out the window long ago." These are worldly figures with a sense of the ridiculous that makes them way of sentiment but that never spills over into paralyzing cynicism.

Barbara di Bernardi has pointed out the significance of an innovative cinematic technique that enforces impressions of the uniqueness and equality of these central figures. Throughout the film, the pace of Walter and Hildy's dialogues is much quicker than those of any of the other characters. It was a conscious directing choice, and it underscores the acumen and the dexterity that set them apart from the others. (Di Bernardi's book *Fast Talking Dames* gives a detailed assessment of the impact of this technique in *His Girl Friday* and other films of the 1930s. It is a crucial work for understanding the place that women carved out for themselves in this genre and in Screwball comedies.) However, even as she is set apart with Walter from the others, Hildy enforces the exceptionality of her nature. Despite the fact that her wit is as sharp as that of her former husband, unlike the callous Walter, Hildy has a sense of humanity that always pushes her to take responsibility for her actions.

This gives the struggle between Walter and Hildy the archetypal shape of Slapstick Comedies like *The Odd Couple* rather than the trappings of a Screwball romance. It turns on Walter's resistance to conventions and Hildy's efforts, ultimately unsuccessful, to adopt those conventions. As Walter tells her during their first encounter, "You've got an old-fashioned idea that divorce lasts forever ... a few words mumbled over you by a judge." A quick initial response might conclude that lines like this make it seem as if romance is a crucial concern for Walter. In fact, he wishes to dispute the validity of the regularized world that Hildy wishes to enter and to reclaim her for the eccentric world of the reporters. (Characters in *M*A*S*H*, *The Blues Brothers*, and *Kingpin* take similar approaches in defending their world against the norm.) Convincing Hildy to write the story of the Earl Williams' (John Qualen) murder case becomes a way for Walter to win back Hildy not so much to their marriage but to the newspaper business.

Indeed, in many ways their marriage seems to have been constructed along the lines of a professional partnership. When Hildy articulates her new-found views of a husband's role by describing the virtues that attracted her to Bruce, Walter sardonically replies: "He sounds more like the man I want to marry." In fact, that remark encapsulates the problem that Hildy faces. Bruce is very domesticated while Hildy, like Walter, is feckless or at least completely committed to the disruptive lifestyle of a reporter.

Certainly, the film turns on Walter and Bruce's struggle for Hildy, but it would be a mistake to see this as a sexual competition. Rather, it reflects the efforts of different lifestyles to claim Hildy as their own (*Trading Places*). When Walter first meets Bruce, we see the clash of perspectives, and the contest begins—not between Walter and Bruce but between Walter and the world that Bruce represents. Walter lays out his approach and showcases his strengths when he intentionally mistakes an older man for Bruce and plays out the scene as a farce. Walter is not trying to make fun of Bruce or the old man. He is performing for Hildy. With a glib tongue and a wicked sense of humor, Walter contrasts life in his world with Bruce's sedate and predictable approach.

As this scene and any number of subsequent ones show, Walter and Hildy are both people who can improvise and are quick to take control of any situation. When Walter tries to manipulate Hildy's abhorrence of injustice to get her to stay and cover the execution of Earl Williams (John Qualen), she immediately discerns the ruse. Tellingly, however, she does not dismiss the proposition, but simply changes the terms of the arrangement so that Walter is forced to pay for what he wants by letting Bruce sell him a life insurance policy. In the next scene, Hildy again shows that she can be a step ahead of Walter when she foils his attempt to get out of his promise to buy lunch. All the while, Bruce stands by as the witless ingénue whose naiveté provides the necessary backdrop to measure the behavior of Walter and Hildy.

All of this demonstrates not only that Hildy is more than a match for Walter. It shows how similar they are. They think alike. They act the same way. (Both Hildy and Walter smoke, drink alcohol at lunch, and continually interrupt people. Bruce does none of these things.) They know each other's temperaments so well as to be able to anticipate each other's behavior. These similarities make clear, early in the film, the inevitability of Hildy's return to reporting. The only thing unresolved is how it will come about.

Hildy's interview with Earl gives the viewer concrete evidence of her skills as a reporter, and it also attests to her qualities as a human being. The scene demonstrates her compassion, but at the same time it never lets us lose sight of her cleverness. She treats Earl humanely, and endeavors to plant ideas that will help him establish his insanity defense. At the same time, her instincts as a reporter never leave her. While Hildy may be trying to offer Earl support, she also realizes that this gives her story the hook that it needs.

In a film filled with men, viewers might find it difficult to get an accurate measure of Hildy's gendered nature, and that is the value of Mollie Malloy (Helen Mack), the woman who briefly sheltered Earl. Mollie is neither as tough nor as intelligent as Hildy, and she certainly is more emotional. Her vulnerability is obvious when, in the courthouse pressroom, she confronts the reporters gathered there over their stories that had distorted her relationship with Earl. Their harsh dismissals of her criticisms shows how callous they feel they need to be, even though their embarrassment when Mollie leaves shows that they too are vulnerable.

Hildy, who has listened to their remarks to Molly, very neatly sets herself apart, by sarcastically addressing them as "Gentlemen of the Press." At the same time, the narrative shows that she is fundamentally no different from the other newspapermen. While Molly chastised the other reporters, the pragmatic Hildy busied herself writing a story based on Molly's remarks.

As the picture goes on, it neatly reverses the conventional roles that Bruce seeks to impose on Hildy and on their life together. She emerges as his protector and support. Hildy goes so far as to trick Bruce into concealing the insurance check in his hatband, telling him to do it because of a newspaper superstition. In fact, she wants it hidden there because she knows that Walter will try to steal the check, yet at the same time she wants to protect Bruce's feelings by not letting him know that he is incapable of defending himself against Walter's schemes. By the time later in the film when Bruce is arrested, he seems well aware of his shortcomings for he turns to Hildy without question as someone who is clever enough to get him out of jail.

Like the best Slapstick characters, Hildy is very much at home in the world around her even as she maintains her distinction from it (*Caddyshack*). In fact, she is able to survive and even prosper in a coarse and brutal environment of newspaper journalism without succumbing to cynicism or despair because she never loses sight of who she is in relation to others. What really sets Hildy apart from everyone else is her morality. Like so many Slapstick heroes, Hildy adheres to certain personal values that govern her behavior and that save her from the morass of sneering pragmatism (*Breaking Away*). In a world full of corruption, Hildy can still find venality reprehensible, whereas Walter simply seeks to make use of it.

Earl's escape and his subsequent reprieve put much of the action in perspective. Hildy and Walter combine to write the story, clearly in their element and obviously enjoying what they are doing. At the same time, a stark contrast between the two obtains. To the end, Hildy's commitment comes from a desire to see justice served, while Walter on the other hand never rises above a willingness to use any means available to secure his ends.

The conclusion, contrasting Hildy and Walter, re-establishes in the minds of viewers the precise delineation of the Slapstick hero. When Earl's case has been resolved, Hildy and Walter begin to reminisce about past escapades. Hildy clearly has a sentimental attachment to those memories, and this gives her second thoughts about leaving. Walter, ever the canny manipulator, seems reluctant to have her disappoint Bruce, and Hildy quickly recognizes his gesture as another effort to trick her. Walter pleads sincerity, and it is not clear just how he feels until Bruce calls to report that Walter has given him counterfeit money. Although Hildy berates Walter, she realizes that she and Walter are meant for each other, at least as a journalistic team. In the end, Hildy does not make a romantic choice but rather a professional one. She does not so much return to Walter as to a newspaper career.

Characters in films in this category represent their differences along a continuum that ranges from gentle eccentricity to stark defiance. The constant in all is the ability of these characters to maintain the integrity of their natures outside the parameters set by society. Other films in the subgroup include the following: any of the Marx Brothers films, *Arsenic and Old Lace, Being There, Gentlemen Prefer Blondes, Breaking Away, Topper, Ghostbusters, 9 to 5, M*A*S*H, Dumb and Dumber, Revenge of the Nerds, Caddyshack, The Blues Brothers, Kingpin, The Odd Couple, Ruthless People, Stripes,* and *Trading Places*.

Animal House

The next category of Slapstick Comedies falls midway between the triumphant renegade of the first group and the downtrodden outcast of the last. It articulates a satirical critique of the world represented in the film, even as it promises eventual reconciliation with it. This group undercuts the validity of both the mainstream and the marginal perspectives, and it leaves one with a sense of the artificiality of both (*The Producers*). The best examples of this group go beyond the spoof or parody of films whose silliness insures that it will have no real satiric impact (*Murder by Death*), to provide acerbic assessments of a complex public environment (*The Great Dictator*).

Animal House's subtle social commentary does not immediately manifest itself. The title of the film, for instance, sends a deceptively simplistic message that it intends to play to common expectations, draw upon familiar stereotypes, and use comic exaggeration to present a broadly focused farce. It does all that, but closer examination shows that it also takes its humor to a more sophisticated level. In fact, through clever inversions, *Animal House* challenges the way viewers see the world simplistically suggested by the title. By the end of the film, both the ham-handed representatives of the dominant culture and the immature rebels who oppose them have been ridiculed for their narrow-minded selfishness, and viewers are challenged to find insights that elude both groups. (A comparison of it with a far more reductive imitation, *Revenge of the Nerds*, gives a clear understanding of the complexity of John Landis' movie.)

The narrative of *Animal House* showcases an ability to operate on multiple levels even when employing familiar types in the main roles. To do so, time and again the movie offers a situation that seems to invite a simple, straightforward interpretation and then goes on to suggest complications that overturn the stability of the initial reading. For example, the opening walk across campus taken by Larry Kroger (Tom Hulce) and Kent Dorfman (Stephen Furst) is accompanied by sentimental music that suggests the intention to burlesque familiar stereotypes. The film seems to underscore this impression of the fatuousness of this world when the camera lingers on the statue of the college founder Emil Faber, and focuses on the near-nonsensically simplistic motto: "Knowledge Is Good." It is a mistake, however, to take the interpretation no further.

The sequence of the narrative tells one a great deal. While in a few moments the film will provide ample evidence of the crassness of college life, the first gesture to undermine common assumptions takes a much subtler tack. The smug obtuseness of the statue's epigram suggests that the unthinking rebelliousness of the central characters will be met with a mindless impulse for conformity by those who represent the dominant culture (*Blazing Saddles*). More significantly, it signals to attentive viewers the smart undercurrent that runs through the film that catches the unquestioning acquiescence of all the figures in the film to the worlds that each has chosen to inhabit.

In quick succession the movie offers graphic illustrations of its contrasting but equally narrow milieus. The snobbish Omega fraternity represents a collection of intolerant and self-congratulatory bigots. The raucous Delta fraternity endorses anarchy, hedonism, and mindless self-gratification as an alternative to the Omegas' approach to the world. In either case, no character gives any thought to the mores defining the environment that he or she inhabits.

However, as is the case in the best examples of this category, the narrative invites viewers to be more reflective. It goes beyond easy dichotomies to sharper social satire (*Waiting for Guffman*). Mocking the inhibited Omegas proves fairly easy. The film exerts its sophistication in its subtle critique of the expressive and unrepressed Deltas. It does both through the socialization (or perhaps desocialization) of Larry and Kent.

At the beginning of the film, Larry and Kent are unsure of the standards to which they should conform, and so are out of place in both worlds. As we watch them clarify their views and become incorporated into the society of the Deltas, we measure the degree to which we can accept the validity of those changes and endorse their new values. Over the course of the film, *Animal House* challenges us to see the shallow self-indulgence of their behavior as corrosive as is the claustrophobic world of the Omegas. (The fact that the movie turns on fraternities creates produces a biting ironic assessment of that any member community. None of the central characters behave as if they were in a band of brothers, but rather without exception each acts in a self-centered, predatory fashion.)

Perhaps the most interesting narrative development moves forward through the interaction of the male couples that populate the motion picture. (This use of pairs has been effectively employed in other films in this category, like *Young Frankenstein*, but rarely has it been taken to such lengths.) While Doug Neidermeyer (Mark Metcalf) and Greg Marmalard (James Daughton) present the expected renditions of stylized villainy—each being "a sneaky little shit" in Dean Wormer's (John Vernon) words—Larry and Kent, Eric Stratton (Tim Mattheson) and Donald "Boon" Shoenstein (Peter Riegert), or Bluto Blutarsky (John Belushi) and D-Day

Lewis (Bruce McGill) offer subtler examples of the corrosive attitudes that characterize the unique and transitory nature of this world.

Larry and Kent stand in for the viewers, experiencing the seductiveness of the feckless lifestyle of the Deltas. Eric and Boon embody the jaded seniors who are beginning to sense uneasily that their hedonistic world might be coming to an end. Bluto and D-Day remain defiantly unrepentant. Like the Lost Boys of *Peter Pan*, they are determined never to grow up. The different ways these couples interact allow us to measure their society, and provide options for responding other than simply accepting their behavior. They discuss their views on life, debate the propriety or impropriety of their behavior, and seek to guide each other towards integration in their world.

Of course, the film very cleverly seems to absolve the Deltas from blame for their behavior by offering no apparent alternative course of action. Dean Wormer is a sadistic tyrant. Greg Marmalard and the others in his fraternity are fascists who fawn upon authority. Professor Jennings (Donald Sutherland) is a self-loathing pedant quick who seduces coeds without a second thought. The mayor of the town (Cesare Denova) is an extortionist with the demeanor of a gangster. The film cavalierly presents immaturity or repression as the only acceptable response to such authority figures, and so it becomes easy for unquestioning viewers to favor the Deltas over all others.

Had *Animal House* gone no further, it would not have developed beyond a film that takes a predictable approach to a conventional topic and milks it for laughs (*Hot Shots*). However, it makes excellent use of the seemingly underrepresented group of characters—women—to show the baseness in the lives of all the major characters. Katy (Karen Allen), Mandy (Mary Louise Weller), Clorette DePasto (Sarah Holcomb), and Marion Wormer (Verna Bloom) provide more than a contrast to testosterone-fueled high jinx. They stand as alternatives to the seductive immaturity and suffocating pomposity of the men. They always operate on their own, and show a real comfort in their independence. While their behavior can be as reckless as any of the Deltas, they also give the impression that they understand and accept the ultimate consequences of flaunting social conventions far better than do any of the young men in the film.

Once the film establishes these polarities, it begins to test the limits of what we will condone. Time and again, Bluto and D-Day alternate between playing the roles of harmless clowns and of dangerous psychopaths. The scene in which they badger Kent into shooting the horse underscores this condition. It also foregrounds the strategy of the film.

(Left to right) Kent (Stephen Furst), Bluto (John Belushi), and D-Day (Bruce McGill) in *Animal House* (1978).

The narrative continually relies upon violence, especially unexpected violence, to produce the cruelty and humiliation that serves as the basis for all of its humor. In scene after scene, *Animal House* seemingly puts viewers in the position of either accepting the outrageous behavior of the Deltas or siding with the priggish attitudes of the Omegas and nearly everyone else in the picture. However, the narrative also shows a good deal of cleverness in raising questions regarding the consequences of everyone's behavior, and over the course of the film sophisticated viewers reject the either/or approach to interpretation.

One finds good examples of this in the way *Animal House* deals with questions of sex. As with violence, while making sex ubiquitous, the movie quickly blurs distinctions between acceptable and unacceptable behavior. The masturbation scene with Greg and Mandy on lover's lane is presented as ludicrous, yet it is difficult to distinguish that form of gratification from what goes on when Bluto peeps into Mandy's window as she undressed. Eric's efforts to pick up the dean's wife in a supermarket seem almost childish, and so have a certain charm: "Mine's bigger than that." At the same time he tries to seduce Kent's date, and does seduce the dean's wife with no thought of the consequences. (Larry Kroger's decision not to assault his drunken date, Clorette Di Pasto, is shown comically as a heroic choice. It is, of course, undermined later when he carries through with intercourse despite finding out the girl is thirteen.) The road trip to Emily Dickinson College becomes simply a challenge to trick strange girls into degrading behaviors. Boon's subsequent hypocritical indignation over Katy's involvement with Jennings allows viewers to sympathize with a point of view not often seen in the film, and it gives us an opportunity to experience the irony of the situation for a character who has shown little sense of anything but himself. A good measure of selfishness, not to say misogyny, motivates such actions, and with a seamlessness that viewers can easily miss, male sexual desire almost inevitably moves from amusing to revolting.

The outrageousness of the Deltas' behavior conveys on them an undeniable charm. However, the narrative never shies away from reminding us how self-centered and cruel these characters can be. When, for example, Kent comes to a full realization of the damage done to his brother's car, the best that Eric can do is to remind Kent how isolated all of the characters really are: "You fucked up. You trusted us."

Expulsion provokes the finale towards which the film has been building. The anarchy of the final scenes as the Deltas turn the college homecoming parade into a shambles seems to represent the triumph of their worldview over the others in the film. Unlike more formulaic Slapstick Comedies, this is not the victory of good over evil but rather the triumph of extreme behavior that the audience condones over extreme behavior that the audience abhors. As noted earlier, scenes of the characters' future interspersed with the final credits underscore this notion by reintegrating the Deltas into society (with, of course, the exception of D-Day who has gone missing) and showing the Omegas' inability to become part of the larger world. It seems to reward non-conformity and punish conformists. However, given what the film has shown us of that larger world—represented by Dean Wormer, Professor Jennings, and the mayor—such integration represents a greater defeat than any other suffered by the Deltas. What the ending shows is that society's rules do not lead to the promised rewards and that unconventional behavior produces no lasting change. It presents a chilling delineation of the artificiality of the entire social structure.

Of course, all parodies are not as cynical as this. At their most lighthearted, such films may seem to embody the carnavalesque, enjoying a temporary dispensation for the misbehavior of the central characters. However, their ability to show the ineffectuality of the dominant culture suggests more than a temporary suspension of order. It presents instead a sardonic, if not cynical, sense of the social structure that the film represents. Resolutions at the end of the film have an aura of artificiality that provokes further criticism rather than ratifies the values of the dominant culture. Other films in the subgroup include the following: *Airplane!*, *Waiting for Guffman*, *Blazing Saddles*, *For Your Consideration*, *The Naked Gun*, *Young Frankenstein*, *Hot Shots*, *This Is Spinal Tap*, *Best in Show*, *The Producers*, *The Great Dictator*, and *A Mighty Wind*.

Clerks

The film *Clerks* is director Kevin Smith's earliest full-length motion picture. (Smith also appears in the movie in the role of Silent Bob.) Despite the coarse language and the explicit sexual topics that give *Clerks* a contemporary feel, it remains a self-conscious evocation of classic Slapstick Comedies, albeit with a heavy dose of shallow teenage nihilism. Filmed in black and white, featuring a character overwhelmed by the routine of daily life, and filled with eccentric individuals, this movie invites associations with the prototypical films of the genre (*Broadway Danny Rose*). At the same time, Smith tests the limits of Slapstick Comedy by focusing on a prosaic day in the life of a convenience store clerk, testing the limits of the audience's patience with a motion picture that both satisfies and overturns their expectations (*Raising Arizona*).

While they fall into the same broad genre, *Clerks*, *Animal House*, and *His Girl Friday* could not be more different in their view of the outsider's place in the world. In contrast to Walter and Hildy's brash self-confidence and the mindless hedonism of Boon and Otter, Dante (Brian O'Halloran) continually questions every aspect of his life and exudes an aura of resignation to defeat. (Of course, his first name ironically calls to mind the circles of suffering depicted in the *Inferno* of his famous namesake.) However, Dante is by no means the sole aberrant figure in the community of the film. Even characters like Randal (Jeff Anderson) or Jay (Jason Mewes), who seem much more at home with their natures, clearly have no place in the world that they inhabit.

Clerks loses no time establishing the atmosphere. In contrast to other subcategories, it introduces an aura of hopelessness and frustration that

Dante (Brian O'Halloran) in *Clerks* (1994).

will dominate the narration. In the opening scene, the jerky movement of the handheld camera as it takes in the disordered room and Dante's whiny tone during the terse phone call enforces the mood of low aspirations, disoriented perspective, and diminished capability. In these few moments, the narrative signals that this movie will make interpretive demands similar to the sophisticated stipulations of a Charlie Chaplin film. Viewers can embrace Dante's role as a put-upon underdog in a world that neither he nor his friends can control. Conversely, they can see all the communal flaws that Dante and the others note, but they can also follow the futility of their anti-social, passive-aggressive responses.

Though *Clerks* follows the events of Dante's day at the convenience store—from the moment he learns that he has to go to work until closing time—the film is really an episodic presentation of loosely connected events, and not so much driven by characterizations as by various articulations on a theme of ennui and despair (*Dazed and Confused*). The movie defines individuals and the nature of their world through a series of confrontations with outsiders and by the broader demands imposed by society. In most instances, these scenes underscore the ineffectualness or indifference of Dante and his friends. Rarely does the motion picture portray one of them as able to cope with the ordinary demands of everyday living, and, for that matter, rarely do events in their lives unfold in a straightforward fashion. They clearly are not part of the ordinary world, but neither are they able to form a satisfactory alternative (*Slackers*).

Early on, the anti-smoking diatribe by the chewing gum salesman posing as a customer highlights the passivity of Dante and the chaos that seems to surround him. The situation spins out of control as the level of abuse relentlessly rises as the chewing gum salesman berates Dante for selling cigarettes to the sheep-like customers. The tone of the episode—emblematic of that of the entire film—teeters between pain and amusement. The action stands as unresolved until Dante's girlfriend, Veronica (Marilyn Ghigliotti), intervenes, spraying everyone with a fire extinguisher. Her act provides a needed release, a comic ending, and an alternative to Dante's somnambulant approach to living.

Veronica's outlook provides a scale against which to measure the legitimacy of Dante's apathy. She sees the world causally, and responds to what is around her. Veronica is integrated into society, demonstrates competence, and rebuts assumptions that the world will inevitably grind down individuals. Dante, on the other hand, finds himself caught in a succession of episodes that he cannot comprehend and for which he has no satisfactory response. He accepts his existence with little more than a whimper, but Veronica shows he has a choice. Dante and Veronica represent the poles of characterization that define the film, and a number of other characters fill the space between them. A variety of customers stream through the convenience store to give a pace to the action and to present diverse attitudes. More significantly, several other supporting characters recur to remind viewers of the options that Dante has chosen not to pursue.

The drug dealers who occupy space in front of the store, Jay and Silent Bob, both contrast and complement Dante. The frenetic Jay is a foul-mouthed, non-stop talker, provides a running monologue articulating the fractured images that run through his brain. His foil, Silent Bob, has only eight seconds of dialogue the near conclusion of the film. By the end of the day, however, as they prepare to stupefy themselves with alcohol and drugs, neither seems any more able to cope with the world than does Dante.

Randal, Dante's best friend and the video store clerk, claims to take a radically different approach to the same occupation. He has a clear sense of the demeaning nature of the job, but attempts to redefine his role, abusing customers when he wishes, closing the store on a whim, and showing a general disregard for any responsibilities. He may have a measure of the independence that Dante claims to crave, but by the end of the film the narrative has presented little evidence to support the idea that he is more than marginally better off than Dante.

Despite the idiosyncrasies of so many characters, the overall normality of the world around them remains a striking constant throughout the narrative. While Randal feels put-upon, Dante feels persecuted, and Jay and Silent Bob emit a confused hostility, in point of fact, the trials they encounter are of their own creation. The tone of the narrative invites us to see the banality of the angst that these characters embrace.

Nowhere is this clearer than in the scenes highlighting Dante's personality through a series of fractured dialectics. His debate with Veronica over what constitutes sexual intercourse is really about the larger issues of intimacy and fidelity, yet he has neither the ability nor the perspicacity to understand the theme or to articulate his deeper sense of sexual insecurity. What we see instead is a conversation balancing the defensiveness of Veronica against the vulnerability and self-absorption of Dante. His pathetic obsession with Caitlin (Lisa Spoonauer) emerges as the most focused element in his life. Indeed, the film shows how trivial his concerns can generally be in his debate with Randal on the morality of destroying the second Death Star in *Return of the Jedi*.

There seem to be few options for Dante. Randal encourages his friend to "vent your frustrations," but Dante seems incapable of letting go of his angst. Playing hockey on the store's roof and going to a high school classmate's wake in the middle of the workday become Dante's acts of rebellion. However, he never can break completely free of the store, and it acts as his albatross: "I'm not even supposed to be here today" is Dante's constant refrain. Caitlin's appearance at the store brings out all of Dante's insecurities, and her obvious shallowness reinforces the impressions of both that the narrative has encouraged viewers to build up. It also underscores the fundamental masochism that drives Dante, and throws into relief the hopelessness of the only relationship that he seems to value.

Even the incident that propels the action towards a conclusion of sorts—the trauma that Caitlin suffers when she realizes that she has had sexual intercourse in the darkened bathroom with a dead man—never goes beyond grotesque humor. It is really a lack of options that push Dante to make a change in his life. Silent Bob, in the only lines that he utters in the film, underscores this when he tries to lay out the value of a girlfriend like Veronica: "You know, dude, there's a million fine looking women in the world, but they don't bring you lasagna. Most of them just cheat on you." This profound insight leads Dante to decide that he loves Veronica, but in true comic fashion Randal has already told her that Dante preferred

Caitlin. Veronica now rejects him, and Dante finally lashes out by attacking Randal in a comical fight.

In the end, at closing time it is Randal who confronts Dante with the fact that he is doing whatever he wants without taking responsibility for what he does. Like the Little Tramp at the conclusion of so many of his films, Dante stands in an ambiguous position with no clear commitment to any course of action. The film, however, refuses to affirm or deny this response in Dante. Instead, it steps back from judgment and leaves to the viewers the decision on how to sort out Dante's behavior.

(It is interesting to note the alternative ending that Smith had filmed. In it, a robber enters the convenience store and shoots Dante. Initially Smith felt that it fit the "independent film" approach, but cut it after deciding that it was not compatible with the rest of the narrative.)

Because films in this group derive their humor from misfits rather than from rebels, they engender little sympathy for the central figures and scant hope that they will ever change. This type of film chronicles the price that such losers must pay for their apathy and social awkwardness, and it invites audiences to laugh not with but at the central character. Other films in this category include *The Seven Year Itch, Dazed and Confused, Eating Raoul, Slackers, Diner, Broadway Danny Rose*, and *Raising Arizona*.

Seven

It Happened One Night
Screwball Comedy/ Romantic Comedies

A General Sense of the Genre

Some film historians have argued that *It Happened One Night*—directed by Frank Capra, starring Clark Gable and Claudette Colbert, and released in 1934—marks the first appearance of a Screwball Comedy.[1] I think one could make an equally strong argument for Capra's 1931 film *Platinum Blonde*—featuring Jean Harlow—as the beginning of the genre. In either case, the term, synonymous with Romantic Comedies, became common currency after a welter of motion pictures appeared in the 1930s, centering on the conflicted romantic relations between men and women and distinguishing themselves for their engaging humor, innovative approaches, and refreshing characterizations.[2]

The deft narrative balance presenting the battles between men and women and between couples and the society around them has always stood out as the primary reason for the ongoing popularity of these movies, but, as in Shakespearian comedies, there is much more to these struggles than simple oppositional disagreements. Screwball comedies have come to prominence because, over the years a range of skilled screenwriters, directors, and actors in the industry have dissected the complex and sophisticated elements of these human interactions with wit and energy that continues to resonate for viewers. Creating such empathy meant going well beyond mere programmatic representations of a brash woman struggling to control an ineffectual and indecisive male or a feckless man-child striving to avoid the responsibilities of domestic life imposed by a far more mature and practical woman. In fact, the most successful Screwball Comedies

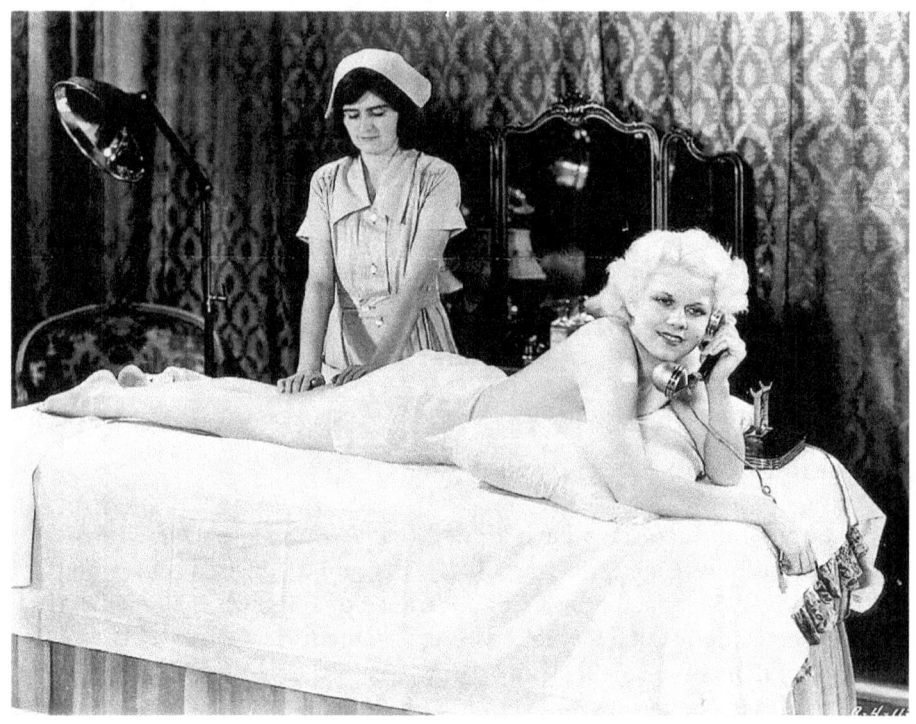

Ann Schulyer (Jean Harlow) in *Platinum Blonde* (1931).

introduce the subversive subtext suggesting that everything undertaken is driven by the need for socialization and that ideas of love merely camouflage the purely pragmatic motivations that drive the process.

Despite story lines that overtly deal with courtship and marriage, the love interests in these films serve as much more a means towards an end. They provide the impetus for Screwball Comedies to examine both the degree to which contemporary society will tolerate the foibles of eccentrics and the ability of those eccentrics to modify their behavior to conform to the mores accepted by the rest of society. Marriage serves as the normalizing institution. Few of these films question its legitimacy as an institution, and it serves as a handy benchmark for a turning point in characters' lives. However, tracing the efforts of individuals to sustain their eccentricities in the face of the impulse to conform emerges as the true central issue for viewers seeking to impose meaning.

Screwball Comedies emphasize this process of domestication, and using the institution of marriage to explore that action makes perfect sense. Thus, from *It Happened One Night* to *Enough Said*, films in this genre all develop

Albert (James Gandolfini) and Eva (Julia Louis-Dreyfus) in *Enough Said* (2013).

characterization through rituals of courtship and the movement towards a stable monogamous relationship, and that can tempt one to a rather narrow interpretive view. Indeed, what make films in this category truly interesting are the negotiations, sometimes successful and sometimes not, of characters who seek to sustain the unique elements of their natures even as they somewhat grudgingly submit to circumscribing forces of domestication. In this genre, however, no matter how outlandish the short-term behavior, they never quite sever connections with the community (*Victor/Victoria*), and in the end resolution comes from their amalgamation into society and not simply from a character's often uneasy accommodation with it.

Just as the cultural contexts of Westerns and Gangster films foreground men in the central roles, marriage as a plot device in this genre puts the activity of women on an equal footing with that of men. Indeed, one can argue that the prominent position of women in the Screwball Comedies produced in the 1930s and early 1940s led to strong female roles in the Film Noir productions of the 1940s and 1950s.[3] Thus, by playing upon audience expectations for prescriptive behavior, the best Screwball Comedies have shown tremendous ingenuity in subverting the cinematic tradition of romance to create singular identities for women and to present a fresh look at conventional male roles.

Cultural and Aesthetic Context

As in any genre, context sets the parameters for the action of Screwball Comedies. Because the central concern, overt or implied, of any film in this genre is domestication, Screwball Comedies play off the broad conventions of courtship imposed in a general way by the society. Nonetheless, significant generic elements make the approach unique in every film in this group.

While it may seem tempting to consider these comedies as simply parodies of traditional love stories, in fact, something more is at work. One sees this in the antics of Cary Grant and Irene Dunne divorcing and then disrupting each other's love lives in *The Awful Truth* or in the efforts of Tom Hanks and Meg Ryan struggling to maintain their own identities even as they come to grips with the inevitability of their love in *You've Got Mail*. The conflict within characters who are desperately trying to resolve the contradictions that grow out of the clash between conventions of normal romantic courtship and their abnormal patterns of behavior is they key feature that drives the plotline in these and other Screwball Comedy. That is where the humor arises.

Screwball Comedies have a genuine esteem, even reverence, for the legitimacy of the love story, but they express their regard in a fashion that differs from traditional representations, accommodating the romantic impulse while taking into account the complexities and contradictions inherent even in seemingly ordinary lives. Most strikingly, they consistently affirm conventional American values and attitudes about courtship and marriage even if their narratives approach both in unorthodox ways.

Screwball Comedies could not begin without the concept of love at first sight (even when the parties involved do not immediately recognize what has happened), and they could not end until they offer some sort of assurance about a couple living happily ever after. Indeed, so many clichés punctuate the discourses of Screwball Comedies that unless eccentricity stands as a dominant feature of at least one of the central characters the films inevitably become cloyingly sentimental. (In fact, Slapstick Comedies, particularly ones made by the Marx Brothers, often use a conventional young couple's traditional approach to courtship and marriage for comedic purposes; see *Monkey Business, The Cocoanuts, Night at the Opera, A Day at the Races.*)

For this reason, many of these films define their central characters in terms of their foibles and peculiarities. However, the narratives carefully circumscribe these attitudes to keep their behavior generally within the bounds defined by society. Unlike figures in Slapstick Comedies—from Fatty Arbuckle to Amy Schumer—who consistently assault communal restraints with maniacal determination, characters in Screwball Comedies have great sympathy for the conventions of the world that they inhabit. No matter how bizarre his or her actions might seem, the Screwball character always remains highly cognizant of society and more often than not defines himself or herself in relation to it. The individual at the center of the action is seeking integration, not trying to sustain independence (*My Favorite Wife*).

Society, in fact, stands as a refuge for many characters in Screwball Comedies. They see its institutions as having the elasticity to allow the measure of uniqueness and independence that individuals need to assert their identities. At the same time, these institutions themselves provide the stability that allows individuals to behave eccentrically without fear of alienation. Unlike their counterparts in Slapstick Comedies, the figures in Screwball Comedies are always seeking affiliation with the community at large, though in some instances their efforts are so ineffectual that they may actually seem to be seeking to escape its bounds.

The feature that consistently centers the Screwball Comedy within the limits of the community is its presumption of a happily ever after ending, frequently linking material rewards to the resolution. Wealth and position often provide a buffer for their protagonists. These conditions let individuals retain a greater measure of eccentricities simply because their money and power usually protects them from the consequences of bad behavior, so long as the characters remain careful to avoid the sort of scandal linked to criminal behavior that might alienate society. Even such insulated figures, however, as the wealthy, sheltered Arthur Bach (Dudley Moore) in learns to his chagrin, must ultimately conform if they wish to gain full acceptance from the world around them. Whatever the characters' economic conditions are at the end of these films, the presumption remains that regularizing their lives through domestic stability is the key to happiness.

In keeping with this tone, the Screwball Comedy provides entertainment through comic deflection, in contrast to the Slapstick Comedy's reliance on the humor of assault. Language stands as the shield for characters in this genre. Here a facility with words blunts criticism, safeguards independence, and negotiates reconciliation with the way that the world operates. Comparing the exchanges between Cary Grant and Rosalind Russell in the Slapstick film *His Girl Friday* and those between Grant and Katharine Hepburn in the Screwball movie *The Philadelphia Story* underscores this trait. In the former, two egos battle for dominance, with neither speaker holding back in efforts to gain supremacy. In the latter, though one may detect a

(Left to right) C.K. Dexter Haven (Cary Grant), Tracy Lord (Katharine Hepburn), and Macaulay Conner (James Stewart) in *The Philadelphia Story* (1940).

measure of hostility in Tracy (Katharine Hepburn) early in the film, by its midpoint one finds a man and a woman seeking to offer criticism with a measure of restraint while sustaining the integrity of his or her position.

This gesture towards affinity also testifies to the Screwball Comedy characters' complicity with society. Because these individuals can use language effectively, they can influence the way that the world works around them. At the same time, their wit functions only within the bounds of society in a symbiotic relationship. Throughout the film, they endeavor to maintain a delicate balance between asserting their individuality and behaving within the conventions of society.

Key Elements in Plot and Characterization

Film historians have tended to emphasize polarities, especially according to gender, when delineating the prototypical characters of

Screwball Comedies, seeing, for example, what Thomas and Vivian C. Sobshack have called "the predatory female who stalks the [naïve and vulnerable] protagonist."[4] Admittedly, some movies seem to play into this tendency by contrasting the innocence and experience, the amiability and misogyny, or the brashness and timidity of the central characters, though individual motion pictures will vary in assigning each role to the male or the female lead. However, despite the tendency to use conventional oppositions to define the parameters of action within the narrative, as the action develops, the best Screwball Comedies distinguish the main characters by the complexities of their natures.

As has been the case in the other genres examined in this study, all Screwball Comedies are to some degree formulaic, with the best using structural familiarity as the starting point for more creative engagement. They take on identities that viewers familiar with the form quickly recognize. Further, the men and women, because they are situated in a fairly prescriptive category, share more similar traits than contrasting ones. More often than not, these individuals are eccentric to a degree that suggests an inability or simply an unwillingness to deal with the mundane routine of the ordinary life. At the same time, the best narratives reiterate a desire to fit into the world that they inhabit. The humor of the film comes from their good luck at surviving despite their ineptitude or their unique approaches to life, usually through the help of a man or woman whom the character pursues or who pursues the character.

In *The Lady Eve* Jean Harrington (Barbara Stanwyck) assumes the predatory role that the Sobshacks have identified, but Stanwyck takes her character well beyond an archetype. Jean stalks and ultimately captures the unwitting Charles Pike (Henry Fonda) not once, but twice. In the process, she brings Charles out of his shell and into the world. Additionally, she makes the audience sympathetic to all of her machinations if for no other reason than because social institutions and conventions make what she is trying to do so difficult and because her manipulation of communal mores and attitudes proves to be so deft. At the same time, she consistently affirms the values of the world against which she struggles. She is not trying to change society but rather to gain a place in it. Thus, the very institutions that she seems to challenge in the end authenticate Jean's identity just as she validates theirs.

For characters not already aware of their subtle relationships to society, Screwball Comedies provide an educating and maturing experience. Individuals at odds with the world become reconciled to it through the mediation of a romantic relationship. Indeed, many films turn

Jean (Barbara Stanwyck) and Charles (Henry Fonda) in *The Lady Eve* (1941).

on the action of a social misfit like Charles Pike being domesticated by a worldly-wise woman like Jean. At the film's conclusion, both Charles and Jean remain distinguished by their determination to accept social institutions on their own terms as much as possible, but to accept them nonetheless.

This pattern of autonomous natures willing to make some accommodation to communal mores runs through most Screwball Comedies. Because the arc of Screwball Comedies moves toward equilibrium, they often begin with disorder. A woman, independent yet well-versed in the requirements of negotiating a complex society, serves as the guide and teacher for the less adept, even child-like, male. Her own techniques strain the limits of social custom (*Adam's Rib*), but she retains a keen sense of how far her behavior can go before reverting to conformity. Further, her *joie de vivre* gives the man whom she pursues a fuller sense of his own life. In many other instances (*My Man Godfrey*), the male character, with equal gusto, provides the instruction. The point is not that one sex is more intelligent, better adapted, or more experienced than the other but rather that figures in these films capture our interest by the consistent attraction that both naïve and sophisticated figures have to the mores of society.

Issues

Screwball Comedies are always about the competition for control in establishing traditional male-female relations, but the stakes and results are not as clear as in non-comedic romances with more conventional individuals. Because idiosyncrasies shape the behaviors of many of the central characters, their struggles usually do not turn on questions of whether or not society will allow the couple to unite but more often on what personal changes they will have to undergo to bring about this unification. While the fundamental values of society are never called into question, the narrative often highlights the foibles of particular traditions. Further, the concept of personal freedom remains a contested topic. Time and again, these comedies privilege the need for eccentric behavior to counteract the stifling effects of convention. At the same time, they underscore the protection that convention ultimately provides as a restraint to dangerous recklessness.

Through all of these struggles, marriage, or in more daring films simply a monogamous romantic union, remains the near-uncontested symbol of the reconciliation of freedom and convention, and rarely does any significant figure successfully challenge its legitimacy as an institution. Instead, the narrative concerns itself with the degree to which traditional marriages can be reconfigured to accommodate the individuality of the film's central characters. In the end, the impulse towards resolution through emotional, psychological, and intellectual balance has the final say. What often begins with an egotistical man vs. woman competition usually ends with the mutual accommodation of both parties, though in some instances one or both may never have a clear sense of how the resolution has come about (*The Philadelphia Story*).

These films also do not ignore the physical side of courtship. At the same time, because men are often infantilized in these comedies, sexual desire and normal sexual activity are either downplayed or represented as adolescent fantasies. This in turn gives complexity to an otherwise programmatic narrative form. With the blurred role of sexuality, the resulting climax, winning the gal or the guy, remains an ambiguous accomplishment whose worth is left to viewers to assess.

This vagueness at the end may trouble some filmgoers, especially those who feel that, despite the cleverness of the principal character, ultimately he or she must settle for a conventional domestic relationship. In fact, time and again the hero (male or female) of a Screwball Comedy shows a dexterous ability to manipulate or ignore conventions as the occasion suits him or her. There is no reason to suspect that marriage will change things. (Although, strictly speaking, not Screwball Comedies, *The Thin Man* series of films exemplifies this. Myrna Loy, playing Nora Charles in all six films, proves herself suited to this genre by being more than capable of handling her feckless and mercurial husband, Nick, played by William Powell. In the process, neither character changes the way he or she interacts with the other.)

Specific Application

All Screwball Comedies turn on the individual's admission of a need for integration into the larger society, but the impetus and degree of success that characterizes that effort can vary significantly. Consequently, the focus of any specific movie will be on the eccentric character or characters who endeavor to be reconciled with society. In each case, the individual to be reclaimed has clearly articulated traits that put him or her at odds with the rest of the world. At the same time, neither the attitude nor the actions of the character are so extreme as to preclude reunification.

In the first category, *Bringing Up Baby* illustrates both the complex narrative demands made by the genre and the distinguishing features of its subgroup. It may seem to highlight the hapless male attempting, ineffectually, to deal with the eccentricities of a strong-willed female. In fact, the action of this film turns upon the determination of the female character to retain her freedom of action even as she works assiduously to bring the resistant male into a conventional relationship.

In some instances, the central characters in Screwball Comedies are more feckless than independent. *Some Like It Hot* represents a category that features both irresponsible and irrepressible males and females. No character has the self-aware commitment to freedom of action so cherished by individuals in the first group. Rather, they simply function on impulse and at an immature level that puts them at odds with the rest of the world.

Not all Screwball Comedies depict their central figures as incapable of change. Indeed, in the third category, *Legally Blonde* wonderfully exemplifies the motion pictures that trace the maturation of the character without presenting the process as a grinding down to conformity. It shows a woman who is completely and unselfconsciously shallow at the beginning of the film but is nonetheless quite capable of dealing with the world as she sees it. By the end of the motion picture, her efforts to meet the standards of one set of values have expanded to include acceptance of another, complementary system. She does not relinquish her idiosyncratic behavior but finds ways to incorporate them into a more traditional lifestyle.

Bringing Up Baby

From the opening scene in the Museum of Natural History, Howard Hawks' 1938 film, *Bringing Up Baby*, announces its reliance on types to move its narrative forward. Dr. David Huxley (Cary Grant), in the role of the absent-minded professor, comes across as a well-meaning but ineffectual man, easily dominated by others, especially women. Alice Swallow (Virginia Walker), his museum co-worker and fiancée, represents the cold, scientific mind intent only on professional success. When, for example, David tentatively suggests plans for a honeymoon, Alice quickly sets him straight on the kind of relations that they will (or will not) have. Pointing to a brontosaurus skeleton that they have been assembling, she says: "Our marriage must entail no domestic entanglements of any kind.... This will be our child."

Given this opening, the conventions that often drive the plotlines of

David (Cary Grant) and Susan (Katharine Hepburn) in *Bringing Up Baby* (1938).

such motion pictures might lead viewers to assume that the action will turn upon David's gradual awakening to the benefits of a freer life personified by a less inhibited woman. To some degree that may be so, but, in fact, the plot places far greater emphasis on transference: the control of David moves from the hidebound Alice to the unconventional Susan Vance (Kathryn Hepburn). As a result, by the end of the movie, despite the prospect of a life full of surprises, David's basic position has not changed in any significant way. As in so many movies in this category (*I Was a Male War Bride*), David remains the weak male dominated by a strong-willed woman. At the same time, Susan, again as in so many films of this type (*The Lady Eve*), has been integrated into society, and that is the point of the motion picture.

Typical of Screwball Comedies, the film turns on the ability of the independent character to upset the orderly routine characterizing the life of the figure who stands as her foil (*Victor/Victoria*). David first meets Susan on a golf course where he has gone to play a round with Alexander Peabody (George Irving) the lawyer of a wealthy museum backer from whom he hopes to get a sizeable contribution. Predictably, nothing goes as planned. In quick succession, Susan hits David's golf ball, damages his car, and then drives off in it with him standing on the running board. All the while she keeps him from talking to Peabody.

The exchange sets the pattern for all of David's subsequent interactions with Susan. His conventional approach to resolving a particular issue is continually derailed by Susan's erratic behavior. That evening, for example, when David runs into Susan at a restaurant, she inadvertently tears his coat and he then accidentally rips off the back of her dress. In both cases the confusion comes from Susan never listening to a thing that David says to her. This too is typical of the independent character in this category who, through intention or caprice, straddles a position in and outside the constraints of society (*Bridget Jones's Diary*).

In short order, it becomes clear to viewers that Susan is trying to keep David's attention. And, when she learns that he intends to be married the next day, she begins to plot to break it up. Most of the remainder of the film covers the next day. It revolves around a series of schemes by hatched by Susan aimed at getting David out of New York City, occupying him for the day, and thus preventing him from getting married. In Screwball Comedies filmmakers typically apply this deferral and deflection to vary the expected form of courtship (*My Favorite Wife*).

To that end, Susan first lures David to her apartment by pretending to be attacked by her pet leopard, Baby. (The leopard's name gives a sardonic flavor to the film's title, for viewers can never be certain that its appearance in the title refers exclusively to the big cat and not to David.) Susan then uses Baby to manipulate David into coming to Connecticut with her. When he tries to resist, she treats his protests as if he were a petulant child: "You've just had a bad day. That's all." Nonetheless, David shows that he has a modicum of humor in the way that he responds: "That's a masterpiece of understatement." Though ostensibly a throwaway line, it gives viewers good insight into how he is being seduced by Susan's mischievousness into patterns of behavior that he would never have previously countenanced (*Desperately Seeking Susan*).

Of course, the film is careful to make this experience seem whimsical. One minor catastrophe after another occurs with regularity whenever Susan is around. Nonetheless, an unshakeable self-confidence and dexterous wit enable her to retain her approach to life, often by compounding her defiance of proprieties, while rarely having to face the consequences of systematically flouting society's conventions (*The Main Event*). To get out of a parking ticket, for example, Susan pretends to own the car next to her own, one that belongs to the man whose wife's purse she took earlier in the film, and she ends up driving off in the stolen car rather than relinquishing control to even a small degree.

David's role as the absent-minded professor, easily distracted by Susan, facilitates the zaniness of the moment. It also gets the audience to accept without question the progressively bizarre actions of characters and the increasingly incredible narrative tendencies towards coincidences. Thus, by the time that George, the dog belonging to Susan's aunt, Elizabeth Random (May Robson), whose money David wants for the museum, steals the bone needed to complete assembly of the brontosaurus skeleton, no chain of events seems impossible or even improbable.

For the rest of the movie, the action turns on trying to find the missing bone and preventing Aunt Elizabeth from learning David's identity and thus possibly withdrawing her support for the museum. The final complication comes when Constable Slocum (Walter Catlett), the man who wanted to give Susan the parking ticket earlier in the film, arrests both her and David for being criminals. When Susan's aunt comes to get them out of jail, more confusion leads to the incarceration of Aunt Elizabeth and her friend Major Horace Applegate (Charles Ruggles). Only the appearance of Mr. Peabody and Miss Swallow to identify everyone leads to an end to the confusion, but when everyone finds out the real identities, it looks as if David will not get the museum money.

The situation quickly sorts itself out in the final few minutes of the picture in a *deus ex machina* fashion that self-consciously underscores the pull of societal mores. Alice Swallow dumps David, in the process giving him an unlikely appellation. "You're just a butterfly." And Susan brings David the bone he has been seeking. She admits that she has been pursuing David, and David admits to enjoying it. "I've just discovered that was the best day of my life." They tell each other that they love one another, and, when Susan climbs up on the brontosaurus, she ends up collapsing it. Of course, the ending defies logical explanation, but the narration of the film has insisted from the very beginning that we will never understand it if we pursue conventional logic (*The Awful Truth*).

Like many characters in this type of Screwball Comedy, Susan Vance wants marriage to David Huxley, but she does not see this aspiration as requiring any major changes in her nature. Their ultimate union comes about when the male accepts the eccentricities of the female while she remains basically unchanged. Indeed her success comes from gaining legitimacy through the institution of marriage more or less on her own terms. Similar films include: *Victor/Victoria, The Lady Eve, The Philadelphia Story, Manhattan, Desperately Seeking Susan, I Was a Male War Bride, What's Up Doc, The Awful Truth, Annie Hall,* and *Bridget Jones's Diary*.

Some Like It Hot

Despite a façade of dizziness, a suave calculation marks Susan Vance throughout *Bringing Up Baby*. Not all characters in Screwball Comedies possess this canniness, and indeed an entire subgroup is made up of ingenuous figures floating through life. Some of the most amusing of these types maintain a false sense of their sophistication while some sustain a Candide-like innocence throughout the narrative. Whatever their public persona, all engage us by their ability to survive, oblivious to the real chaos around them.

Billy Wilder's 1959 film, *Some Like It Hot*, reflects this category, and the ineptitude of its characters makes it at times seem closer to Slapstick. In fact, this motion picture both follows the conventions of Screwball Comedy and pushes the limits of what a filmmaker can include in this type of motion picture. Most particularly, the narrative replaces the relatively harmless upheavals of a film like *Bringing Up Baby* with more dramatic situations. The movie opens with a running gun battle as Prohibition-era police pursue a phony hearse used to transport bootleg liquor, and it quickly moves to the subsequent raid on a saloon disguised as a funeral parlor. Despite all of the shooting and breaking of glass and furniture, relatively little harm is done, and, at this point at least, the violence still seems more comic than menacing. It announces a world of anarchy rather than one of danger.

The criminal activity does, however, serve as a way of introducing Joe (Tony Curtis) and Jerry (Jack Lemmon) as near destitute members of the band at the speakeasy. Their escape from the raid signals the first of many close calls and harebrained situations that will punctuate the action of the film. Like Susan Vance in the previous group of Screwball Comedies, Joe and Jerry continually take risks that they think will provide shortcuts to success. However, as is the case with many other characters in this group, they lack the intelligence and polish that distinguish Susan Vance, and consequently they consistently find themselves in deeper trouble. For example, because they have not been paid, they lose their overcoats betting on a dog race. Trying to get to a job playing for a college dance leads them to the Clark Street garage where the St. Valentine's Day Massacre takes place. As witnesses to murder desperate to get out of town, Joe and Jerry dress as women and join the all-girl band on its way to Florida.[5]

The appearance of Marilyn Monroe, already an icon of sexuality when the film was made, shifts the tone from Slapstick to Screwball and foregrounds issues of gender that always function within the genre. As Sugar Kane, Monroe provides a wonderful contrast to the boys in drag. She also plays to the stereotype of dumb blond (neatly reversed in *Legally Blonde*) that most of the best Screwball Comedies have avoided since Jean Harlow gave the lie to that label in *Platinum Blonde.* Indeed, the challenge of the film—and one not always met by Billy Wilder's direction—is to show an identity in Sugar that goes beyond physical attraction and sexual availability (something accomplished far more deftly in Garson Kanin's *My Favorite Wife*).

In any case, the idea of two men surrounded by women who do not know the men's sex provides the basic source of humor as well as sexual tension between Joe and Jerry. It allows Wilder to explore the conventions of male/female, male/male, and female/female relations in a deft but not very rigorous fashion. The party in Jerry's Pullman car berth illustrates how difficult it is to manage affairs, and it raises some issues regarding how women can and cannot behave if they are to avoid sanctions of society.

One might go so far as to say that the film invites us to ask the question what it means to be a woman. Sugar's adventures with men embody this, though arguably the investigation never goes beyond the topic of sexual attraction. That, of course, is the point. The seemingly farcical approach taken by the narrative leaves it to the viewer to decide how far the film goes as a critique of sexual mores.

In fairness, Screwball Comedies rarely set themselves up as social commentaries. Rather, they show a fascination for the foibles of human behavior (*Bridget Jones's Diary*). That is not to say that they cannot provide sharp insights (*Adam's Rib*), but more often than not they glory in the superficiality of male/female relations (*The Palm Beach Story*). If *Some Like It Hot* concentrates on sexuality, it is no more shallow at its heart than other films that focus on the problem of being a famous woman (*Woman of the Year*), how to negotiate between love and friendship (*When Harry Met Sally*), or how political or social necessity can propel a relationship (*Green Card*).

Certainly, the film never backs away from the issue of physical desire and the implications that surround it. The attraction that Sugar feels for Joe and that Osgood Fielding (Joe E. Brown) feels for Jerry calls into question the very nature of sexuality and sexual attraction. Comparing notes on what they have to endure as women, Joe says to Jerry: "Now you know how the other half lives." Thus, while the film never demonstrates any genuine sympathy for what women must endure, it does highlight the inherent incongruities in male-female relations.

Even in traditional courtship roles, the men in the film experience the kind of tribulations generally expected to fall on women. When Joe,

(Left to right) Marie (Carrie Fisher), Jess (Bruno Kirby), Harry (Billy Crystal), and Sally (Meg Ryan) in *When Harry Met Sally* (1989).

for example, tries to pursue Sugar, he must reconfigure himself to conform to her expectations. He has to take on another disguise, with an exaggerated Cary Grant accent (in a heavy-handed, parodic effort that comes as little more than a cheap shot on the part of Curtis and Wilder), on top of the one that he has already assumed, to appeal to what the materialist Sugar has said would be her ideal millionaire.

Despite touching on the socialization of the courtship ritual, however, the narrative never strays very far from the issue of sexuality. Indeed, in the use of Monroe, the approach is often shockingly blatant. Sugar's dress on the night she goes out with Joe is cut in a fashion that makes it look as if she is topless. It shows how a clever director could skirt the restrictions on what one could or could not show an audience, but more to the point it offers a blunt statement regarding what attracts males.

Joe's behavior brings out similar feelings regarding what attracts women. He works to seduce Sugar by whetting her need to prove her sexual desirability. In a fey accent that suggests a stereotypical representation of homosexuality, he claims that a trauma has made it impossible to find women attractive. With this statement, he implicitly challenges Sugar to arouse him, and she readily complies.

In juxtaposing this exchange with Osgood's courtship of Jerry, the film adds a note of ambiguity, especially when Jerry seems willing to marry Osgood: "Why would a guy want to marry a guy," asks Joe. Jerry replies with a single word: "Security." True enough, Wilder tempers the sexual and gender implications of the scene when he reveals that Jerry plans to extort money from Osgood after the wedding.

In the end Joe, Jerry, Sugar, and Osgood escape to Osgood's yacht. On the trip out, Joe and Sugar announce their commitment to each other, though in a fashion that does not promise any greater durability than any of Sugar's previous liaisons. Jerry and Osgood come to a more interesting accommodation. Osgood remains intent on marriage, even as Jerry gradually lists a series of increasingly serious impediments. None of which faze Osgood. Finally, in desperation he reveals his true identity: "I'm a man." With perfect aplomb, Osgood dismisses the problem—"Well, nobody's perfect"—and the film ends leaving the viewer to sort matters out.

That adds a crucial element of ambivalence as the conclusion to an otherwise straightforward seeming film. *Some Like It Hot* can work perfectly well as a silly send-up of cross-dressing ne'er-do-wells. Conversely, it can function equally effectively as a corrosive view of male and female relations. Courtship and marriage are societal rites of passage that repre-

Joe/Josephine (Tony Curtis, left) and Jerry/Daphne (Jack Lemmon) in *Some Like It Hot* (1959).

sent the transition from child to adult, but, although these characters often marry by the end of the film, in terms of their maturity and ability to cope with the word nothing really changes. Though not every central character has the lack of maturity that one sees in Joe and Jerry, they all nonetheless have a diminished grasp of the demands of adult society.

In these films, characters trust to luck and the understanding of others rather than undergo any modification in the way that they see the world. They find ways to accommodate themselves within society, though any long-term integration seems unlikely. Similar films include: *The Palm Beach Story, Pat and Mike, French Kiss, My Favorite Wife, Adam's Rib, When Harry Met Sally,* and *Green Card.*

Legally Blonde

The first two categories of Screwball Comedies have emphasized characters whose integration with society takes place in spite of themselves. The final group highlights characters who very much wish to fit into the pattern of ordinary life. These motion pictures derive their humor from the character's lack of awareness of how far removed his or her life is from being part of the normal routine.

The charm of *Legally Blonde* (2001) reflects an inversion of the premise of *Some Like It Hot*. It challenges the stereotype of the dumb blond, but it does so in a very clever fashion that affirms as much as it rebuts. Rather than making the central character the antithesis of the stereotype, the movie shows that she possesses all of the shallow values that seem to condemn that type of individual as frivolous, even as it highlights her ability to succeed. (It leaves viewers to determine whether this comes in spite or because of her superficiality.)

Like Claudette Colbert's character in *It Happened One Night*, and with an equally clear-eyed yet accepting sense of the narrow confines of her wealthy environment, Elle Woods (Reese Witherspoon), the central character, lives a cloistered material existence. Her enjoyment of such a life and her success at negotiating the pitfalls of that society have left her unprepared for the shocking news that one might wish to enter that larger

(Left to right) Elle Woods (Reese Witherspoon), Emmett Richmond (Luke Wilson), and Brooke Taylor Windham (Ali Larter) in *Legally Blonde* (2001).

world and that her boyfriend, Warner Huntington III (Matthew Davis), perceives her to have no place in it. In the process of dumping Elle, Warner explains his behavior by evoking two contrasting icons of American femininity: "If I'm to be a senator, I need to marry a Jackie, not a Marilyn." Elle responds by evoking her own pop icon to establish her credibility and worth. "I grew up in Bel Air ... across the street from Aaron Spelling."

Unlike *Clueless*, a film to which it bears some superficial resemblance, *Legally Blonde* shows a depth and intensity that co-exists with its shallowness. The charm and fascination that Elle evokes from viewers comes not from her willingness to change but from her desire to expand. In the end, she proves to be an engaging character because she can cope with the demands of the so-called serious world of Harvard Law School without having to sacrifice her love of consumerism and her commitment to superficiality. (Katharine Hepburn, in *Bringing Up Baby*, shows the same steadfastness when confronted with the larger world but unlike Elle she give no indication that, beyond marrying David, she will adopt or even more than minimally adapt to its conventions.)

The opening scenes play upon viewer expectations by evoking all of the markers found in a world characterized by reflexive materialism. At the same time, while highlighting the mindless hedonism of fraternity/sorority life in a predictable manner, they show Elle's meticulous preparations for her date with Warner, at which she expects him to propose to her. Time and again, the narration emphasizes a shallow concern for appearance, but it also underscores her scrupulous attention to detail. In an early indication of the perils of any quick assumptions about Elle, the narration undercuts these views in the dress shop scene where Elle shows how much she knows about clothing and proves that the saleswoman has grossly misjudged her as nothing more than "a dumb blonde with daddy's credit card."

Elle's effort to get into Harvard Law School at first seems little more than a desperate and wacky ploy for pursuing her ex-boyfriend. Certainly, the videotape that she makes to accompany her application underscores this attitude. However, as the scene in the dress shop demonstrates, Elle has a keen eye, a sharp wit, and a deft awareness of things that are important to her. Further, she is not accepted into the Harvard Law School by mistake, a typical ploy in lesser comedies of this type. Rather, as the admissions committee takes pains to note, her grades and test scores meet the school's requirements, and her eccentricity charms the admissions committee.

In moving from Bel Air to Cambridge, however, Elle steps out of the sheltered environment that supported her views and allowed her to excel while she was an undergraduate. (In this way, she exerts a very different appeal than someone like Julia Roberts' character in *The Runaway Bride* who knows exactly what society expects and flees from it.) Because it sets out to do more than bring Elle into the mainstream way of seeing the world, the film turns on its ability to sustain the balance of Elle's naiveté, determination, and intelligence without ever denying her shallowness: "Whoever said orange was the new pink was seriously disturbed."

At first, the narrative wisely makes it seem as if the world of Harvard Law School cannot be swept along by the bubbly lack of concern that characterizes Elle's view of life. Indeed, in her first class, she is humiliated when her professor (Holland Taylor) refuses to succumb to her zaniness. The experience leads to a real crisis of confidence, causing Elle to question whether she has the attributes that would enable her to make her way in the study of law. Again, this sets the film apart from the other two categories. Characters in this group very much want acceptance by the mainstream and are shocked by the idea that they do not already fit in with the rest of society.

A chance meeting with a former law student and current lawyer, Emmett Richmond (Luke Wilson), saves Elle from despair. Emmett's take on law classes and his kind-hearted encouragement provide a balance to the general snobbishness of the class and to the particular cattiness of Vivian (Selma Blair), Elle's rival for Warner's affections. A trip to the nail salon as a temporary escape from the Harvard environment provides a nice proletarian connection, and it reminds us of the combination of grit and sweetness that gives her character depth and charm. Elle comforts the stylist, Paulette Bonofonte (Jennifer Coolidge), offering advice on dealing with a missing dog and finding a new boyfriend

The charm of the film turns on its affinities to a fairy tale. The isolated stranger from the West is at the mercy of the monsters on the East Coast. Indeed, the party where Elle comes dressed as a Playboy Bunny, after being tricked into thinking she must wear a costume, has a Cinderella-like quality. She does not leave the scene pursued by the handsome prince, but she does come away from it with a determination to succeed despite the odds against her.

This twist in the narrative underscores both her vulnerability and her resilience. Elle refuses to be cowed by efforts to humiliate her. When Warner again tells her that she is not smart enough for law school, it is a real revelation: "I'm never going to be good enough for you, am I?" The challenge then becomes not winning Warner back but showing that she is better than he is. Like Greta Garbo's *Ninotchka*, Elle must cope with the shocking fact that her conception of the world can no longer meet the challenges that she encounters in society, and to survive and eventually prosper she must change.

Here the film is at its best, for it refuses to succumb to expectations or conventional plotlines. Though Elle decides to take her law studies with a seriousness that she had previously dismissed, she does not become a new person. From the color of her laptop to the décor of her room, she retains the same identity that she had in California. Even as she buckles down to study, she continues to maintain all of the shallow pursuits that characterized her at first.

At the same time, a series of artfully plotted scenes enforce the idea that Elle is fundamentally a very good person, that she empathizes with others, and that she remains committed to a shallowness that is part of her charm. The trailer park confrontation with Paulette's ex-boyfriend shows Elle's quick wit and pluck. Her performance in class, emphasizing common sense and good humor, demonstrates her ability to use her mind. And, the bend-and-snap exercise she teaches Paulette as a way of attracting a man's attention reminds us of her ongoing commitment to male manipulation and her endorsement of relatively shallow goals.

Perhaps most revealing in these transition sequences is the demonstration of Elle's humanity and of her humanizing effect upon others. The scene where she helps her classmate David Kidney (Oz Perkins), who is trying to get a date, shows a sense of compassion and playfulness. (This is immediately followed by a sympathetic scene showing that Vivian also has a human side that sees beyond stereotypical romantic rivalry.) All in all, the film deflects without completely rebutting the dumb blond stereotype: fashion may seem a shallow pursuit, but she has a sophisticated sense of design and construction. While caught up in her own way of seeing the world, she shows time and again an abiding sympathy for any vulnerable women and men whom she encounters. Finally, despite her materialism, she deeply resents objectification of any woman.

If *Legally Blonde* went no further than this, it would establish itself as an amusing, if not very ambitious, film. What it does, however, is show a willingness to confront Elle with complexity to underscore her ability to succeed in the world. Although Elle is initially elated by being chosen by Professor Callahan (Victor Garber) to assist on a high-profile murder case, she quickly realizes that she has only gotten as far as she has because of her looks. When her female professor chastises her about quitting, it puts in motion a series of events that makes Elle the lead defense attorney in a murder case. Of course, the plot is improbable, but that is the point of a comedy.

Once committed to the murder trial, the events of the narrative become predictable, though no less engaging. Elle's ability to succeed in the case turns not on her legal experience but on her fashion knowledge. An awareness of male heterosexual knowledge of women's shoes allows her to know immediately that the poolboy, the so-called lover of her client, Brooke Taylor Windham (Ali Larter), is gay. A sense of how one manages a permanent is essential for her scheme to get Chutney Windham (Linda Cardellini), the murdered man's daughter, to confess to the murder with which her client has been charged.

The film comes to its conclusion in apt Screwball Comedy fashion. When she rebuffs Warner, who is now attracted by her successes and re-thinking his options, Elle uses the same lines that he used to dump her when they were in college. With that, she shows that she has developed, if not changed, over the course of her experiences at Harvard. At the end, her address to her graduating classmates reaffirms the consistency of her character and the whimsicality of the genre.

One might be tempted to sum up the plot by saying that Elle retains a measure of shallowness while experiencing a better self-image, but there is much more to the film and to the best in this category. *Legally Blonde* plays off the contrast between conformity and individuality, and it comes to a more optimistic conclusion than does either of the two preceding categories. In the end it explores the range of individuality that one can assert while still enjoying society's approval. Similar films include: *It Happened One Night, Woman of the Year, It Had to Be You, Runaway Bride, While You Were Sleeping, Ninotchka,* and *Clueless.*

Now What Am I Looking At?

In this study, I have tried to offer an overview of Classic Hollywood Cinema, and a detailed plan for talking about films that fall into the categories examined here. Nonetheless, I cannot end without acknowledging what was left unexamined. In the process, I want to underscore what I tried to do and to leave to my readers the judgment of how useful that will be for future viewing.

What may seem chauvinistic in my emphasis on movies made in America reflects the profound influence that films made in this country have had on ordinary viewers around the world. Almost every feature length, non-documentary film that goes into distribution relies on the framework of Classic Hollywood Cinema. Many documentaries, overtly or implicitly follow its structure as well. In addition, with the stunning exception of Bollywood productions, most films shown in the United States are centered in American culture.[1] Even seeming exceptions prove the rule: They either rely heavily on archetypes and familiar storylines without much social complexity—*Babette's Feast*—or present a world with cultural markers suppressed or diluted—*Amélie*.

Understanding how Classic Hollywood Cinema functions in motion pictures will help shape awareness of not only that type of movie but of a range of non–American films work as well. Further, a sense of how these motion pictures are structured will facilitate understanding movies in other categories.

As noted in the Prologue, number of significant genres do not appear in this study—Documentaries, Animation, Musicals, Action Films, War Movies, Profession-related movies (about Medicine, Journalism, Law, Business, et al.) Each evokes distinctive characteristics worthy of study and each has produced stunning examples of the type, and their structures follow the same general format of those in the categories given consideration in this volume. With this in mind, one can apply the lessons learned on understanding other categories as useful starting points for further exploration of a large range of other types of movies.

This same impulse towards extrapolation applies as well to the groups of movies that I have examined over the course of the book. My aim has always been to encourage independent responses rather than to inculcate single ways of seeing. When I present detailed interpretations in each of the chapters, I am not offering definitive explanations for others to recapitulate. Rather, I seek to provide examples of what a thoughtful moviegoer can say about films. I feel it useful to see how someone puts together interpretations of various motion pictures in a range of categories, and I hope that these examples will stimulate readers to articulate their own opinions.

In the end, the most important lesson that can come from reading this work is that the best films, like the best works of literature, offer numerous opportunities for response. They continue to engage and delight us with each repeated viewing. And they pay us each the individual compliment of seeing every viewer as a participant in the full creative representation of the film.

Thank you for reading this book. I hope you have enjoyed reading it as much as I enjoyed writing it.

Glossary

A note before beginning: I have compiled this section as a handy lexicon to supplement informal film appreciation discussions. To that end, I have tried to mix annotations of useful technical terms with familiar descriptive labels often invoked when talking about film. In both cases I have limited my selections to common working terms. I have consciously adopted an informal tone for most definitions. My aim is to give readers a working sense of how various terms can be used while allowing them the freedom for a liberal and at times subjective application of them. More detailed glosses can be found in books listed in the General Film Studies portion of the For Further Reading section that follows.

against type: An actor playing a role that runs contrary to that in which the public expected him to take, as in *A Bronx Tale* when Robert De Niro played a reserved, law-abiding New York City bus driver worried about his young son coming under the influence of a neighborhood gangster.

aleatory techniques: Techniques which depend on the element of chance. Scenes are composed on the spot by a director who often acts as his or her own camera operator.

ambient sounds: The usual sounds of a place that people tend not to notice: street sounds in a city; sounds of nature in the countryside; machines in a factory; etc.

anamorphic lens: A lens that squeezes a wide image onto a film frame in the camera, making everything look tall and thin. They were primarily created so that a wider range of aspect ratios could fit within a standard film frame. That is, it changes the way an image can fit into that standard frame.

animatronic: A puppet likeness of a human, creature, or animal whose movements are directed by electronic, mechanical, or radio-controlled devices (*Jurassic Park*).

anti-hero: The central character, generally in an action film, whose values run counter to those of a conventional hero. Clint Eastwood's character in *A Fistful of Dollars* embodies this persona.

aperture: (1) The opening in the camera lens that permits the operator to regulate how much light passes through the lens to the film. (2) The opening in a motion-picture projector that regulates light sent from the projector to the screen.

arc lamp or **arc light**: A system of illumination used early in the film industry for interior shots.

arc shot: The effect achieved when the camera moves around the subject in a single take.

art design: see set design.

art director, also **production designer**: The individual responsible for designing and overseeing the construction of sets for a movie.

art house film: Usually a low budget, independent film, often foreign, that focuses on issues outside the subjects presented in most Hollywood movies. These motion pictures generally attract a coterie audience though some, like François Truffaut's *The 400 Blows*, have achieved wide acclaim.

aspect ratio: The proportion of the width to the height of the image on a TV or movie screen or on the individual frames of the film. Most movies shown in theaters have an aspect ratio of 1.85:1.

asynchronous sound: A sound from a source on-screen that precedes or follows its source, such as words that are not synchronized with lip movements.

auteur theory: A critical approach that assumes that the major creative decisions of a film are the responsibility of one person, normally the director.

available lighting: The use of only that illumination that actually exists on a location.

avant-garde film: A film that rejects the conventions of mainstream movies often self-consciously highlight the act of filmmaking. Sometimes called **experimental film**, **underground film**, or **independent film**.

back lot: Parts of motion picture studio lots where standing exterior sets of common locales like a frontier town, a turn-of-the-century city block, a European village, and so on could be used as settings in various films.

backlight or **backlighting**: Lighting from behind the subject.

backstory: Events shaping the life of individual in a film. They do not always form an overt part of the narrative but may only be alluded to obliquely. In either case, the backstory gives an actor guidance in forming the character of a particular role.

best boy: Assistant to the chief electrician, **gaffer**, on a film set.

B-film: A low-budget movie that was usually shown as the second feature during the big studio era in America.

Biopic: A biographic film, often one tempered with fictionalized events or characters (*Malcolm X*).

bird's-eye view: Camera angle that films the subject from directly overhead.

bit part: A small acting role, usually no more than a scene or two.

bit player: An actor in a **bit part**.

black comedy: A style that shows the humorous possibilities in subjects previously considered off-limits to comedy, such as war, murder, and death (*Dr. Strangelove or: How I Learned to Stop Worrying and Love the Bomb*).

Blaxploitation film: Films appearing in the 1970s that featured the urban experiences, sometimes self-consciously hyperbolic, of young and generally male African Americans (*Shaft*).

blocking: The planned movements of the actors within a given playing area.

Bollywood: Informal designation of the Hindu language film industry of India.

boom: See crane.

bridge: Music used to link two or more scenes. Often used to enhance continuity. Sometimes called **sound bridge**.

bridging shot: Connects one scene or even one shot to another by showing a change in time and/or location.

buddy film/buddy picture: A film in which the narrative turns on the interaction of two close friends, often dealing with difficult situations as in *Butch Cassidy and the Sundance Kid* or *Thelma and Louise*.

cameo: A brief appearance in a film by a well-known person, usually a famous actor, whose name is often not included in the credits or publicity.

canted framing: See Dutch angle.

cel: A thin sheet of clear plastic on which images are painted for use in making some animated films.

character actor: An actor who specializes in well-defined secondary roles.

chiaroscuro lighting: Dramatic use of light and dark, with little use for midrange grays. Often used in **Film Noir**.

cineaste: An avid film enthusiast with a deep knowledge, real or imagined, of the intricacies of motion pictures.

Cinema Noir: See Film Noir.

cinematographer: Person responsible for the photography during the making of a film. Often called **director of photography**.

cinematography: Motion-picture photography, including technical and artistic concern with such matters as choice of film stock, camera distance and angle, camera movement, and choice and use of lenses.

cinéma vérité: Literally "film truth." A style of documentary filmmaking which also shaped fictional narratives developed in France during the late 1950s and early 1960s, the aim of which was to capture events as they happened (*Children of Hiroshima*). It evolved parallel to **new wave cinema**, and at times the terms have been used synonymously.

Cinerama: A wide-screen process involving the use of three synchronized projectors showing three contiguous images on a wide, curved screen. Cinerama was first used commercially in the early 1950s and was available only in selected theaters in large cities.

Classical Hollywood Cinema: A term used by some film scholars to describe the type of narrative film dominant throughout most of world movie history. Classical Hollywood cinema shows one or more distinct characters with clear goals who overcome many problems in reaching them (*The Wizard of Oz*). See the introduction for a detailed examination of this form.

claymation: Animation that uses clay figures and stop action instead of drawings to produce the action of the film.

close-up: An image in which the subject fills most of the frame and little of the surroundings are shown.

colorization: The process of using computers to replace the black, white, and grays of films on videotape with color. An earlier form of this process was called **tinting**.

compilation film: A film made by editing footage shot by others.

composition: The arrangement of settings and subjects (usually people and objects) within the frame.

computer generated imagery (CGI): The creation or enhancement of images in a film through computer graphic programming.

continuity: A narrative consistency within the film. If a well-established character behaves in a fashion completely different from our expectations that is never adequately explained, then the continuity has been violated. On a more mundane term, if the level of a character's drink goes up and down during a scene or if a cigarette inexplicable grows longer despite being smoked, there has been a slip in continuity.

continuity editing: Film editing that maintains a sense of uninterrupted action and continuous setting within each scene of a narrative film.

contrast: The difference between the brightest and darkest parts of an image. In low-contrast images there is little difference between the intensity of the brightest part of the image and that of the darkest part. In high-contrast images the intensity is extreme in both dark parts the bright parts.

crane: A mechanical device used to move a camera through space above the ground or to position it at a place in the air. A shot taken from a crane gives the camera operator many options: different distances and angles from the subject, different heights from the surface, and fluid changes in distance and angle from the subject. Sometimes called a **boom**.

credits: A listing of individuals on and off camera whose work contributed to the making of a film.

cross-cut: Alternating shots between events at different settings and often presumably transpiring at the same time. Sometimes called **intercut**. See **parallel editing**.

cult film: A movie panned or ignored by critics and general audiences that develops a following based on its quirkiness. At times the popularity comes from the sheer badness of the film as in Ed Wood's *Plan 9 from Outer Space*.

cut: (1) The transition between shots, made by splicing or joining the end of one shot to the beginning of the following shot, so that the transition from the first shot to the next appears to be instantaneous. (2) Any act of editing a movie.

cutaway: A shot that briefly interrupts one image to show another through a different camera angle or location.

cutting continuity: A written description of a finished film. It often contains information regarding scene divisions or shots within the scenes and descriptions of settings, events, dialogue, and camera set up. See also **screenplay** and **shooting script**.

dailies: The prints made from a day's filming. The director, cinematographer, and perhaps editor usually check the dailies to see if the recently filmed shots are satisfactory and if additional takes or shots are needed. Also called **rushes**.

deep focus: A technique that puts subjects near the camera, those in the distant background, and those in between are all in sharp focus. Achieved in photography by use of wide-angle lenses or small lens aperture or both. In low illumination, fast lenses and fast film stock also help create deep focus. Opposite of **shallow focus**.

depth of focus: The furthest distance from the camera in which all objects are in focus.

depth of field: The closest distance to the camera in which all objects are in focus.

desaturated color: Drained, subdued color approaching a neutral gray. Opposite of **saturated color**.

designer or **production designer**: The person responsible for much of what is photographed in a film, including architecture, locations, sets, costumes, makeup, and hairstyles.

diffuser: (1) Material such as spun glass, granulated or grooved glass, or a silk or thin nylon stocking placed in front of the camera lens to soften the image's resolution. (2) Translucent material such as silk or spun glass placed in front of a light source to create soft light.

digital format: Recording a motion picture using digital image sensors rather than film stock. Images are captured by photodetectors, digitized, and stored as computer files.

direct cinema: A type of documentary film developed in the United States during the 1960s in which actions are recorded as they happen, without rehearsal, using a portable 16 mm camera with a zoom lens and portable magnetic sound recording equipment (*Dont Look Back*). See also **cinéma vérité**.

director: The individual who oversees filming. Strong directors, like Alfred Hitchcock, gave an indelible personal imprint to the movies they made. Other directors, especially during the height of the **Studio Era**, followed a very mechanistic, workman-like approach to their jobs.

director's cut: Usually, the rough version of a film before its final editing. It has also come to mean a version of the film including scenes favored by the director but taken out at the behest of producers or others in charge. Canny marketers have extended the value of a popular film by releasing the director's cut after the initial release has run its course.

director of photography (DP): See **cinematographer**.

dissolve: See **lap dissolve**.

docudrama: A film that dramatizes occurrences from recent history by blending fact and fiction.

documentary film: A film that presents a version of events that viewers are intended to accept not as the product of someone's imagination but primarily as fact (*Harlan County, USA*).

Dogme 95: A film collective founded in Denmark in 1995. It advocates an egalitarian filmmaking philosophy directly opposed to the structure of Hollywood style films. Their movies rely on hand-held cameras, natural lighting, and eschew props.

Dolby sound: Trade name for a system that reduces noise on optical and magnetic sound tracks.

dolly: (1) A wheeled platform most often used to move a motion-picture camera and its operator around while filming. (2) To film while the camera is mounted on a moving dolly or wheeled platform.

double exposure: The superimposition of two literally unrelated images on film.

dub: (1) To add sound after the film has been shot. Sometimes used to supplement sounds that were recorded during filming. (2) To replace certain sounds, for example, to substitute native speaking voices for the original voices of a foreign-language film.

Dutch angle: Camera angle in which the vertical and horizontal lines of the motion-picture image are in an oblique relation to the vertical and horizontal lines of the film's frame. For example, in a Dutch angle shot, the vertical lines of a door frame will appear slanted. Often used to suggest disorientation by the subjects filmed or to disorient the viewers or both (*The Cabinet of Dr. Caligari*).

edit: To select and arrange the processed segments of photographed motion-picture film. To edit a film is sometimes called "to cut a film."

effects: (1) A shortened form of **sound effects**. (2) A shortened form of **special effects**. In both cases, "effects" is often represented by the abbreviation FX.

ensemble film: A movie whose narrative features a number of prominent roles generally played by well-established actors (*The Women*).

epic: A film **genre** characterized by bold and sweeping themes, usually in heroic proportions. The protagonist is usually an ideal representative of a culture—national, religious, or regional (*Lawrence of Arabia*).

episodic plot: Story structure in which some scenes have no necessary or probable relation to each other; many scenes could be switched without strongly affecting the overall story or audience response (*Pulp Fiction*).

establishing shot: A shot, usually a long shot or extreme long shot, used at the beginning of a scene to show where and sometimes when the action that is to follow takes place (see opening of *The Third Man*).

experimental film: See **avant-garde film**.

expressionism: A style of film not as concerned with representing external realities as with conveying characters' states of mind (*Nosferatu*).

exterior: A scene filmed outdoors.

extreme close-up: Image in which part of the subject completely fills the frame and the background is largely or completely excluded. If the subject is someone's face, only part of it is visible.

extreme long shot: Image in which the subject appears to be far from the camera. If a person is the subject, the entire body will be visible (if not obstructed by some intervening object) but very small in the frame, and much of the surroundings will be visible. Usually used only in the outdoors, often to establish the setting of the following action (see the end of *The Good, the Bad and the Ugly*).

eye-level angle: A camera angle that creates the effect of the audience being on the same level as the subject.

eyeline match: A transition between shots in which the first shot shows a person or animal looking at something off screen, and the following shot shows what was being looked at from the approximate angle suggested by the previous shot.

fade-in: Optical effect in which the image changes by degrees from darkness (usually black) to illumination. Frequently used at the beginning of a film and sometimes at the beginning of a new sequence.

fade-out: Optical effect in which the image changes by degrees from illumination to darkness (usually black). In old movies this technique is frequently used at the conclusion of a sequence and at the end of a film as a gradual exit from its world.

fade-out, fade-in: A transition between shots in which a shot changes by degrees from illumination to darkness (usually to black); then, after a pause, the image changes from darkness to illumination. Sometimes used to indicate the passage of time.

fake documentary: See **mock documentary**.

fast cutting: Editing characterized by many brief shots, sometimes shots less than a second long. Most recent American action movies, music videos, and trailers have extensive fast cutting. Opposite of **slow cutting**.

fast film (stock): Film stock that requires relatively little light for re-creation of images. Opposite of **slow film (stock)**.

fast motion: Motion in which the action depicted on the screen occurs more quickly than its real-life counterpart, as soldiers marching in World War I news reels. Opposite of **slow motion**.

feature (film): A film usually regarded as being at least sixty minutes long.

fill light: A soft light used to fill in unlit areas of the subject or to soften any shadows or lines made by other, brighter lights.

film continuity: See **cutting continuity (script)**.

Film Noir: A genre that emerged in the United States during and after World War II, characterized by frequent scenes with dark, shadowy (low-key) lighting; (usually) urban settings; most of its characters are motivated by self-interest and lack a sense of morality; social institutions have become corrupted. Generally, the central character adheres to moral codes disdained by the rest of society (*Touch of Evil*). Sometimes called **cinéma noir**. See Chapter Three for a detailed discussion of the form.

final cut: The last version of an edited film.

fisheye lens: An extreme wide-angle lens that captures nearly 180 degrees of the area before the camera and causes much curvature of the image, especially near the edges.

flashback: A brief scene that interrupts a narrative to show earlier events.

flashforward: A scene that interrupts a narrative to show events that happen in the future.

Foley artist: Sound specialist who uses various objects, usually in a Foley studio, to simulate sound effects and synchronize them with their corresponding movie images.

form cut: See **match cut**.

frame: (1) A separate, individual photograph on a strip of motion-picture film. (2) The borders of the projected film or TV set or monitor. (3) To position the camera in such a way that the subject is kept within the borders of the image.

frame enlargement: A photograph of an individual frame from a motion picture, enlarged) to reveal its details.

freeze frame: A projected yet unmoving motion-picture image, which looks like a still photograph, achieved by having the film laboratory reprint the same frame or two repeatedly (*Tom Jones*).

French new wave cinema: See **new wave cinema**.

full shot: A type of **long shot** which includes the human body in full, with the head near the top of the frame and the feet near the bottom.

FX: See **effects**.

gaffer: Chief electrician on a film set. See also **best boy**.

genre: A commonly recognized group of fictional films that share characteristics and conventions. Western, science fiction, horror, gangster, musical, and comedy are film genres.

graphic match: A technique used in continued editing in which the major features of the composition in one shot are duplicated or matched in the next shot, providing continuity between the two.

hard light: Light that has not been diffused or reflected before illuminating the subject. Opposite of **soft light**.

Hays Code: See **Motion Picture Production Code**.

head shot: A full face upper shoulder photograph used by actors as part of their audition portfolio.

high angle: View of a subject from above, created by positioning the camera above the subject.

high contrast: An image with few gradations between darkest and lightest parts of the image. Opposite of **low contrast**.

high-key lighting: High level of illumination on the subject. With high-key lighting, the bright frontal key lighting on the subject prevents dark shadows. Often used to create or enhance a cheerful mood, as in many stage and movie musicals. Opposite of **low-key lighting**.

homage: A tribute to an earlier film or part of one, for example, by including part of the original film or re-creating parts of it or respectfully imitating aspects of it. It is often, and somewhat pretentiously, given the French pronunciation with the h silent and the accent on the final syllable.

hook: An element in the film's narrative that grabs the viewers' attention, usually in the opening scenes as in Will Munny chopping wood against a fiery sunset at the beginning of *Unforgiven*.

IMAX: System of high projecting film horizontally rather than vertically to enhance a film's resolution, show expansive panoramas, and blur the distinction between viewers and film.

independent film: Film made without support or input from the dominant, established film industry. Usually an independent film is made without costly stars, director, and writer(s) and thus has a budget far below the big studio-backed movies. Sometimes called an **indie**.

inter-cut: See **cross-cut**.

inter-cutting: See **parallel editing**.

interior: A site of a scene filmed indoors.

inter-title (card): See **title card**.

iris-in: An optical effect usually functioning as a transition between shots in which the image is initially dark, then a widening opening—often a circle or an oval—reveals more and more of the next image, usually until it is fully revealed.

iris-out: An optical effect usually functioning as a transition between shots in which the image is closed out as a constricting opening—usually a circle or an oval—closes down on it. Normally the iris-out ends with the image fully obliterated.

iris shot: Shot in which part of the frame is masked or obscured, often leaving the remaining image in a circular or an oval shape. The iris shot was widely used in silent films, but is rarely used today except as a homage.

Italian neorealism: See **neorealism**.

jump cut: A discontinuous transition between shots, used to shorten the depiction of an event or to disorient viewers or both. It sometimes results unintentionally from careless editing or missing footage. Opposite of **continuity editing**.

key light: (1) The main light in a shot. (2) The lighting instrument used to create the main and brightest light falling on the subject.

lap dissolve: A transition between shots in which one shot begins to fade out as the next shot fades in, overlapping the first shot before replacing it. Usually used between scenes or sequences to suggest a change of setting or a later time or both. Also frequently known as **dissolve**, but lap dissolve conveys what happens: (over)lapping (by the second shot) and dissolving (of the first).

letterbox format: Videotape, videodisc, and DVD format that retains the film's original theatrical aspect ratio by not using a portion of the top and bottom of the analog TV or monitor screen.

limbo: An indistinct setting that seems to extend to infinity. This can often appear in horror films, musicals, and science fiction films. Also called **limbo background** or **limbo set**.

location: Any place other than a constructed setting that is used for filming. For example, the Monument Valley region in Utah and Arizona was a location for the 1939 *Stagecoach* and other Westerns, and *Schindler's List* was filmed on location in Poland, not on a studio set built to resemble Poland. See **set**.

long lens: See **telephoto lens**.

long take: An uninterrupted shot of long duration.

loose framing: Techniques in which the subject is far from the edges of the frame. Such framing can be used to give a sense of the subject's freedom of movement or of the subject being lost in or engulfed by a large environment. Opposite of **tight framing**.

low angle: View of the subject as seen from below eye level.

low contrast: An image with many gradations between darkest and lightest parts of the image. In black-and-white film, low-contrast images have many shades of gray. Opposite of **high contrast**.

low-key lighting: Lighting with predominant dark tones, often deep dark tones. By using little frontal fill lighting, the filmmakers can immerse parts of the image in shadows. It is often used to contribute to a dramatic or mysterious effect, as in many detective and crime films and in many horror films. Opposite of **high-key lighting**.

masking: Technique that was fairly common in silent films used to block out extraneous details and focus viewer attention, to elongate or widen the viewed image, or to censor certain details.

master shot: A shot, usually made with an unmoving camera, that records an entire scene. Parts of the master shot plus other shots of the same scene may be used as the final version of the scene, or the entire master shot may be used.

match cut/match on action: A transition between two shots in which an object or movement (or both) at the end of one shot closely resembles (or is identical to) an object or movement (or both) at the beginning of the next shot. Also known as **form cut**.

matte: A partial covering placed in front of a camera lens so that another image (usually a matte painting) can be added to the unexposed area of the image. A matte shot is made by using one or more mattes in front of the camera lens and later by filling in the unexposed areas with images from other sources. Today, matte shots are usually made entirely in a film laboratory.

medium close-up: Image in which the subject fills most of the frame, though not as much as in a close-up. When the subject is a person, the medium close-up usually reveals the head and shoulders. As with the close-up, medium close-ups are used to direct viewer attention to a part of something or to show facial expressions in detail.

medium shot: Shot in which the subject and surroundings are given about equal importance. When the subject is a person, he or she is usually seen from the knees or waist up.

medium long shot: A shot similar to a **medium shot** but accommodating larger objects.

method acting: Acting in which the performer studies the background of a character in depth, immerses himself or herself in the role, and creates emotion in part by thinking of the emotional situations from his or her own life that resemble those of the character.

mise en scène: French for "staging." It has come to mean the materiality of the filmmaking process: setting, lighting, sound, costumes, props, characters, and composition.

mix: (1) To select sound tracks of music, dialogue, and sound effects; adjust their volumes; and combine them into a composite sound track. (2) A final composite sound track consisting of a blend of other sound tracks.

mo-cap (Motion Capture): recording the movement of actors and using that to digital characters. Gollum, in *The Lord of the Rings*, is created through mo-cap.

mock documentary/mockumentary: A fictional film that parodies or amusingly imitates documentary films. Because mock documentaries use some of the techniques of many documentary films—such as interviews, handheld cameras, and the absence of stars—at first viewers may think they are seeing a documentary (*Best in Show*). See also **fake documentary**.

montage: This can be a slippery term, so I will use the very helpful three-part explanation given by my colleague, Andrew Strycharski.

> (1) It can be an arrangement of discontinuous shots meant to create a single overriding impression. This meaning applies to instances like the breakfast montage in *Citizen Kane*, where we see in a series of separate shots Kane (Orson Wells) and his wife Emily (Ruth Warrick) sitting at a breakfast table over a period of years with the change in their emotional life reflected by subtle details, a succession of clips from various films shown at the Oscars as part of the Academy's celebration of the achievements of one of its members, or the mandatory 'training montage' in a film whose central character movies from a novice to an experienced professional. (2) Another meaning is just editing. In that sense a number of non–American films will use Montage (or linguistic equivalent) in their credits to identify the movie's editor. (3) In the Soviet context, it is usually used to distinguish dialectical editing principles from continuity editing.
>
> The overarching idea of this concept is that rather than seeing editing in terms of how to tell a linear narrative, Montage, as a theoretical editing principle, outlines the ways assemblies of shots create impact. It does not necessary contradict **continuity editing** (indeed, some of the principles of Soviet montage can enhance continuity editing). But it is not tied to **continuity** either, so forms of discontinuity like **jump cuts** are also covered. (Late in his career, Eisenstein listed the terms ideological or intellectual montage, among his several categories of dialectal montage).

morphing: Alteration of a film image by degrees by use of sophisticated computer software and multiple advanced computers. This has become a common feature of Horror Films (*Men in Black*).

Motion Picture Association of America: A trade organization, founded in 1922, to represent the interests of major Hollywood studios.

Motion Picture Production Code: A set of industry guidelines, popularly known as the Hays Code, that sought to set standards for the content of American films. It was adopted in 1930 by the **Motion Picture Association of America**, though strict enforcement did not begin until 1934. It was aimed at curbing explicit depictions of sex, violence, and controversial topics. A comparison of pre–Code films, or at films released before strict adherence began—*Little Caesar* or *Baby Face*, for example—with those made shortly after—*Angels with Dirty Faces* or *Dark Victory*—give a clear sense of the Code's impact. It's influence continue through the mid–1950s but its force eroded progressively from then until 1968 when it was replaced by far less influential a rating system (still in use) devised by the **Motion Picture Association of America**.

narration: See **voice-over**.

narrator: A character, person, or unidentifiable voice that provides commentary before, during, or after the main body of a film, or a combination of these options.

neorealism: A film movement in Italy at the end of and after World War II whose films are a mixture of imaginary and factual occurrences usually located in real settings and showing ordinary and believable characters caught up in difficult social and economic conditions (*La Strada*). Other characteristics of this "new realism" are a heavy but not exclusive reliance on nonprofessional actors, available lighting, chronological narratives, few close-ups, straightforward camera angles and other unobtrusive filmmaking techniques, and natural dialogue that includes a range of dialects. It is most usually associated with directors Roberto Rossellini, Luchino Visconti, Frederico Fellini, and Vittorio De Sica.

new wave cinema: A diverse group of French fictional films made in the late 1950s and early 1960s created by directors committed to **auteur theory**. It developed in parallel to **cinéma vérité**, though it focused more or less exclusively on fictional representations rather than on documentary style. New wave films resisted conventional approaches in narrative, cinematography, and editing. Examples of new wave cinema are the early feature films of Truffaut (*Shoot the Piano Player*), Godard (*Breathless*), and Claude Chabrol (*Handsome Serge*).

nickelodeon: Literally, "five-cents theater." Small storefront movie theater popular in the United States from 1905 to roughly 1915. The successor to one-person peephole machines and the forerunner of large, elaborate movie theaters that were sometimes called "movie palaces."

nonnarrative documentary: A film that presents primarily factual information without using a narrative or story (*Timescapes*).

nouvelle vague: See **new wave cinema**.

objective camera: Camera placement that allows the viewer to see the subject approximately as an outsider would, not as someone in the film sees it. Opposite of **point-of-view shot**.

offscreen: Area beyond the frame line.

offscreen sound: Sound that does not derive from any on-screen source, such as an unseen dog barking or music that is not played by anyone within the frame.

180-degree rule: An imaginary line that separates the subject and the camera. Crossing over this imaginary line creates a jump which gives the appearance that the subject has reversed directions. See **shot/reverse shot**.

on-screen sound: Sound that derives from an on-screen source, such as a character viewers see and hear sneezing.

optical effect: Special effect usually made with an optical printer. Examples are lap dissolves, wipes, and freeze frames.

outtake: A take or shot not included in a film's final version, although occasionally outtakes are included during the ending credits, especially in a comedy (*Anchorman*).

overhead shot: A camera perspective that looks directly down on the action of a scene.

pace: A viewer's sense of a subject (such as narrative developments or factual information) being presented rapidly or slowly. A highly subjective experience that is influenced by many aspects in a film, such as the film's editing (fast cutting or slow cutting) and the frequency of new and significant subjects.

panning: Effect achieved when a motion-picture camera on a stationary base pivots horizontally during filming, often to the vastness of a setting. Panning too rapidly results in a blurred image called a **swish pan**.

parallel action: The action highlighted by **parallel editing**.

parallel editing: Editing that alternates between two or more subjects or lines of action. Sometimes called **cross-cutting** or **intercutting**. See also **montage**.

plotline: A narrative or series of related events usually involving only a few characters or people and capable of functioning on its own as an entire story. Short films tend to have one plotline. Feature films may combine two or more, but in **Classic Hollywood Cinema**, the plotlines are always related.

point-of-view editing: An editing technique that uses the perspective of a character or characters as the basis for shaping the narrative. *Lady in the Lake* presented strictly from the point of view of the detective, illustrates this approach.

point-of-view shot (p.o.v. shot): Camera placement at the approximate position of a character or person (or occasionally an animal) that gives a view similar to what that creature would see. It is almost as if someone in the film had a camera strapped on. Sometimes called **p.o.v. shot** or **subjective camera**. Opposite of **objective camera**.

postproduction: Work done on a particular film after the completion of principle photography.

preproduction: Work done on a particular film before the initiation of principle photography.

prequel: A narrative film made after the original film that tells a story that happens before the original. *Solo* in the *Star Wars* series is an example of such a film.

pre–Code: A period between 1930 and 1934 when the **Motion Picture Production Code (Hays Code)** though ostensibly established was not in fact enforced.

producer: A person in charge of the business and administrative aspects of making a film. Depending on the level of responsibility, a producer can be given a variety of titles from executive producer to assistant producer.

production: The making of a film or video, which typically involves three stages: **preproduction** (which may include planning, budgeting, scripting, designing and building sets, and casting); **production** (filming and taping); and postproduction (which includes editing and mixing sound).

production still: See **publicity still**.

product placement: The practice of including commercial products, such as Coca-Cola cans or bottles, in films so that viewers can notice them. This approach is used both to promote the product and to help finance the making of the film.

product plug: See **product placement**.

publicity still: A photograph taken, usually during production, to help publicize a film. It usually replicates a moment in one of the movie's scenes, though that is not always the case.

pull focus: See **rack focus**.

rack focus: Changing the sharpness of focus during a shot from foreground to background or vice versa. Also known as **pull focus**.

ratings: Classification of films developed by the Motion Picture Association of American. They rank films as suitable for different age groups according to a fixed set of standards.

reaction shot: A shot, usually of a face, that shows someone or occasionally an animal presumably reacting to an event. Used frequently in fictional films to intensify a situation and to cue viewers how they should react.

rear(-screen) projection: The process of projecting (usually moving) images on a screen behind actors seen in the foreground. This was often used in the early cinema to create the illusion of characters in a moving vehicle.

reel: (1) A metal or plastic spool to hold film. (2) One thousand feet of 35 mm motion-picture film stored on a spool. Since the speed of projection was not standardized before the late 1920s, early films were measured in terms of the number of reels.

remake: A version of a previously released film with a new cast, director, and in some cases significant script changes. *The Thing*, *Ocean's 11*, and *True Grit* are typical examples of this kind of film.

rough cut: An early version (usually the first complete or nearly complete version) of an edited film. See **fine cut**.

running time: The time that elapses when a film is projected.

rushes: See **dailies**.

saturated color: Intense, vivid, or brilliant color. Opposite of **desaturated color**.

scene: A section of narrative film that gives the impression of continuous action taking place in continuous time and space.

Schüfftan process: Method for combing into a single shot live action and artwork as in *Who Framed Roger Rabbit*.

scope lens: See **anamorphic lens**.

screenplay: The earliest version of a script, a script written before filming begins. Usually a finished film varies considerably from the original screenplay. See **shooting script** and **cutting continuity**.

serial: A form of cinema popular in theaters from the 1910s until the early 1950s. It signified an action film divided into chapters or installments, one of which was shown each week.

set: Constructed setting where action is filmed; it can be indoors or outdoors. See also **location** and **soundstage**.

set design: The plan for the physical representation of the film's environment, usually integrated with the director's conception of the project.

setting: The place where filmed action occurs. It is either a set, which has been built for use in a film, or a location, which is any place other than one built for use in a movie.

shallow focus: A term that identifies a shot that puts a sharp focus on the foreground leaving the background out of focus. Opposite of **deep focus**.

shock cut: A sudden shift juxtaposing two sharply contrasting scenes like people praying in a church and a couple having sexual intercourse.

shooting script: The version of the script used by the director and other filmmakers during filming. Because of frequent changes during filming and editing, the finished film usually varies considerably from the shooting script. See **screenplay** and **cutting continuity**.

short film: Variously defined, but usually regarded as a film of less than sixty minutes.

short lens: See **wide-angle lens**.

short subject: See **short film**.

shot: The presentation of a subject, perhaps even a blank screen, during an uninterrupted segment of time.

Shot/reverse shot: Alternating shots between two actors to enhance the sense of an exchange taking place between them.

simulated documentary: See **fake documentary** or **mockumentary**.

slasher film: A horror film, often low budget and featuring actors playing the roles of teenagers, with a heavy emphasis on sex and violence. *Scream* is an example of a movie that follows the conventions of the subgenre but that also makes a sophisticated comment on its strengths and weaknesses.

slow cutting: Edited film characterized by frequent lengthy shots. Opposite of **fast cutting**.

slow film (stock): Film stock that requires a large camera aperture or bright light for appropriate recreation of images. Slow film produces images with fine grain and sharp detail. Opposite of **fast film (stock)**.

slow motion: Motion in which the action depicted on the screen is slower than its real-life counterpart, as when people are seen running slowly. Achieved whenever the projector runs at a slower speed than the speed at which the camera filmed. Opposite of **fast motion**.

socialist realism: A Soviet doctrine and style in force from the mid–1930s to the 1980s that decreed that all Soviet creative works, including films, must promote communism and thus the working class and must be "realistic" and thus understandable to working people.

soft light: A light that has been reflected before illuminating the subject, giving shadows a softer edge and somewhat obscuring surface details. Opposite of **hard light**.

sound bridge: See **bridge**.

sound dissolve: A transition in which the first sound begins to fade out as the next sound fades in and overlaps the first sound before replacing it.

sound effect: A sound in film other than vocals or music that is usually added after filming is completed.

sound mixing: Process of re-recording and editing multiple sound tracks to produce one final soundtrack, which includes all dialogue, "looped" dialogue (ADR), music, sound effects and foley, and narration (if any), for each reel of picture.

sound stage: A permanent enclosed area for shooting film and recording sound. It enables filming without the intrusion of unwanted sights and sounds.

Soviet montage: See **montage**, definition 3.

special effect: Shot unobtainable by live-action cinematography. Includes split screen (one subject in part of the image, another subject in another part of the image); most superimpositions; freeze frame; and many others.

staged documentary: See **fake documentary** or **mockumentary**.

standard aspect ratio: Until the 1950s, the usual shape of motion-picture screens throughout the world and still the usual shape of analog TV screens. In the standard aspect ratio, the width to height ratio is 4:3 or 1.33:1.

Steadicam: A lightweight and portable mount for holding a motion-picture camera and stabilizing camera movements during handheld shots.

still: See **publicity still**.

stock footage: Footage stored for possible duplication and use in other films. Often stock footage is of subjects and locations difficult, impossible, or costly to film anew, such as warfare.

stop-motion cinematography: The process of filming a subject for only one or a few frames, stopping the camera and changing something in the *mise en scene*, then filming again, and repeating this process many times. This technique may be used to create a continuous movement, as in most animated films made with stop-motion cinematography, or discontinuous or jumpy movement, as in pixilation. See **time-lapse cinematography**.

storyboard: A series of drawings of each shot of a planned film or video narrative, usually accompanied by brief descriptions.

story time: The amount of time covered in a film's narrative or story. Nearly always the story time for a movie is much longer than its running time with a film like *High Noon* being an exception.

Studio Era: A period, roughly from the turn of the last century to its midpoint in which major Hollywood Studios—MGM, Paramount, Fox, RKO, and Warner Brothers—controlled almost every aspect of filmmaking, including production, financing, distribution, and the careers of almost all actors.

studio system: See **Studio Era**.

subjective camera: See **point-of-view shot**.

superimposition: Two or more images photographed or printed on top of each other. Can be achieved in the camera during filming or, more often, by using an optical printer. At the beginning of many movies, the credits are superimposed on the opening action. During a lap dissolve, one image is momentarily superimposed on another.

swish pan: Effect achieved when a motion-picture camera (usually on a stationary base) pivots horizontally during filming so rapidly that the resultant image is blurred. Occasionally used within a shot; sometimes used as a transition between shots. Sometimes called a zip pan.

swoop: A camera movement that moves from a high angle to a close-up in a single rapid take.

take: A version of a shot. More than one take of each shot is usually made because of some mistake or to improve on previous takes.

telephoto lens: A lens that makes subjects appear closer and larger than a normal lens does. With its long barrel, a telephoto lens resembles a telescope. Not to be confused with a **zoom lens**, which is capable of varying by degrees from telephoto range to normal, sometimes even to wide-angle range, while the camera is filming.

THX sound: A multispeaker sound system developed by Lucasfilm and used in selected motion-picture theaters to increase frequency range, audience coverage, and dialogue intelligibility while decreasing low bass distortion.

tight framing: A shot in which the subject is close to the edges of the frame. Uses for such framing include giving a sense of the subject's confinement or lack of mobility.

tilting: Effect achieved when a camera on a stationary base pivots vertically during filming. Often used as a way of slowly revealing information, as when we first see someone's shoes, then the camera tilts to reveal the wearer. See also **panning**.

time-lapse cinematography: The process of filming the same subject one frame at a time at regularly spaced intervals, for example, one frame every thirty minutes or one frame every twenty-four hours. When the processed film is projected at normal speed, any movement that was photographed is much accelerated, perhaps even blurred. See **stop-motion cinematography**.

tinting: The process of dyeing a film with color. Sometimes used before the adoption of color film stock in the late 1930s. In such movies, often each scene or sequence would be tinted one color.

title card: A card or thin sheet of clear plastic on which is written or printed information in a film. Before the late 1920s, title cards were used to give credits, exposition, dialogue, thoughts, descriptions of actions not shown, the numbered parts of a movie, and other types of information. In contemporary films they generally refer to an image at the film's beginning bearing its title. Less frequently intertitle cards are sued to give a particular atmosphere to the film as, for example, in *The Sting*.

track: (1) To film while the camera is moving. Sometimes the camera is mounted on a cart set on tracks; sometimes it is handheld and the camera operator moves or is moved about in a wheelchair or on roller skates or by some other means. In some publications, "to track" and "to dolly" are used interchangeably.

trailer: A brief compilation of clips from a particular film. It was usually shown in motion-picture theaters, before some videotaped movies, or on TV to advertise a movie or video release. Sometimes called a preview or a preview of a coming attraction.

treatment: A condensed written description of the content of a proposed film, often written in paragraphs and without dialogue.

typecasting: Choosing an actor for a role based on a series of similar roles, like Victor McLaughlin as a veteran soldier in John Ford's cavalry films or selecting an actor for types of roles based on his or her physical appearance, as with Marilyn Monroe's frequent casting as a dumb blonde. See **against type**.

underground film: See **avant-garde film**.

vocal: Any sound made with the human voice, including speech, grunts, whispers, screams, and countless other sounds. Along with silence, music, and sound effects, one of the components of the typical film soundtrack.

voice-over: Commentary about some aspect of the film or subject in the film, usually exposition and often from someone off screen. See Sid Hudgens' (Danny DeVito) description of Los Angeles that opens *L.A. Confidential*.

wide-angle lens: A camera lens (significantly shorter than 50 mm on a 35 mm camera) used, for example, to photograph more of the sides of a setting than is possible with a normal lens.

wide-screen film: Any film with an aspect ratio noticeably greater than 1.33:1 (a shape wider than that of an analog TV screen). Most current films shown in U.S. commercial theaters have a wide-screen aspect ratio of 1.85:1. Wide-screen film formats have been tried out since nearly the beginning of cinema but have been used in most theaters only since the 1950s.

wipe: A transition between shots, usually between scenes, in which it appears that a shot is pushed off the screen by the next shot. Many kinds of wipes are possible; perhaps the most common is a vertical line (sharp or blurred) that moves across the frame from one side to the other, seemingly "wiping away" a shot and replacing it with the next one.

zip pan: See **swish pan**.

zoom: To cause the image of the subject to either increase in size as the area being filmed seems to decrease (zoom in) or to decrease in size as the area being filmed seems to increase (zoom out).

zoom lens: A camera lens with variable focal lengths; thus it can be adjusted by degrees during a shot so that the size of the subject and the area being filmed seem to change.

Chapter Notes

Prologue

1. My definition of Classic Hollywood Cinema is distilled from a number of sources and focuses on the fundamental features familiar to most thoughtful viewers. More formal, academic delineations can be found in any number of film books like David Bordwell, Janet Steiger, and Kristen Thompson, eds., *The Classic Hollywood Cinema: Film Style and Mode of Production to 1960* (New York: Columbia University Press, 1985).

Introduction

1. The term is sometimes used pejoratively, but I find that a snobbish reaction that ignores how effective the form has been.
2. The most detailed account of the American film industry is the University of California Press's ten-volume series *History of American Cinema*. It begins in the late nineteenth century and covers through 1989.
3. George Vecsey, "Wooden as Teacher: The First Lesson Was Shoelaces," *New York Times*, 4 June 2010. nytimes.com/2010/06/05/sports/ncaabasketball/05.
4. Glen Frankel, "John Ford's Monument," *Washington Post Magazine*, 14 September 2008. washingtonpost.com/wp-dyn/content/article/2008/09/05/AR2008090502090.

Chapter One

1. There are a number of good surveys of the development of the Western. See, for example, Scott Simon, *The Invention of the Western Film* (Cambridge: Cambridge University Press, 2003).
2. William Indick, *The Psychology of the Western: How the American Psyche Plays Out on Screen* (Jefferson, NC: McFarland, 2008).

Chapter Two

1. I use the label Gangster Film rather that Crime Film, Detective Movie, or Police Procedural to underscore the driving force and central focus of attention in movies of this category.
2. The code had been instituted by the industry in 1930 to forestall government intervention. It ostensibly regulated depictions of violence and sexuality, but it was only sporadically enforced in the early years. For further reading, see Thomas Doherty, *Pre-Code Hollywood: Sex, Immorality, and Insurrection in the American Cinema, 1930–1934* (New York: Columbia University Press, 1999).

Chapter Three

1. Nino Frank, "A New Kind of Police Drama: the Criminal Adventure," *L'Ecran francais* (August 1946): 15–19.
2. See E. Ann Kaplan, ed., *Women in Film Noir* (London: British Film Institute, 1998).

Chapter Four

1. I have not included films like *Psycho* in this genre. While Hitchcock and directors like him often have a masterful sense of how to shock audiences, the absence of the preternatural puts such films in a different category: police procedurals, melodramas, or perhaps even Noir.

2. For a good overview, see Kendall Phillips, *Projected Fears: Horror Films and American Culture* (Santa Barbara: Praeger, 2005).

3. The best overview of the impact of fairy tales is still Bruno Bettelheim, *The Uses of Enchantment: The Meaning and Importance of Fairy Tales* (New York: Alfred A. Knopf, 1977).

4. See, for example, Barry Keith Grant, *The Dread of Difference: Gender and the Horror Film* (Austin: University of Texas Press, 2015).

5. It is perhaps relevant here to note one element in the movie that shows a connection to cinematic tradition through its lasting effect upon the way that horror characters comport themselves. Bela Lugosi, in his role as Dracula, uses the same impressionistic acting style common to the demeanor of an actor in the silent films—like *The Cabinet of Dr. Caligari* and *Nosferatu*—that produced such a formative impact upon the industry just a few years prior to the filming of *Dracula*. The impassiveness of his facial expressions and the slow, deliberate gestures when he moves heighten his awesomeness, and this manner sets the mold for the way such creatures behave even in contemporary films. Indeed, although the halting speech of Lugosi may now seem awkward, through its pauses, its deferrals, its hesitancies, *Dracula* evokes a sense of disorientation and of complexity often only imperfectly perceived by those engaged in the action.

6. The role of Renfield as Dracula's slave is undeveloped, due both to editing and to the screenplay itself. According to Browning's biographers, David Skal and Elias Savada, "scenes showing Van Helsing and Seward's discovery of one of Dracula's hiding boxes, and Renfield's role in protecting the others—the film's only explanation of precisely what services the slave is providing—simply disappeared." *Dark Carnival: The Secret World of Tod Browning, Hollywood's Master of the Macabre* (New York: Doubleday, 1995), p. 148. This may be a link to Van Helsing's vague promise. Also of note is that a Spanish language version of the same film was shot at the same time as Browning's. The Spanish crew used the same sets after the Americans had finished for the day. The script for the Spanish version was translated from Garrett Fort's screenplay for Browning's film. The Spanish version is longer and truer to the screenplay, but even after comparing the two films, as Joslin notes, "one is forced to conclude that Garrett Fort's screenplay adapts this aspect of Stoker's novel—i.e., the nature of Renfield's involvement in the Count's depredations—poorly." Lyndon Joslin, *Count Dracula Goes to the Movies: Stoker's Novel Adapted, 1922–2003* (Jefferson, NC: McFarland, 2006), p. 40. As for Mina, there isn't a clear explanation for why she doesn't have to die. One possibility is that Dracula's death has freed her from her slavery. This is the case in *Bram Stoker's Dracula* (1992); in that film Mina receives a scar after being bitten by Dracula, and when he dies, the scar fades.

7. Though it cannot justify the final results, economics provides an explanation for the abrupt and somewhat disconnected ending of the film. Browning was faced with studio demands for budget cuts, and that led to rough and crude editing. Van Helsing's line at the end of the film, for example, has something to do with Renfield. The critic Lyndon Joslin explains it as follows: "As John and Mina depart in the light of dawn, Van Helsing, for whatever reason, tells them he'll be along 'presently.' In the screenplay, he says, 'I shall remain, and fulfill my promise to Renfield.' Even in the context of the original screenplay, it can only be guessed what 'promise' he's talking about [probably to kill Renfield]." *Count Dracula Goes to the Movies: Stoker's Novel Adapted, 1922–2003*, p. 30.

8. Discussion of this film is based upon the version that has restored some of the previously cut scenes, like Regan's spider-walk down the front staircase.

Chapter Five

1. Mordaunt Hall, "*Metropolis*: A Technical Marvel," *The New York Times*, 7 March 1927.
2. For a contextualizing look at this issue, see M. Keith Booker, *Alternate Americas: Science Fiction Film and American Culture* (Santa Barbara: Praeger, 2006).
3. For a detailed study of this condition, see Steven D. Bloom, *The Physics and Astronomy of Science Fiction* (Jefferson, NC: McFarland, 2003).
4. The spacecraft takes as its name the title of a novel written by Joseph Conrad in 1904, and the narrative of *Alien* subtly reflects themes that run through *Nostromo*. Conrad's book focuses on the responses of a range of characters caught up in a political revolution in a fictional South American country. A number of subplots complicate its digressive narrative. However, as in *Alien*, the threat to order is a constant, and the insistent refusals of individuals to suppress personal ambition and cooperate effectively punctuates the action and continually frustrates efforts to resolve the threats posed to the community.
5. Like the ship in *Alien*, Morpheus' craft has a name with powerful references. It refers to the Biblical king of the Chaldean empire who destroyed the Temple of David and sent the Jews into exile in Babylon. Given the mission of liberation that Morpheus and his companions have undertaken, the name adds a note of irony to the narrative.

Chapter Six

1. For a more detailed look at this issue, see the following: Kristen Anderson Wagner, *Comic Venus: Women and Comedy in American Silent Film* (Detroit: Wayne State University Press, 2018); Kathleen Rowe, *The Unruly Woman* (Austin: University of Texas Press, 2011); Maria di Batista, *Fast-Talking Dames* (New Haven: Yale University Press, 2001); and Maggie Hennefeld, *Specters of Slapstick and Silent Film Comediennes* (New York: Columbia University Press, 2018).
2. Martin A. Gardner, *The Marx Brothers as Social Critics* (Jefferson, NC: McFarland, 2009).
3. The issue, of course, is far more complex than one can fully convey in a single paragraph summary, and the reference to it here should be a starting point for further study.

Chapter Seven

1. Cele Otnes, Elizabeth Hafkin Pleck, *Cinderella Dreams: The Allure of the Lavish Wedding* (Berkeley: University of California Press, 2003), p. 168.
2. This films also are often labeled Romantic Comedies. Neither term is set in stone, and the debate over which is more appropriate continues. I prefer the term Screwball, for it retains the sense that one or more of the central characters has an independent nature and some sense of the irony that surrounds them, traits that more traditional romance films, like *The Shop around the Corner*, often lack. See, for example, Wes D. Gehring, *Romantic vs. Screwball Comedies* (Metuchen, NJ: Scarecrow Press, 2002).
3. Compare Barbara Stanwyck's Jean Harrington in the 1941 film *The Lady Eve* with her Phyllis Dietrichson in the 1944 motion picture *Double Indemnity*. Though the results of her behavior differ greatly from one film to the other, the single-minded determination motivating her actions remains strikingly similar.
4. Thomas Sobchack and Vivian C. Sobchack, "Chapter 4: Genre Films," in *An Introduction to Film* (Boston: Little, Brown, 1980), p. 208.
5. George Raft, as Spats Colombo, is head of the criminal gang that pursues Joe and Jerry after the St. Valentine's Day Massacre. Raft manages to play a convincing gangster without slipping into parody. However, the film does offer some inside jokes about gangster films: when a young hoodlum ostentatiously flips a coin, just as Raft's character did in *Scarface*, Raft asks him: "Where did you pick up that cheap trick?" Later, at a banquet for an association of criminals who have gathered in Miami, Raft threatens to push a grape-

fruit half into the face of one of the thugs, as James Cagney memorably did to Jean Harlow in *The Public Enemy*.

Now What Am I Looking At?

1. For a breakdown of the upsurge in Bollywood screenings, see Rob Cain, "Indian Movies are Booming in America," *Forbes*, 5 May 2017. www.forbes.com/sites/robcain/2017/05/05/these-are-the-best-of-times-for-indian-movies-in-america.

For Further Reading

General Studies of Film

Bazin, Andre. *What Is Cinema?* Berkeley: University of California Press, 1967.
Bordwell, David, Janet Staiger, and Kristin Thompson, eds. *The Classic Hollywood Cinema: Film Style and Mode of Production to 1960.* New York: Columbia University Press, 1985.
Cain, Rob. "Indian Movies Are Booming in America." *Forbes*, 5 May 2017. www.forbes.com/sites/robcain/2017/05/05/these-are-the-best-of-times-for-indian-movies-in-america.
Cook, David A. *A History of Narrative Film*, 5th ed. New York: Norton, 2016.
Doherty, Thomas Patrick. *Pre-Code Hollywood: Sex, Immorality, and Insurrection in the American Cinema, 1930–1934.* New York: Columbia University Press, 1999.
Ebert, Roger. *Your Movie Sucks.* New York: Andrews McMeel, 2007.
Gaines, Jane M. *Pink Slipped: What Happened to Women in the Silent Film Industries?* Urbana: University of Illinois Press, 2018.
Haskell, Molly. *From Reverence to Rape: The Treatment of Women in the Movies*, 3d ed. Chicago: University of Chicago Press, 2016.
Hoberman, J. *Film After Film: Or, What Became of 21st Century Cinema?* New York: Verso, 2012.
Kael, Pauline. *I Lost It at the Movies.* 1965; New York: Marion Boyars, 1994.
Kaminsky, Stuart M., ed. *American Film Genres*, 2d ed. Chicago: Nelson-Hall, 1985.
Karlyn, Kathleen Rowe. *The Unruly Woman: Gender and the Genres of Laughter.* Austin: University of Texas Press, 2011.
Lynch, David, and Kristine McKenna. *Room to Dream.* New York: Random House, 2018.
Perkins, V.F. *Film as Film: Understanding and Judging Movies.* New York: Da Capo Press, 1993.
Sarris, Andrew. *The Primal Screen: Essays on Film and Related Subjects.* New York: Simon & Schuster, 1973.
Smith, William G. *Plato and Popcorn: A Philosopher's Guide to 75 Thought-Provoking Movies.* Jefferson, NC: McFarland, 2004.
Sobchack, Thomas, and Vivian C. Sobchack. *An Introduction to Film.* Boston: Little, Brown, 1980.
Wagner, Kristen Anderson. *Comic Venus: Women and Comedy in American Silent Film.* Detroit: Wayne State University Press, 2018.

Westerns

Cawelti, John. *The Six-Gun Mystique Sequel*, rev. ed. Madison: University of Wisconsin, 1999.
Indick, William. *The Psychology of the Western: How the American Psyche Plays Out on Screen*. Jefferson, NC: McFarland, 2008.
Lusted, David. *The Western*. New York: Routledge, 2003.
Rollins, Peter C., and John E. O'Connor. *Hollywood's West: The American Frontier in Film, Television, and History*. Lexington: University Press of Kentucky, 2005.
Sarris, Andrew. "The Spaghetti Westerns." *Confessions of a Cultist: On the Cinema, 1955–1969*. New York: Simon & Schuster, 1971, pp. 386–391.
Simon, Scott. *The Invention of the Western Film: A Cultural History of the Genre's First Half Century*. Cambridge: Cambridge University Press, 2003.
Smith, Thomas Brent, and Mary-Dailey Desmarais, eds. *Once Upon a Time ... The Western: A New Frontier in Art and Film*. Milan: 5 Continents Editions, 2017.
Tuska, John. *The American West in Film: Critical Approaches to the Western*. New York: Praeger, 1985.
Walker, Janet, ed. *Westerns: Films through History*. New York: Routledge, 2001.

Gangster Films

Grieveson, Lee, Esther Sonnet, and Peter Stanfield, eds. *Mob Culture: Hidden Histories of the American Gangster Film*. New Brunswick: Rutgers University Press, 2005.
Larke-Walshe, George S. *Screening the Mafia: Masculinity, Ethnicity, and Mobsters from The Godfather to The Sopranos*. Jefferson, NC: McFarland, 2010.
Leitch, Thomas M. *Crime Films*. Cambridge: Cambridge University Press, 2002.
Mason, F. *The American Gangster Film: From Little Caesar to Pulp Fiction*. New York: Palgrave Macmillan, 2002.
McCarty, John. *Bullets over Hollywood: The American Gangster Picture from the Silents to The Sopranos*. New York: Da Capo Press, 2005.
Munby, Jonathan. *Public Enemies, Public Heroes: Screening the Gangster from Little Caesar to Touch of Evil*. Chicago: University of Chicago Press, 1999.
Shadoian Jack. *Dreams and Dead Ends: American Gangster/Crime Films*. Boston: MIT Press, 1977.
Wilson, Ron. *The Gangster Film: Fatal Success in American Cinema*. New York: Wallflower Press, 2014.

Film Noir

Copjec, Joan, ed. *Shades of Noir*. New York: Verso, 1993.
Damico, James. "Film Noir: A Modest Proposal." *Film Reader* (February 1978): 48–57.
Durgnat, Raymond. "Paint It Black: The Family Tree of Film Noir." *Cinema* (U.K.). Nos. 6–7 (August 1970): 49–56.
Frank, Nino. "A New Kind of Police Drama: the Criminal Adventure." *L'Ecran français*. (August 1946): 15–19.
Hare, William. *Early Film Noir: Greed, Lust, and Murder Hollywood Style*. Jefferson, NC: McFarland, 2003.
Hirsh, Foster. *The Dark Side of the Screen: Film Noir*, 2d ed. New York: Da Capo Press, 2008.
Kaplan, E. Ann, ed. *Women in Film Noir*, 2d ed. London: British Film Institute, 1998.
Naremore, James. *More Than Night: Film Noir in Its Contexts*. Berkeley: University of California Press, 1998.

Pippin, Robert B. *Fatalism in American Film Noir: Some Cinematic Philosophy*. Charlottesville: University of Virginia Press, 2013.
Schwartz, Ronald. *Houses of Noir: Dark Visions from Thirteen Film Studios*. Jefferson, NC: McFarland, 2014.
Silver, Alan, and James Ursini, eds. *The Film Noir Reader*. New York: Limelight Editions, 1996.
Spicer, Andrew. *Film Noir*. Harlow, England: Pearson Education Limited, 2002.

Horror Films

Benshoff, Harry M. *Monsters in the Closet: Homosexuality and the Horror Film*. Manchester: Manchester University Press, 1997.
Berenstein, Rhona. *Attack of the Leading Ladies: Gender, Sexuality, and Spectatorship in Classic Horror Cinema*. New York: Columbia University Press, 1995.
Carroll, Noel. *The Philosophy of Horror: Or, Paradoxes of the Heart*. New York: Routledge, 1990.
Grant, Barry Keith. *The Dread of Difference: Gender and the Horror Film*, 2d ed. Austin: University of Texas Press, 2015.
_____, and Christopher Sharrett, eds. *Planks of Reason: Essays on the Horror Film*, rev. ed. Metuchen, NJ: Scarecrow Press, 1984.
Jancovich, Mark. *Horror, The Film Reader*. New York: Routledge, 2001.
Joslin, Lydon W. *Count Dracula Goes to the Movies: Stoker's Novel Adapted, 1922–2003*. Jefferson, NC: McFarland, 2006.
Leeder, Murray. *Horror Film: A Critical Introduction*. London: Bloomsbury Academic, 2018.
Phillips, Kendall R. *Projected Fears: Horror Films and American Culture*. Santa Barbara: Praeger, 2005.
Skal, David J., and Elias Savada. *Dark Carnival: The Secret World of Tod Browning, Hollywood's Master of the Macabre*. New York: Doubleday, 1995
Weishaar, Schuy R. *Masters of the Grotesque: The Cinema of Tim Burton, Terry Gilliam, the Coen Brothers, and David Lynch*. Jefferson, NC: McFarland, 2012.
Worland, Rick. *The Horror Film: An Introduction*. Hoboken, NJ: Wiley-Blackwell, 2006.

Science Fiction Films

Bloom, Steven D. *The Physics and Astronomy of Science Fiction: Understanding Interstellar Travel, Teleportation, Time Travel, Alien Life and Other Genre Fixtures*. Jefferson, NC: McFarland, 2003.
Booker, M. Keith. *Alternate Americas: Science Fiction Film and American Culture*. Santa Barbara: Praeger, 2006.
Cornea, Christine. *Science Fiction Cinema: Between Fantasy and Reality*. New Brunswick: Rutgers University Press, 2007.
Hall, Mordaunt. "*Metropolis*: A Technical Marvel." *The New York Times*, 7 March 1927.
Nama, Adilifu. *Black Space: Imagining Race in Science Fiction Film*. Austin: University of Texas Press, 2008.
Redmond, Sean, ed. *Liquid Metal: The Science Fiction Film Reader*. New York: Wallflower Press, 2005.
Sanders, Steven. *The Philosophy of Science Fiction Film*. Lexington: University Press of Kentucky, 2009.
Sobchack, Vivian. *Screening Space: The American Science Fiction Film*. New Brunswick: Rutgers University Press, 1997.
Telotte, J.P. *Science Fiction Film*. Cambridge: Cambridge University Press, 2001.

Slapstick Comedies

Austerlitz, Saul. *Another Fine Mess: A History of American Film Comedy*. Chicago: Chicago Review Press, 2010.
DiBattista, Maria. *Fast-Talking Dames*. New Haven: Yale University Press, 2001.
Gardner, Martin A. *The Marx Brothers as Social Critics: Satire and Comic Nihilism in Their Films*. Jefferson, NC: McFarland, 2009.
Hennefeld, Maggie. *Specters of Slapstick and Silent Film Comediennes*. New York: Columbia University Press, 2018.
King, Geoff. *Film Comedy*. New York: Wallflower Press, 2002.
Mast, Gerald. *The Comic Mind: Comedy and the Movies*, 2d ed. Chicago: University of Chicago Press, 1979.
Paulus, Tom, and Rob King. *Slapstick Comedy*. New York: Routledge, 2010.
Trahair, Lisa. *The Comedy of Philosophy: Sense and Nonsense in Early Cinematic Slapstick*. Albany: SUNY Press, 2007.
Tueth, Michael V. *Reeling with Laughter: American Film Comedies: From Anarchy to Mockumentary*. Metuchen, NJ: Scarecrow Press, 2012.

Screwball Comedies

Byrge, Duane, and Robert Milton Miller. *The Screwball Comedy Films: A History and Filmography, 1934–1942*. Jefferson, NC: McFarland, 2004.
Carlson, Erin. *I'll Have What She's Having: How Nora Ephron's Three Iconic Films Saved the Romantic Comedy*. New York: Hatchette, 2017.
Cavell, Stanley. *Pursuits of Happiness: The Hollywood Comedy of Remarriage*. Cambridge: Harvard University Press, 1984.
Everson, William K. *Hollywood Bedlam: Classic Screwball Comedies*. New York: Citadel Press, 1994.
Gehring, Wes D. *Romantic vs. Screwball Comedies: Charting the Difference*. Metuchen, NJ: Scarecrow Press, 2002.
Harvey, James. *Romantic Comedy in Hollywood: From Lubitsch to Sturges*. New York: Da Capo Press, 1998.
McBride, Joseph. *How Did Lubitsch Do It?* New York: Columbia University Press, 2018.
McDonald, Tamar Jeffers. *Romantic Comedy: Boy Meets Girl Meets Genre*. New York: Wallflower Press, 2007.
McGraw, Onalee. *Men and Women in Love: the View from Classic Hollywood*. Front Royal, VA: Educational Guidance Institute, 2016.
Mortimer, Claire. *Romantic Comedy*. New York: Routledge, 2010.
Rybin, Steven. *Gestures of Love: Romancing Performance in Classical Hollywood Cinema*. Alban: SUNY Press, 2017.
Sikov, Ed. *Screwball! Hollywood's Madcap Romantic Comedies*. New York: Random House, 1991.

Of Additional Interest

Bettelheim, Bruno. *The Uses of Enchantment: The Meaning and Importance of Fairy Tales*. New York: Alfred A. Knopf, 1977.
Frankel, Glen. "John Ford's Monument." *Washington Post Magazine*, 14 September 2008. washingtonpost.com/wp-dyn/content/article/2008/09/05/AR2008090502090.
Otnes, Cele, and Elizabeth H. Pleck. *Cinderella Dreams: the Allure of the Lavish Wedding*. Berkeley: University of California Press, 2003.
Vecsey, George. "Wooden as Teacher: the First Lesson Was Shoelaces." *New York Times*, 4 June 2010. nytimes.com/2010/06/05/sports/ncaabasketball/05.

Index

Numbers in *bold italics* indicate pages with illustrations

action films 196
Adam's Rib (1949) 180, 187, 190
The Adventures of Frank and Jessie James (1980) 54
Airplane! (1980) 147, 168
Al Capone (1959) 65
Alien (1979) 20, 128, 131, 135–*138*, 139–140
Alien Versus Predator (2004) 135
Altered States (1980) 99
The Amazing Dr. Clitterhouse (1938) 71
Amélie (2001) 196
American Gangster (2006) 56, 60–*61*
An American Werewolf in London (1981) 107, 120
The Angel and the Badman (1947) 39, 43
Angels with Dirty Faces (1938) 66, 211
Animal House (1978) 20–21, 156, 162–*166*, 167–168
animation films 196
Annie Hall (1977) 186
Arrival of a Train at the Ciotat Station (1896) 14, *15*
Arsenic and Old Lace (1944) 162
The Asphalt Jungle (1950) 73
Astor, Mary *78*
Audrey Rose (1977) 115
The Awful Truth (1937) 176, 186

Babette's Feast (1987) 196
Baby Face (1933) 211
Bacall, Lauren *80*
Bad Girls (1994) 54
Badlands (1973) 56, 73
Bancroft, George *38*
Barbershop (2002) 153

Barnes, Justin D. *23*
Basic Instinct (1992) 78, 86
Beetlejuice (1988) 12, 154
Being There (1979) 162
Belushi, John *166*
Bern, Rosie *150*
Berron, Bluette *122*
Best in Show (2000) 168, 210
Bettelheim, Bruno 97
The Big Heat (1953) 71
The Big Sleep (1946) 77, 79–*80*, 81, 87, 90, 91
Biograph Studios 5
Black, Maurice *64*
Blade Runner (1982) 121, *123*–124, 140, 144
The Blair Witch Project (1999) 100, *101*
Blazing Saddles (1974) 147, 164, 168
Blood Simple (1984) 25, 78, 86
Bloody Mama (1970) 73
The Blue Dahlia (1946) 78
Blue Velvet (1986) 79, 91, 93
The Blues Brothers (1980) 153, 160, 162
Body Heat (1981) 86
Bogart, Humphrey *78*, *80*
Bolger, Ray *6*
Bollywood 196
Bond, Ward *11*
Bonnie and Clyde (1967) 55, 73
Booth, Elmer *56*
Bootstrap Theory 35–36, 41–42, 56, 66
Bowen, Michael *76*
Boyz n the Hood (1991) 65
Brando, Marlon *67*
The Bravados (1958) 48
Brazil (1985) 130
Breaking Away (1979) 162

Index

Breathless (1960) 211
Bride of Frankenstein (1935) 102, 111
Bridesmaids (2011) **150**
Bridget Jones's Diary (2001) 184, 186, 187, 190,
Bringing Up Baby (1938) 147, 182, **183**–186, 192
Broadway Danny Rose (1984) 168, 172
Broken Arrow (1950) 33, 48
A Bronx Tale (1993) 58, 66, 199
Brother Orchid (1940) 65
Bullets or Ballots (1936) 71
Bunker, Edward **72**
Buscemi, Steve **72**
Butch Cassidy and the Sundance Kid (1969) 25, 54, 201

Caan, James **67**
The Cabin in the Woods (2010) 97
The Cabinet of Dr. Caligari (1920) 104, 205
Caddyshack (1980) 162
Cagney, James **60**
camera angles 75
Campbell, Neve **120**
Candy, John **148**
Cape Fear (1962) 86
Capone, Al 62
Carradine, John **38**
Carrie (1976) 99, 102, 112, 115
Casino (1995) 59–60, 65, 66
The Cat People (1942) 102, 120
Catholic Church 70, 111–112, 113, 114–115
Chaplin, Charlie 150
Children of Hiroshima (1952) 201
Children of the Corn (1984) 102, 115
Child's Play (1988) 95, 120
Chinatown (1974) 75–76, 81, 86–**87**, 88–90
Christine (1983) 99, 100
Churchill, Burton **38**
Citizen Kane (1941) 210
Clarke, Mae **60**
classic Hollywood cinema 4–21, 196–197
Clerks (1984) 156, 168–**169**, 170–172
Clockers (1995) 57, 65
A Clockwork Orange (1971) 144
Close Encounters of the Third Kind (1977) 128, 135
Clueless (1995) 195
The Cocoanuts (1929) 176
commedia dell' arte 145
The Conversation (1974) 93

Cooper, Gary 26, 43–**46**, 47–48
Cop Land (1997) 71
Corsitto, Salvatore **67**
Costner, Kevin 33–**34**
Cotton, Joseph **8**
The Cowboys (1972) 31, 40, 43
Crabbe, Buster 121
Criss Cross (1949) 88, 90
Cromwell, James **91**
Crowe, Russell **91**
Crystal, Billy **188**
Curse of the Zombies (1966) 111
Curtis, Tony **190**

Damien: Omen II (1978) 112, 115
Dances with Wolves (1990) 33, **34**, 41, 43
Dark City (1998) 79
The Dark Planet (2009) 136, 140
Dark Victory (1939) 211
A Day at the Races (1937) 176
The Day the Earth Stood Still (1951) 124
Dazed and Confused (1993) 169, 172
Desperately Seeking Susan (1985) 185, 186
The Detective (1968) 71
Devil in a Blue Dress (1995) **75**–76
Devine, Andy 38
de Wilde, Brandon **30**
Diner (1982) 172
DiNiro, Robert **59**
Dirty Harry (1971) 61, 131
The Distinguished Gentleman (1992) 153–**154**
Django Unchained (2012) 17
D.O.A. (1949) 81, 90
Donohue, Heather **101**
Dr. Jekyll and Mr. Hyde (1931) 116, 118, 120
Dr. Strangelove or: How I Learned to Stop Worrying and Love the Bomb (1965) 201
documentaries 196
Dog Day Afternoon (1979) 73
Donnie Brasco (1997) 61
Don't Look Back (2009) 204
Double Indemnity (1944) **73**, 74, 81, 82–83
Dracula (1931) 102, 103–**105**, 106–111
Dragnet (1987) 91
Drums Along the Mohawk (1939) 24
Dumb and Dumber (1994) 162

Earth Vs. the Flying Saucers (1956) 28
Eastwood, Clint 25–**26**, 49–**52**, 53–54, 199

Index

Eating Raoul (1982) 172
Edison Studios 5, 55
Elysium (2013) 127, 128
Enough Said (2013) 174–*175*
E.T. the Extra-Terrestrial (1982) 132, 135
The Evil Dead (1981) 96, 115
The Exorcist (1973) 103, 111–*114*, 115

Fahrenheit 451 (1966) 127, 130
fairy tales 96–97
Fallen (1998) 99, 115
Farewell, My Lovely (1975) 79, 90
Fargo (1996) 79, 85, 86
Ferris Bueller's Day Off (1986) 153
Fields, W.C. *151*
The Fifth Element (1997) 127
The Fighting Kentuckian (1949) 24
film noir 2, 30, 31, 74–93, 145, 175
Fishburne, Laurence *142*
Fisher, Carrie *188*
A Fistful of Dollars (1964) *26*, 28, 199
flashback 1
The Fog (1980) 110
Fonda, Henry *11*, 26–27, *180*
For Your Consideration (2006) 168
Forbidden Planet (1956) 130, 140
The Force of Evil (1948) 86
Ford, Francis 38
Ford, Harrison *123*, *128*
Ford, John 17–18, 26, 31
Fort Apache (1948) 10–*11*, 43
48 Hours (1982) 71
The Four Hundred Blows (1959) 199
1408 (2007) 95
Frank, Nino ("A New Kind of Police Drama: the Criminal Adventure") 74
Frankenstein (1931) 100, 102, 107, 110, 117
Freeman, Morgan *52*
The French Connection (1971) 71
French Kiss (1995) 190
Friday the 13th (1980) 95, 117, 120
The Front Page (1931) 157
Furst, Stephen *166*

G Men (1935) 57, 71
Gandolfini, James *175*
gangster movies 2, 29–30, 35, 55–73, 145, 175
Garland, Judy *6*
Gentlemen Prefer Blondes (1953) 157, 162
Get Out (2017) 102
Get Shorty (1995) 86
Ghostbusters (1984) 162

Giant (1956) 25
Gish, Lilian *56*
Goddard, Drew 97
The Godfather (1972) 14, 62, 66–*67*, 68–71, 73
The Godfather II (1974) 56, 66, 69
The Godfather III (1990) 66
The Good, the Bad, and the Ugly (1966) 32, 205
GoodFellas (also identified as *Goodfellas*) (1990) 58–*59*, 66
Grant, Barry Keith 97
Grant, Cary *158*, *178*, *183*
The Great Dictator (1940) 163, 168
The Great Northfield Minnesota Raid (1972) 49–50, 54
The Great Train Robbery (1903) *23*, 55
Green Card 187 (1990) 190
Greenstreet, Sidney *78*
Grier, Pam *76*
The Grifters (1990) 77–78, 86
Guest, Christopher *147*
Gun Crazy (1950) 55, 73
The Gunfight at the O.K. Corral (1957) 45, 48

Hader, Bill *151*
Haley, Jack *6*
Halloween (1978) *95*, 96, 100, 120
Handmaid's Tale (1990) 144
Handsome Serge (1958) 211
Harlow, Jean *174*
Hansen, Curtis 75
Harlan County, USA (1976) 204
Harper (1966) 66
Harry Potter and the Sorcerer's Stone (2001) 122
The Haunting (1963) 100, 116
Have Gun, Will Travel (1957–1963) 34
Hawks, Howard 26, 31, 37–43
Heaven's Gate (1980) 33
Hellraiser (1987) 102
Hepburn, Katharine *178*, *183*
Hereditary (2018) 99
Heydt, Louis Gene *80*
High Noon (1952) 13, 36–37, 43–*46*, 47–49, 52, 216
High Sierra (1941) 66
His Girl Friday (1940) 9–10, 156–*158*, 159–162, 168, 176
Holt, Tim *38*
Hombre (1967) 34
horror films 2, 94–120, 145
Hot Shots (1991) 168

House on Haunted Hill (1959) 107, 110
House Un-American Activities Committee 45
How the West Was Won (1962) 33
The Howling (1981) 108, 111
Hud (1963) 25
The Hunger Games (2012) 130, 144

I Am the Law (1938) 71
I, Robot (2004) 129
I Was a Male War Bride (1949) 184, 186
Identity Thief (2013) 151
In the Mouth of Madness (1994) 112, 115
Independence Day (1996) 124, 133, 135
Insomnia (2002) 90
Internal Affairs (1990) 71
Interview with the Vampire (1994) 105
Invaders from Mars (1953) 127, 135
Invasion of the Body Snatchers (1957) 125–126, 127, 130, 131–**132**, 133–135
The Invisible Man (1933) 116
It (2017) 100
It Came from Outer Space (1953) 135
It Had to Be You (2015) 195
It Happened One Night (1934) 173, 174–175, 191, 195
It's a Wonderful Life (1946) 122

Jackie Brown (1997) **76**–77, 90
Jaws (1977) 14
The Jazz Singer (1927) 14
Jeepers Creepers (2001) 95
Jeremiah Johnson (1972) 23, 43
Juice (1992) 73
Jurado, Katy 47–48
Jurassic Park (1993) 128, 135, 199

Kalem Company 5
Keaton, Michael **76**
Kelly, Grace 43–48
Kemper, Elie **150**
The Killers (1946) 74, 90
King of the Roaring 20s (1961) 66
Kingpin (1996) 160, 162
Kirby, Bruno **188**
Kiss Kiss Bang Bang (2005) 81
Kiss Me Deadly (1955) 81, 93
Kitel, Harvey **72**

L.A. Confidential (1997) 75, 81–82, 90–**91**, 92–93, 217
Ladd, Alan 29, **30**
The Lady Eve (1941) 179–**180**, 184, 186
The Lady from Shanghai (1947) 76, 90

Lady in the Lake (1946) 13–14, 88
Lahr, Bert **6**
Larter, Ali **191**
The Last Jedi (2017) 121
The Last of the Mohicans (1936) 24
The Last Picture Show (1971) 25
Laura (1944) 74
Lawrence of Arabia (1962) 11, 205
Legally Blonde (2001) 182–183, 187, 190–**191**, 192–195
Lemmon, Jack **190**
Leone, Sergio 25–26
Lestina, Adolph **56**
The Lights of New York (1928) 55
Like Me (2014) 118, 120
Lillard, Matthew **120**
Liota, Ray **59**
Little Caesar (1931) 55, 56, 58, 65, 210
The Long Goodbye (1973) 75–76, 79, 93
The Long Riders (1980) 50–51, 54
The Lord of the Rings (2001) 122, 210
Lorie, Peter **78**
Lost in Space (1965) 124
Louis-Dreyfus, Julia **175**
Lugosi, Bela **105**
Lumière, Auguste 15
Lumière, Louis 15

Machine-Gun Kelly (1958) 73
Mack Sennett Studios 145
MacMurray, Fred **83**
Mad Max (1979) 129
Madigan (1968) 131
Madonna 72
Madsen, Michael **72**
The Magnificent Seven (1960) 35, 48
Malcolm X (1992) 200
The Maltese Falcon (1941) 16–17, 74, 78, 82, 86
A Man Called Horse (1970) 33, 43
The Man Who Shot Liberty Valence (1962) 17, 31, 36, 43
Manhattan (1979) 186
Manhattan Melodrama (1934) 71
Manifest Destiny 33, 35, 41–42
Mars Attacks! (1996) 129, 135
Marvin, Lee 36
Marx Brothers 149, 155
M*A*S*H (1972) 153, 160, 162
The Matrix (1999) 121, 125, 126, 131–**142**, 143–144
McCabe & Mrs. Miller (1971) 25, 44, 48
McCarthy, Kevin **132**
McCarthy, Melissa **150**

McDonnell, Mary *34*
McGill, Bruce **166**
McKean, Michael **147**
McLendon-Covey, Wendy **150**
Mean Streets (1973) 66
Meek, Donald *38*
Memento (2000) 81, 82, 86
Men in Black (1997) 129, 135, 210
Metropolis (1927) 121, 125, **126**
A Mighty Wind (2003) 168
Miller, Walter **56**
Miller's Crossing (1990) 66
Minority Report (2002) 127
misé en scene: actor 9–10; props and costumes 12; setting 10–11
The Missouri Breaks (1976) 54
Mitchell, Thomas 37–**38**, 47
Monkey Business (1931) 176
montage 1
Moran, Tony **95**
Morley, Karen **64**
Moss, Carrie-Anne **142**
Motion Picture Production Code 55
Mulholland Drive (1999) 77, 90, 92–93
Mulholland Falls (1996) 71, 79,
The Mummy (1932) 100, 107, 110, 116
Muni, Paul **64**
Murder by Death (1976) 163
Murder, My Sweet (1973) 74, 77, 90
Murnau, F.W. 97
Murphy, Eddie **154**
musicals 196
The Musketeers of Pig Alley (1912) 55, **56**
My Darling Clementine (1946) 32, 45, 48
My Favorite Wife (1940) 176, 184, 187, 190
My Little Chickadee **151**
My Man Godfrey (1936) 189

The Naked City (1948) 61–62, 71, 90
The Naked Gun (1988) 147, 168
The Naked Spur (1953) 44, 48, 49
Natural Born Killers (1994) 56, 73
New Jack City (1991) 73
Nicholson, Jack **87**
A Night at the Opera (1935) 149, 176
Night of the Hunter (1955) 86
Night of the Living Dead (1968) **94**, 110
Nightmare on Elm Street (1984) 100, 118, 120
nihilism 62
9 to 5 (1980) 162

1984 (1956) 144
Ninotchka (1939) 194, 195
No Country for Old Men (2007) 25
North by Northwest (1959) 10
Nosferatu (1922) 97, 98, 104, 111, 205
The Nutty Professor (1963) 153

Ocean's 11 (1960) 213
The Odd Couple (1968) 159, 162
O'Halloran, Brian **169**
O'Hara, Maureen *18*
The Omega Man (1971) 129
The Omen (1976) 101, 112, 115, 120
Once Upon a Time in America (1984) 58, 66
Once Upon a Time in the West (1968) 26, 43
One-Eyed Jacks (1961) 49–50, 54
The Others (2001) 111, 118, 120
Out of the Past (1947) 76, 81, 86
The Outlaw Josie Wales (1976) 54
The Ox-Bow Incident (1943) 26–27, 44, 48

Pale Rider (1985) 33
The Palm Beach Story (1942) 187, 190
Pantoliano, Joe **142**
Pat and Mike (1952) 190
Pat Garret and Billy the Kid (1973) 32, 50–51
Pearce, Guy **91**
Peckinpah, Sam 25–26
Penn, Chris **72**
A Perfect World (1993) 56, 72
Perkins, Osgood **64**
Pesci, Joe **59**
The Philadelphia Story (1940) 14, 176–177, **178**, 181, 186
Plan 9 from Outer Space (1959) 203
Planet of the Apes (1968) 128, 130, 140, 144
Platinum Blonde (1931) 173, **174**, 187
Platt, Louise *38*
The Player (1992) 77–78, 86
Polanski, Roman 86–88
Poltergeist (1982) 102, 109
Posse (1993) 39, 43
The Postman Always Rings Twice (1946) 84, 86
Predator (1987) 135
Prizzi's Honor (1985) 66
The Producers (1967) 163, 168
profession-related movies 196
Psycho (1960) 117

The Public Enemy (1931) 55, 57, 58–59, **60**, 73
Pulp Fiction (1994) 72, 73, 93, 205

Q & A (1990) 71
The Quiet Man (1952) 17–**18**

Raising Arizona (1987) 25, 168, 172
Rancho Notorious (1952) 54
Rear Window (1954) 12
Red River (1948) 31, 40, 43
Reeves, Keanu **142**
The Reptile (1966) 111
Reservoir Dogs (1992) 62, 71–**72**, 73
Return of the Jedi (1983) 171
The Revenant (2015) 24, 54
Revenge of the Nerds (1984) 162, 163
Rio Bravo (1959) 24–25, 44, 48
Rio Grande (1950) 10, 43
The Rise and Fall of Legs Diamond (1960) 73
The Road to Perdition (2002) 56, 66
The Roaring Twenties (1939) 57, 65
Robinson, Edward G. **83**
RoboCop (1987) 129, 143, 144
romantic comedies *see* screwball comedies
Rooster Cogburn (1975) 31
Rosemary's Baby (1968) 95, 115
Roth, Tim **72**
Rudolph, Maya **150**
rugged individualism 32, 33–35, 56, 66
Runaway Bride (1999) 195
The Running Man (1987) 129, 140, 144
Russell, Rosalind **158**
Ruthless People (1986) 162
Ryan, Meg **188**

Scarface (1932) 55, 62–65, 68
Schindler's List (1993) 208
Schreck, Max **98**
Schumer, Amy **151**
Schwarzenegger, Arnold **125**
science fiction 2, 121–144, 145
Scream (1996) 95, 98–99, 103, 115–**120**, 129
screwball comedy 2, 145, 173
The Searchers (1956) **27**–28, 30, 41, 43
The Seven Year Itch (1955) 172
Shaft (1971) 201
Shane (1953) 29, **30**, 33
She Wore a Yellow Ribbon (1949) 10, 40
Shearer, Harry **147**
The Shining (1980) 95

Shoot the Piano Player (1960) 211
The Shootist (1976) 25, 31, 131
Siegel, Don 31, 131
Signs (2002) 135
Silent Running (1972) 128, 140
Silverado (1985) 39, 43
Sin City (2005) 75, 79
The Sixth Sense (1999) 98, 110
Slackers (2002) 170, 172
slapstick comedy 2, 145–172
Solo (2018) 212
Some Like It Hot (1959) 182, 186–**190**, 191
Sorvino, Paul **59**
Soylent Green (1973) 140, 144
Spacey, Kevin **91**
special effects 12–15; camera position 13–14, 75; crosscutting 1, 70; editing 14–15, 70, 124–125; lighting 12–13, 74–75; sound 14, 75–76
Stagecoach (1939) 31, 36–37, **38**–43, 43–44, 46, 47, 50, 208
Stanwyck, Barbara **180**
Star Trek series 130, 138, 140
Star Wars series 121, 125, **128**, 140, 212
Starship Troopers (1997) 135, 140
Stewart, James 26, 36, 49, **178**
Stigmata (1999) 99, 113, 115
The Sting (1973) 19–20, 217
La Strada (1954) 211
Strange Invaders (1983) 128
Stripes (1981) 162
Sunset Boulevard (1950) 75–76, 82, 86, 90–91

Tarantino, Quentin 71–**72**, 73
Taxi Driver (1976) 14
The Terminator (1984) 124, **125**, 140, 144,
Thelma and Louise (1991) 201
Them (1954) 124
The Thin Man series 182
The Thing (1982) 134, 213
The Third Man (1949) 7–**8**, 86, 205
The 39 Steps (1935) 16
This Is Spinal Tap (1984) **147**, 168
The 3:10 to Yuma (1957) 44, 48
Tierney, Lawrence **72**
The Time Machine (1960) 128, 144
Timecop (1994) 135
Timescapes (2012) 211
Tom Jones (1963) 207
Tombstone (1993) 17, 32, 45, 48
Topper (1937) 162
Total Recall (1990) 128, 143, 144

Index

Touch of Evil (1958) 77, 91, 92–93, 206
Trading Places (1983) 151, 160, 162
Training Day (2001) 71
Trainwreck (2015) **151**
Trevor, Claire **38**
True Grit (1969) 31, 32, 213
Truffaut, François 199, 211
28 Days Later (2002) 121
Two Mules for Sister Sara (1970) 131
2001: A Space Odyssey (1968) 121, 125, 130, 136, 144

Ulrich, Skeet **120**
Uncle Buck (1989) 147–**148**
Unforgiven (1992) 36–37, 49–**52**, 53–54, 207
The Untouchables (1987) 19, 57, 61, 66, 71
The Usual Suspects (1995) 66

Victor/Victoria (1995) 175, 184, 186 186
The Virginian (1941) 35
voiceover 1
von Sydow, Max **114**
Le Voyage dans le lune (A Trip to the Moon) (1902) 121–**122**

Waiting for Guffman (1996) 164, 168
war films 196
The War of the Worlds (1953) 123, 134, 135
Warner Brothers 55
Washington, Denzel **61**, **75**
Wayne, John **11**, **18**, 20, **27**, 30–31, 36, 37–**38**, 39–43

Wells, Orson **8**
West, Mae **152**
The Westerner (1940) 17, 49, 54
Westerns 2, 23–54, 145, 175
What's Up Doc (1972) 186
When Harry Met Sally (1989) 187, **188**, 190
While You Were Sleeping (1995) 195
White Heat (1949) 59, 71, 73
Who Framed Roger Rabbit (1988) 214
The Wicker Man (1973) 100
Wiig, Kristen **150**
The Wild Bunch (1969) 25, 50–51, 54
Willard (1971) 99
Williams, John 75–76
Wilson, Luke **191**
Winchester '73 (1950) 34
Witherspoon, Reese **191**
The Wizard of Oz (1939) 5–**6**, 7, 17, 122, 202
Wolf (1994) 99
The Wolf Man (1941) 95, 107, 120
Woman of the Year (1942) 187, 195
The Women (1939) 205
Wooden, John 8–9
Woolvett, Jaimz **52**
Wyatt Earp (1994) 38, 45, 48
Wynter, Dana **132**

Young Frankenstein (1974) 147, 164, 168
You've Got Mail (1998) 176

Zinnemann, Fred 26, 43–49

www.ingramcontent.com/pod-product-compliance
Lightning Source LLC
Chambersburg PA
CBHW061346300426
44116CB00011B/2018